ERRATA - FIRST PRINTING

ERRORS AND TYPOS THAT ESCAPED THE PROOFREADER:

References to Toledo, Ohio, should read Chicago, Illinois

P. 7, 3rd sentence: "of" should be "or."

P. 87, 1st paragraph, should read "military."

P. 97, last paragraph, should read "United."

P. 203, 1st paragraph, should read "civilization."

Dedicated to the world's children and grandchildren.
May their futures be peaceful, blessed, and bright.

DIRECT DEMOCRACY

And the
Curse of the Boiled Frogs

Joseph Jenkins

ISBN: 978-1-7336035-7-7
Library of Congress Control Number: 2024915424

First paperback printing: September 2024
Printed in the United States of America

Published by Joseph Jenkins Inc.
143 Forest Lane, Grove City, PA 16127 USA
JosephJenkins.com

Cover design by DTPerfect Book Design

Distributed by:
Chelsea Green Publishing
White River Junction, Vermont, USA
London, UK
www.chelseagreen.com

TABLE OF CONTENTS

Introduction

This book is written not only for "we the people" of today but for our children and grandchildren when they become adults. They should have the opportunity to understand what happened in the 2020s from a working-class perspective rather than from what's filtered through the lens of government, medical, or academic institutions.

Working-class people have built almost everything around the world and have done so for millennia. We represent much of humanity. We have similar values, no matter where we live on the globe, or what we do for a living. We value our children, as they are the future. We will do anything to protect them. We devote many years of our lives to making sure our children grow up healthy, safe, educated, and stable. We also value our own personal health. Without it, we have little or nothing.

There are many things working people find to be repugnant. War is at the top of the list. War is when innocent children are slaughtered, families destroyed, villages leveled, hopes vanished. Working people toil for generations to create magnificent monuments, bridges, highways, tunnels, and all parts of the built environment that we rely on and value. What takes years, even centuries, to create, war destroys in minutes. War represents the worst of humanity, while *those who lead us into needless warfare represent the worst of leadership*. War, like many if not most human crimes, is fed by greed. Greed breeds corruption, heartless cruelty, injustice, inequality, tyranny, and madness.

In the 2020s, Western humanity was in the midst of a mass insanity. Governments in the Western world were corrupt at the highest levels. The TV-watching world had become slowly and certainly brainwashed. The science of propaganda had reached a zenith unimaginable just a generation earlier.

Humanity had reached a crossroads. One path would lead humans into another world war, followed by generations of suffering, unspeakable crimes against humanity, and unimaginable destruction of the natural world — a path being pushed by wealthy individuals. Their sense of humanity had died and had become replaced by a lust for power and control.

Each of us really needs very little. The Earth can provide comfortable, safe, healthy lives for all of us. The future could be magnificent for human beings, with happy families, strong communities, clean environments, creative and constructive livelihoods, and governance dedicated to the protection of human rights. The future of humanity must be built on a foundation of cooperation, not conflict. That's the direction where the other fork in the road could take us. There is currently a deep streak of greed infecting humanity like a malignant cancer. We can cure it, or it can destroy us. Direct democracy focuses on that cure.

The left-handed pages in this book contain sidebars, quotes, excerpts, screenshots, illustrations, and media headlines that were almost all current at the time this book was written in the 2020s. These are added according to 17 U.S. Code § 107, which states that fair use of copyrighted material for purposes such as criticism, comment, news reporting, or research, is not an infringement of copyright. These wide-ranging illustrations represent a snapshot of society in the first half of the 2020s. The information they reveal is critical to the thesis of this book, especially for those who are reading it in the future. In a sense, this is like two books in one.

Many of today's public *don't see the information on the left-side pages* because most of it is censored by mainstream media outlets. It is unfortunate that a large percentage of the American population is constantly bathed in information that is censored and propagandized. Many seem to be totally unaware of what's happening to them, their families, and their country.

We need to cooperatively rethink the way our government is structured. The system currently in use does not work. It is broken. Today, we are witnessing a government that is a slow-motion train wreck. How do we fix this problem? Let's discuss some ideas.

1
America's Pretend Democracy

"For if Men are to be precluded from offering their Sentiments on a matter . . .
reason is of no use to us; the freedom of Speech may be taken away, and, dumb
and silent we may be led, like sheep, to the Slaughter."
George Washington, March 15, 1783

If you think America's government is a democracy, you're wrong. We have a "Constitutional Republic," an outdated form of "democracy."

If you think you have the "right to vote" in America, you're wrong again. When you vote for a representative, you're not exercising your right to vote, you're *sacrificing* your right to vote.

Allowing someone to vote on your behalf *takes away* your vote and the votes of millions of people, handing them instead to a tiny minority of politicians. Such an unfair and antiquated system doesn't make sense in our modern times. Instead, we need to wrest the decision-making power out of the hands of that tiny minority and put it where it belongs, directly into the hands of our tax-paying citizens.

This is called *Direct Democracy*, and the concept is simple. It is based upon four foundational principles:

1. **The purpose of government is** *to serve the people*. Government exists as a tool that we the people create and use to protect and preserve our basic inalienable rights. We do not serve the government; the government serves us.

2. **Citizens** *vote directly* **on legislation.** We're past the point of needing representatives to vote on our behalf.

3. **"Representatives"** are *randomly selected* using an intelligent filtration process. Their role as esteemed public servants is to coordinate, organize, and execute the legislative processes and record the collective, binding votes of the citizens. Representatives have one vote, the same as everyone else.

America's Dangerous Election Cycle

Just as the crowned heads of state in Europe beheld the onset of World War I with paralyzed dread, aware it would ruin them but powerless to stop it, there is a deep fatalism to American politics today. The basic legitimacy of the electoral system is being undermined, the 2024 election likely won't be accepted by around half of all Americans, and the consequences both in the short and long term of this escalating polarization look disastrous. Everyone can sense that a crash is coming, but even if we try to slam on the brakes, it may be that they gave out long ago.

The West's Descent Into Madness

If it is possible to watch a society—an entire civilization—go insane, we are watching that phenomenon in real time. Across all forms of media, the headlines bring fresh evidence daily.

Western civilization—that aggregation of cultural, political, social, and religious traditions that has formed the basis for European societies and those of their current and former colonies and territories—is committing suicide, using every weapon—philosophical, legal, political —at its disposal.

THE PRICE OF POWER

"It is unhealthy for our country and our democracy for money to be such a critical component of how legislative leaders are selected. This dirty secret has metastasized into a major cancer afflicting our legislative process. The time to combat this is now. Nothing less than the public's trust in government itself is at stake."

Supreme Court Rejects Attempt to Expand No-Excuse Mail-in Ballots in Texas

"Unless the people, through unified action, arise and take charge of their government, they will find that their government has taken charge of them. Independence and liberty will be gone, and the general public will find itself in a condition of servitude to an aggregation of organized and selfish interest." —Calvin Coolidge

THE POWER OF THE PEOPLE IS STRONGER THAN THE PEOPLE IN POWER

4. **Citizens** *directly engage in crafting legislation*, including proposing and developing bills, legislative documents, legislative policy, and protocols.

Humans are the creator species; we can create the future we want; we can evolve our "democracy." Voting is needed; what we don't need are a tiny minority of politicians voting on behalf of everyone else. That scenario has become a recipe for disaster, as indicated by the impending collapse of the United States of America, and much of the Western world, in the twenty-first century.

Selection by Intelligent Filtration

Citizens interested in pursuing a position as a public representative can *opt in on their tax return*. There can be no forced selection, no involuntary government servitude. Eligible citizens who *want* to play a constructive role in the legislative process can choose to throw their hat into the ring. If they're eligible, qualified, and fortuitous, they will be selected at random in the first round of candidates.

Candidates should be selected *based on their Social Security numbers* or other government identification number. Imagine a selection process that eliminates all irrelevant factors such as political party, religion, race, gender, and sexual orientation. Imagine a selection process that eliminates outside money. We all know that outside money has shamefully corrupted our government.

The selections are *filtered through a series of intelligent processes* that screen out ineligible candidates. You can't opt in on your tax return if you don't pay taxes. You can't be in the selection pool if you don't have an official identification number. These are initial filters.

For the U.S. House of Representatives, a candidate must be a legal citizen, age 25 or older, at least seven years a citizen of the United States, and a resident of the constituency of which he or she will represent. For the U.S. Senate, they must be at least 30 years old and have been a U.S. citizen for nine years. These criteria are specified in the United States Constitution.

Counterfeit Cash Financed Midterm Democrats

If you thought Republicans were the party of big business

and the heartless rich, you might be wondering how Democrats managed to outspend Republicans in key races this year, like John Fetterman raking in nearly $48 million in his Pennsylvania U.S. Senate campaign, while the GOP opponent he defeated, Mehmet Oz, took in only about $12 million, (augmented by loaning himself $21 million). Or incumbent New Hampshire U.S. Sen. Maggie Hassan being re-elected after raising $38 million, while her GOP challenger, Trump-backed retired Gen. Don Bolduc, pulled in a mere $2.2. million. A big part of the answer is that Democrats are now the party of the snake oil mogul.

Before his financial scam came crashing to an end this month and over $2 billion in FTX clients' investments dissolved, Bankman-Friend had handed Joe Biden $10 million during the 2020 presidential election and gave Democrats over $40 million in this year's midterms, likely buying the party a majority in the U.S. Senate in the next Congress. Now ruined, he was the second-biggest donor to the party's campaigns, behind only Hungarian-born leftist billionaire currency manipulator George Soros.

Scant Election Reforms Since 2020 Forebode a Repeat in November

Massive voter fraud allegations that marred the 2020 election spurred a political and grassroots movement from coast to coast to pursue an array of election reforms designed to increase election integrity. However, with just months left ahead of the 2024 election, Republicans say little was mended, especially in contested states where they thought fixes were needed most. Much concern is centered around five key swing states that became the focus of 2020: Georgia, Pennsylvania, Arizona, Michigan, and Wisconsin.

Prominent Democrat Official Charged over Mail-In Ballot Fraud Scheme During 2022 Election

A Democrat operative and ex-president of the Atlantic City council has been arrested on charges of allegedly orchestrating a mail-in ballot fraud scheme in the New Jersey city.

Two Weeks to Flatten Became Eight Months to Change the Election
March 2020: The CDC and the CARES Act Meddle in the Election
April and May 2020: Voter Fraud Skyrockets

In May 2020, New Jersey held municipal elections and required all voting take place via mail. The State's third largest city, Paterson, held its election for city council. The results should have been a national scandal that ended the push for mail-in voting. Shortly after the election, the Postal Service discovered "hundreds of mail-in ballots" in one town mailbox. Paterson resident Ramona Javier never received her mail-in ballot for the election. Neither did eight of her family members and neighbors, yet they were all listed as having voted. "We did not receive vote-by-mail ballots and thus we did not vote," she told the press. "This is corruption. This is fraud."

All qualified selected candidates would be required to take a comprehensive test to prove they have an acceptable understanding of how government functions. Those who refuse to take the test of who fail it are filtered out. Those who score highest on the test remain in the final, randomly selected group. It is this final cut from which the representatives and backup candidates are selected, based on their identification numbers, general qualifications, and test results.

We no longer need to vote for representatives. For the legislative body, no elections would be needed, no political parties would be in control; there would be no gender considerations, the process would be color blind, there would be no rejections based on socio-economic status, no outside money would be involved.

Citizens can and should develop and propose legislation, either as individuals or in organized groups (think church groups, trade unions, parent groups, community organizations, and so on). Our randomly selected representatives and committee members would coordinate and execute the legislative process. The votes of the citizens must be counted, and they must be binding.

This is called "direct democracy," and we need it. If we want to change the face of a nation, then change how its decisions are made. Take the power away from a wealthy minority and put it squarely where it belongs: in the hands of all the people. No matter how we describe the problem of a democracy gone awry, a solution must be found. Direct democracy is one that must be considered.

Brainwashing Machines

Currently, in 2024, in the United States of America, our government is mired in corruption, division, animosity, injustice, and frustration. Government fraud and malfeasance are undeniable, despicable, and disgusting. Much of it surrounds one issue: elections. American elections have become rigged, corrupt, and sleazy. No thinking person trusts them.

The exceptions, perhaps, are the "weak-minded TV watchers." brainwashed masses of people whose minds have become weak and corrupted by the endless stream of propaganda fed directly to them by their "brain-

California Voters Report Ballot Mix-Ups, Share Concerns About Election Integrity

"There have been multiple people who experienced this," a poll worker said. "We don't know how or why their party affiliation was changed."

Conservative Group Files FEC Complaint Alleging Coordinated Election Influence for Biden

Arizona Mohave County Board of Supervisors to Discuss Litigation Against Maricopa County following Fraudulent Election

Complaint alleges campaign finance violation involving Secretary of State Antony Blinken and 51 former intelligence officials over Hunter Biden laptop letter.

Colorado Secretary of State's Office Admits It Mailed Over 31,000 Voter Registration Instruction Cards to Non-Citizens

In a Jan. 5, 2023 press release, the Public Interest Legal Foundation (PILF), said, "The Secretary of State's office blamed a 'data analytical error' for the non-citizens in 58 counties receiving voter registration materials."

5 states decided the 2020 Election. All 5 stopped counting at the same time with Trump holding commanding leads. When counting resumed each state dumped 100,000s of ballots that broke almost exclusively for Joe Biden. Only a fool wouldn't ask questions. **David Giglio**

Elections Department Sends Out Wrong Ballots to 'Undetermined Number' of People

Officials in a Montana county said an unknown number of wrong ballots were sent out recently.

Virginia's General Assembly Elections Drawing Intense National Interest, Money

The general consensus is about $100 million will ultimately be spent by campaigns, PACs, and interest groups by Nov. 7, more than double 2019's General Assembly election spending.

washing machines," otherwise known as televisions, social media platforms, and search engines.

A clandestine group of billionaires, employing an army of clever hackers, subservient media operatives, paid ballot box stuffers, and a host of other illicit accomplices, can shift votes by the millions one way or another, hack voting machines, control search engines, send private election data to foreign destinations, block opposition voices, censor free speech, and propagandize the public in a manner that our founding fathers could never have imagined.

The playbook is well known — divide and conquer. Us versus Them. Right versus Left. Democrats versus Republicans. Liberals versus Conservatives. Male vs Female. Straight vs Gay. Neighbor against neighbor, brother against brother, families torn apart with no healing in sight. So long as a conflicting dichotomy is maintained, the public will easily be misled, controlled, conquered, and subjugated, like sheep in a pasture, with the barking dogs of mainstream propaganda herding them one way or the other.

At this dark hour, now is not the time to get drawn into the petty issues that are floated before us as a distraction by the media and its owners. We the people must think for ourselves, think outside the box, find solutions, and act on them. New ideas must be proposed, discussed, developed, and realized. Direct democracy offers a way out of the corner we have painted ourselves into. The idea, which is totally legal, practical, and doable, offers a starting point, allowing us to imagine and create a future for humanity based on truth, justice, and real democracy, rather than greed, corruption, and conflict.

Civil War Must Be Avoided

Nobody wants a civil war other than those who will profit from it in one way or another. If severe population reduction and the elimination of basic human rights and freedoms are goals of a group of deranged billionaires, then goading private citizens into violence against each other will serve their purpose.

However, responsible citizens must work together *cooperatively* and

Catastrophic "Loss of Control" Data Breach in NY Elections

A peer-reviewed study in the Journal of Information Warfare (JIW) confirms a "Loss of Control" breach has occurred in the NYSVoter Database.

"Through auditing the voter roll databases, obtained directly from state and local boards of elections, we have uncovered millions of invalid registrations, hundreds of thousands of votes cast by legally invalid registrations, hundreds of thousands of votes cast by legally invalid registrants, massive vote discrepancies, and the clear presence of algorithmic patterns we reverse engineered from within the state's own official records.

To be absolutely clear, there is no known innocent purpose or explanation for why these algorithms exist. I am told by cyber-intelligence experts they indicate a 'Total Loss of Control' data breach, the most severe kind of data breach recognized by our federal government. The law says it renders the affected NYSVoter database completely untrustworthy."

Maricopa County Files Response to Kari Lake Claims Tabulators Were Working as Intended When 60% FAILED on Election Day

Judge OVERTURNS Bridgeport, CT mayoral primary election after Democrat clerk busted for ballot stuffing

Connecticut Judge William Clark overturned the results of Bridgeport's Democratic mayoral primary on Wednesday after a video emerged showing a supporter of current Mayor Joe Ganim allegedly stuffing ballots into an absentee ballot drop box.

The videos, Clark said, "are shocking to the court and should be shocking to all the parties."

Trump Supporters Targeted by FBI as 2024 Election Nears

The federal government has created a new category of extremists, President Trump's MAGA followers, to track and counter the threat of violence and major civil disturbances around the 2024 U.S. presidential election.

Refutation of Georgia Secretary of State Brad Raffensperger's False Election Claims

creatively to allow democracy to unfold in a non-violent manner. We must never turn our guns against each other. When a snake is biting you, chop off the head, don't shoot your brother or sister. Cut the strings of the puppet masters, then bring the puppet masters to justice. We do not need to be foolishly led into a war against ourselves.

The human race is a creator species. We create things that otherwise would not be found in nature: plastic, steel, glass, music, art, harnessed nuclear energy, electric motors, aircraft, and so on. Why can't we also create a better democracy? When we *elect* a "representative," we terminate our right to vote, handing it over to someone else, a person who spends incredible amounts of money to become "elected." Sometimes, that representative is nothing more than a political prostitute, owing favors to special interests and opulent backers who expect the representative to support and pass legislation that favors *them*. The oligarchs expect favors, and if they are not forthcoming, their money spigot is shut off.

Representatives consequently spend much of their time in the congress or senate (at both state and federal levels), groveling for money to run for reelection. For generations, U.S. representatives were almost entirely wealthy white men. They primarily voted to advance the interests of wealthy white men. They did not represent their constituents, except on paper. Blacks and Native Americans were pushed out of the legislative process altogether. Women had the right to vote in the Soviet Union before they did in the United States. This is an inconvenient fact that is not taught in American public schools.

Today, Congressional representatives include a greater balance of females and more ethnic diversity, but these people are almost all controlled by a political party, primarily Democrat or Republican. Representatives still don't represent their constituents, nor can they. Republican and Democrat congresspersons should be impartial to political leanings to be fair, since about half of their constituents are likely to be Democrat and half Republican. Fair representation isn't happening. Many representatives instead vote lockstep with their political party.

It's no longer 1776. We no longer have to choose a representative from our village to ride a horse over miles of dirt roads to get to a central location to cast a vote on behalf of our community. We live in the twenty-first

Judge Issues Huge Decision On Georgia Voting Machines

Judge Amy Totenberg has issued a decision concurring there is sufficient reason to believe that the electronic voting machines used by the State of Georgia have substantial flaws.

The District Court Judge found that there is sufficient cause to believe that there may be "cybersecurity deficiencies that unconstitutionally burden Plaintiffs' First and Fourteenth Amendment rights and capacity to case effective votes that are accurately counted."

Bombshell Report Exposes Voting Scheme In Michigan, Cover-Up By State Officials

How Long Has Election Corruption Been Going On?

Widespread election manipulation can only occur with corrupted voter rolls, centralized technology infrastructure, and sophisticated data collection, all combined with loose practices like no-excuse mail and early voting, and corrupt practices like ballot harvesting and drop boxes amplifying the cheating.

Absentee Voting From Abroad Presents Myriad of Fraud Vulnerabilities in US Elections

Ballots Cast Without Proof Of Citizenship 'Exploded' After Lawfare Crippled Arizona Election Laws

About 1,700 people in Arizona voted in 2018 with a federal-only ballot. Two years later, the number grew to 11,600 individuals.

Georgia election server wiped after suit filed

It's not clear who ordered the server's data irretrievably erased. Wiping the server "forestalls any forensic investigation at all," said Richard DeMillo, a Georgia Tech computer scientist following the case. "People who have nothing to hide don't behave this way."

Filmmaker: Documentary Proves Rampant Illegal Vote Trafficking in 2020

California City Council Member Arrested on Voter Fraud Charges: Sheriff

century, and it's time to update our political system instead of trying to fit a square 1776 election model into a round twenty-first century hole. It isn't working. Let's use the technology we have to move civilization forward, to evolve our governmental processes, and fortify our basic, common interests.

The U.S. Declaration of Independence, signed on July 4, 1776, states:

"We hold these truths to be self-evident, that all men are created equal, that they are endowed by their Creator with certain unalienable Rights, that among these are Life, Liberty, and the pursuit of Happiness. That to secure these rights, Governments are instituted among Men, deriving their just powers from the consent of the governed. **That whenever any Form of Government becomes destructive of these ends, it is the Right of the People to alter or to abolish it, and to institute new Government,** *laying its foundation on such principles and organizing its powers in such form, as to them shall seem most likely to affect their Safety and Happiness."*

The preamble to the Constitution of the United States, effective since March 4, 1789, states:

"We the People of the United States, in Order to form a more perfect Union, establish Justice, ensure domestic Tranquility, provide for the common defense, promote the general Welfare, and secure the Blessings of Liberty to ourselves and our Posterity, do ordain and establish this Constitution for the United States of America."

The United States government was created *as a tool to serve the people.* Period. The people do not serve the government; our ancestors created it to be used as a tool for our benefit. It exists to protect and secure our inalienable rights: *Life, Liberty, and the pursuit of Happiness.* We have strayed so far from this intent. Even though most government employees are good and decent people, our federal government has become a criminal enterprise at the highest levels. Our "representatives" rob our treas-

150,000 Votes in the 2020 Election Not Tied to a Valid Address in Wisconsin

Election Watch (EW), a Wisconsin election integrity watchdog organization, has discovered that more than 150,000 votes cast in the 2020 presidential election cannot be connected with a valid address. That's illegal in the state of Wisconsin.

IT IS HARD TO IMAGINE A MORE STUPID OR MORE DANGEROUS WAY OF MAKING DECISIONS THAN BY PUTTING THOSE DECISIONS IN THE HANDS OF PEOPLE WHO PAY NO PRICE FOR BEING WRONG -THOMAS SOWELL

Predetermined Algorithms Source of Widespread Election Fraud in Arizona

Arizona Secretary of State Says Resolution Banning the Use of Voting Machines Will Not Be Enforced

Bombshell Report Exposes Election Rigging with Voting Machines
The Forensic Investigator's Credentials Must Be Taken Seriously

My name is J. Alex Halderman. I am Professor of Computer Science and Engineering, Director of the Center for Computer Security and Society, and Director of th Software Systems Laboratory at the University of Michigan in Ann Arbor. I hold a Ph.D. (2009), a master's degree (2005), and a bachelor's degree (2003), summa cum laude, in computer science, all from Princeton University.

Georgia a Prime Target for Election Fraud

Hackers Can Compromise Not Only Elections, But Audits

Georgia's Current Voting Machines Worse in Some Ways Than Previous Models

Remote Hackers Can Install Malware to Compromise Elections in Numerous Ways

Attackers Can Obtain Root Privileges and Rig Elections for Parties, Candidates

Installing Malware Locally is Easy, Requires No Special Expertise

QR Codes are Not 'Encrypted' in the Way Georgia Election Officials Had Claimed

Voting Machines are Plagued by Weak Security

Fulton County Questions More Serious After Forensic Investigation

Fulton County Sent Test Scanner That Failed Even Rudimentary Security Precautions

ury by starting useless, pointless, offensive wars, shuffling billions, even trillions of dollars into their pockets or the pockets of their handlers.

Not content to rely on messy, drawn-out warfare to drain the people's treasury, criminals cleverly came up with a new idea in 2019: plan and orchestrate "pandemics." The 2020 COVID "pandemic" crashed the stock market, then quickly funneled $4 trillion out of the U.S. treasury into the pockets of the people who orchestrated it.

Propaganda platforms kept the population so scared they didn't even know they were being robbed, even though it was in broad daylight and right in front of their eyes. When the stock market hit bottom, people who were already wealthy bought up stocks at bargain prices, causing the stock market to revive, while making trillions of dollars in profits in the process.

Our national debt has skyrocketed to $35 trillion and continues to rise exponentially. Our politicians have done this to us. Our "representatives" have created this obscene debt while pretending to serve their constituents. They are robbing us blind. Who is expected to pay that money back? Our grandchildren?

Who collects the interest on this gargantuan debt, to the tune of a trillion dollars of interest payments per year? Where are those payments going? *Who is pocketing that money?* Imagine being able to rake in a trillion dollars a year by doing nothing at all, just sitting back and gaming the system. A billion is a thousand million dollars. A trillion is a thousand billion dollars.

Imagine if you could rob someone of four trillion dollars in just one year. Our treasury, the money we collect from the working class in the form of taxes, has become a pot to pilfer, to rob, and to be drained by criminal masterminds while we keep on working, keep on paying taxes, and keep on watching our money vanish while we remain distracted, censored, frightened, threatened, entertained, and propagandized by the brainwashing machines. Working people are like cows being milked by billionaires sitting back on their private islands playing us all like a giant video game.

We haven't had the technology to create a random intelligent selection process until now. You can sit on your couch, pull out your phone,

Election Fraud Happens - In Addition
to Widespread Election Rigging

Evidence for this rigging is now ubiquitous. Just recently Congressional investigators discovered emails from the White House to Amazon, requesting, and then getting; the suppression of books negative about the government's response to Covid. Individuals were "shadow banned" and outright banned, from major social media outlets. Twitter, before Elon Musk, was one of the worst offenders, even staffing itself with former government agents. Sounds like something out of Communist China. Former intelligence officials said that the Hunter Biden laptop was "Russian disinformation" while recently the FBI admitted the laptop and its contents were real. The whole "Russia gate" scandal was made up and paid for by Democratic Party operatives and Hillary Clinton. **Mark Zuckerberg gave almost half a billion dollars to pay off local election officials.** The J6 Committee hearings we now know were orchestrated by a former executive for ABC News and evidence on many important issues (such as to what extent Federal agents were involved in manipulating the crowd) have been suppressed.

Users Outraged by Instagram and Threads Limiting Political Content Ahead of Election

Democrats Want To Criminalize Republican Election Challenges

Florida County Supervisor of Elections Placed Under State Oversight for Mail-In Ballot Violations

Osceola County's Mary Jane Arrington has been ordered to stop sending out illegal mail-in ballot envelopes.

41 Times Google Has Interfered in US Elections Since 2008

Data findings show that the number of votes shifted by Google's actions grew from 2.6 million in 2016 to at least 6 million in 2020, a 140 percent increase. Findings in 2016 showed that "Google's search algorithm likely shifted at least 2.6 million votes to Hillary Clinton. Findings further showed that Google's results and get-out-the-vote reminders favored Democrats and shifted the 2020 election results by at least 6 million votes.

AllSides data show that Google's own news site ("Google News") completely eliminated all links to right-leaning media outlets while generously linking to left-leaning media outlets for articles relating to Trump, Biden or "elections," according to its 2022 study. The data are as follows for articles on these topics:

Trump (88% of articles were left-leaning; 0% were right-leaning)

Biden (68% of articles were left-leaning, 0% were right-leaning)

Elections (96% of articles were left-leaning; 0% were right-leaning)

put your feet up, sip a Mexican beer, order a coffee table made in Thailand, and have it at your door within a week. We all have Social Security Administration web pages listing our income, year by year, and our Social Security "benefits." Why not include on that website, or another similar publicly funded service, another section listing pending legislation which we can all review, provide input to, and vote on? All eligible citizens should be able to vote directly on legislation and those votes must be binding. Any taxpaying citizen of eligible age should also be able to propose legislation easily and directly. Then, we the people can control our government, our lives, and our collective pocketbook.

Direct democracy would remove money from legislative politics, eliminate the need for political parties in the houses of representatives, provide equal opportunities for everyone, no matter your gender, your skin color, age, or socio-economic status, and create true democracy for the very first time in the history of the United States.

There's a lot to unpack here, so let's get started.

> We the people are the rightful masters of both Congress and the Courts, not to overthrow the Constitution but to overthrow those who would pervert the Constitution.
>
> Abraham Lincoln

34,000 Illegal 2020 Election Ballots Found in Michigan during Forensic Study

Tens of thousands of illegal ballots have been found in Detroit, Michigan during an explosive criminal forensic study into the 2020 election results.

43,000 Absentee Ballot Votes Counted In DeKalb County 2020 Election Violated Chain Of Custody Rule

43,907 of the 61,731 absentee ballots deposited in drop boxes in the November 2020 presidential election in DeKalb County, Georgia—72 percent—were counted in official tallies certified by the county and the state, despite violating chain of custody requirements set forward in Georgia Emergency Rule 183-1-14-1.8-.14 promulgated by the Georgia State Election Board at its July 1, 2020, meeting.

After Durham: One Crucial Question
How do we keep the FBI out of the next election?

Remember from the Durham report: The entire Russian collusion hoax was a complete fabrication from a Hillary Clinton campaign plan to subvert Donald Trump in 2016. As Mr. Durham reported: "There was never any actual evidence of collusion between the Trump campaign and Russia."

Never. Any. Evidence.

Then, in the next election in 2020, you have all these retired CIA intel types with this Gang of 51 letter that denied the Hunter Biden laptop ever existed and called it a Russian disinformation campaign — even though, of course, the FBI was in possession of the Hunter Biden computer starting in December 2019. And the FBI lied. And the CIA lied.

Utah Election Official Hit with Felony Charges for Illegally Shredding, Mishandling Ballots

A 'Well-Funded Cabal' Influenced the 2020 Election

In a laudatory 2021 article in Time titled "The Secret History of the Shadow Campaign That Saved the 2020 Election," author Molly Ball detailed a "well-funded cabal of powerful people, ranging across industries and ideologies, working together behind the scenes to influence perceptions, change rules and laws, steer media coverage, and control the flow of information."

The "conspiracy," as Ms. Ball described it, included DNC operatives, union leaders, tech and social-media companies, Wall Street bankers, and a network of nonprofit donor funds that pooled hundreds of millions of dollars to finance "armies of poll workers and got millions of people to vote by mail for the first time."

2
Representation by Intelligent Selection

The purpose of the representative is to *represent* their constituency, not to replace them. The constituencies are already established at the federal, state, county, and local levels. Representatives should not vote on behalf of their constituency. Individual representatives should have one vote on any matter, the same as any other citizen.

All citizens who want to exercise their civic duty should vote directly on legislation. It is the responsibility of the representatives to make sure that their constituents are informed of all pending legislation, know how and when to comment on it or to vote on the drafts, and make sure the votes of the citizens are duly recorded, honored, and binding. There would be *no need for people to vote for their representatives*. People would vote directly *on legislation*. The selected representatives, public servants all, make sure this process flows smoothly, legally, and correctly.

Many citizens may not be interested in voting on legislation. It generally holds true that only a minority of people care enough to get involved in organizational affairs, maybe 15%. But the ones who do care are the ones who will make the decisions for the overall group. More citizens will likely become involved over time as they realize that they actually have a vote that means something. The opportunity to get directly involved in legislation should be open to all eligible citizens and that involvement should be easy to execute.

There were 162 million registered voters in the United States in 2022. If only 15% of them voted on legislation, over 24 million people would be weighing in on the issues. This is in contrast to the U.S. House of Representatives, which includes only 535 congresspersons. As mentioned, many in this small group may be ethically compromised due to the grotesque need for financial backing required to run for office. Why should only 535 people make important decisions on war and peace, on how our tax dollars are spent, how much debt we should accumulate, and on other matters that affect 330+ million citizens? Where is *our* say in all of this?

The answer is "nowhere." It doesn't exist! Sure, you can call your representative, big deal. Many of them don't care about their constituents.

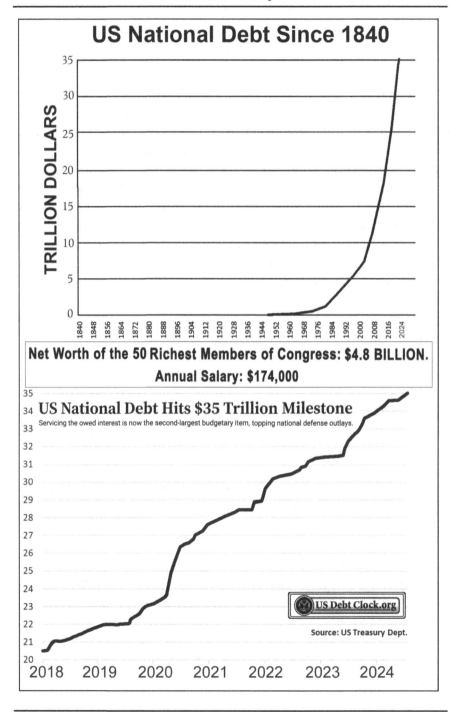

US National Debt Since 1840

TRILLION DOLLARS

Net Worth of the 50 Richest Members of Congress: $4.8 BILLION.
Annual Salary: $174,000

US National Debt Hits $35 Trillion Milestone

Servicing the owed interest is now the second-largest budgetary item, topping national defense outlays.

US Debt Clock.org

Source: US Treasury Dept.

They only care about who is going to fund their reelection campaign. This is the cold, hard, truth. Citizens must stand up and say enough is enough! We need to understand that the current system is obsolete, and we need to amend, evolve, and update our legislative process. All concerned, eligible citizens must be able to vote on legislation. That very idea is enough to scare the crap out of the people currently in power today. Their power would be taken away and placed in the hands of the citizens.

Our national debt is outrageous. Running a government is like running a business, and the people running our government are certainly incompetent, if not utterly corrupt thieves. We're going bankrupt; dollars are flying out of our national bank account like bats out of hell, shoveled into the pockets of the military industrial complex, the medical industrial complex, the censorship industrial complex, the deep state, the shadow government, the black ops, and all the minions who surround them waiting for crumbs to drop at their feet.

As of August 2023, the average monthly social security check was $1,700. People who work all their lives and pay into Social Security can try to live on an annual income of $20,400, which, as of 2024, is classified as poverty level for a family of two. Yet our representatives are only too eager to spend billions of our dollars fueling foreign wars.

Why has the Pentagon never passed a yearly audit? Why can't it account for trillions of dollars in assets? Do we the people really want to be involved in yet another war? The crooks raking in the money certainly do. Why can't we, all of us, vote on it? Do we want political prostitutes to continue to create money-laundering schemes, like foreign wars and public health scams? Let grandma have a vote. Let the people who actually work for a living, unlike career politicians, have a say in how their money is spent. That would be real democracy.

In a direct democracy, representatives would have a variety of important responsibilities. Citizens submit legislation through their representatives. The representatives and their committees are responsible for screening proposed legislation for appropriateness, accuracy, and completeness. Committee members could also be randomly selected from the final pool of initial candidates. Once proposed legislation passes committee review, it is presented to all constituents for review and vote. If the

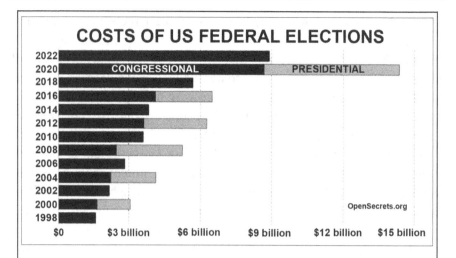

COSTS OF US FEDERAL ELECTIONS

19,000 Dead People Registered to Vote in Virginia, Election Officials Admit

Election officials in Virginia have announced this week that they found 19,000 dead people registered to vote in the state.

"If you want to serve on a committee in Congress, you have to pay for the privilege," wrote Rep. Ken Buck, a Republican from Colorado, in his new book Drain the Swamp: How Washington Corruption is Worse than You Think. *"Committee assignments, then, are less about qualifications than they are about cash — or, to put it another way, cash is the chief qualification you need."*

Local lawmaker: Congressional committees 'all have prices'

WASHINGTON — Rep. Thomas Massie has an unpaid bill for $240,000 sitting on his desk in Washington — a debt GOP leaders say he owes to the House Republicans' campaign operation.

"They told us right off the bat as soon as we get here, 'These committees all have prices and don't pick an expensive one if you can't make the payments'," Massie told The Enquirer. *"That's part of the orientation."* Massie, a Republican who represents Northern Kentucky, has likened the dues system to "extortion."

legislation passes the local level of voting, then it is elevated to a higher level for consideration.

For example, if a county level of proposed legislation passes a county vote, then it is elevated to state level, providing the issue involves the entire state, not just the county. The legislation, if it passes the state level by direct vote of the citizens, then moves on to federal level, and so on. It is the responsibility of the representatives to guide this process.

If proposed legislation does not pass a committee screening, perhaps because it is unconstitutional, it is sent back to the person or group of people who submitted it, to be reviewed, reworked, then resubmitted, or abandoned.

In a direct democracy, representatives can be elevated to higher levels of responsibility, committee chairpersons for example, on a *meritocracy* basis. Currently, access to political committees at the federal level depends on how much money you can pay "the swamp."

Representatives can gain merit points when their constituency succeeds in submitting successful legislation; when they responsibly conduct their duties; when they maintain open contact and communication with their constituency, and so on. They receive demerits when they fail to attend committee meetings, or when they engage in misconduct or collect too many legitimate complaints on record.

In this manner, representatives can truly represent their constituents. Instead, our current representatives are forced to spend much of their time raising money, both for reelection and for committee participation. The money they raise often comes from well-heeled special interests that have business before the committees. This is a conflict of interest that reeks of corruption.

Rep. Zach Wamp (R-TN), who was the top member of two subcommittees on the House Appropriations Committee during his eight terms in Congress, stated: *"The current 'party dues' system is a recipe for corruption that disconnects members of Congress from their constituents. The current 'dues' system puts legislators under immense pressure to make appeals to special interests to gain and maintain their committee assignments. The factors that determine who serves on which congressional committees should include your expertise, passion, and experience — not just how dedicated you are to raising money."*

Thousands of Votes in 2020 Election Misreported, Virginia Officials Say

Problem stemmed from a failure to properly program result tapes, officials say

"The harsh truth is that our elections are extremely vulnerable to attack: Forty-two states use voter registration databases that are more than a decade old. Laughably, in 2019, some still use Windows 2000 and Windows XP. Twelve states still use paperless machines, meaning there's no paper trail to verify vote counts. Some states don't require post-election audits. And ten states don't train election officials to deal with cybersecurity threats."

Elizabeth Warren

LOS ANGELES COUNTY

The team at electionfraud20.org, a collective of software developers, data scientists, and engineers who study election system vulnerabilities, say that Los Angeles county's network diagram shows that "you are giving massive back-door access to all the critical election subsystems that are required to rig the election, in a way that no one will ever notice. And you are giving it to Chinese developers."

"If PollChief is compromised, this diagram shows that the whole election management system is compromised."

In that case, one can easily imagine why Los Angeles prosecutors allege that "astounding" amounts of data were breached in what is "probably the largest data breach in United States history."

According to IssueOne.org, *"The exact amount of money that members of Congress are expected to raise is secret, albeit a secret that occasionally leaks to the public. In 2017, conservative Rep. Ken Buck (R-CO) published a book that said chairs of the most powerful House committees were expected to raise $1.2 million apiece over two years for the National Republican Congressional Committee (NRCC) — and that the Republican House Speaker was expected to raise $20 million."*

Instead of a handful of wealthy individuals voting on behalf of everyone else, men and women 18 years of age and older who are citizens of the United States and who pay taxes, should be able to vote on legislation if they choose to do so. Instead of a small group of wealthy elitists passing legislation that primarily benefits a small group of wealthy elitists, the common people and the working class should have the final word.

Want to be a representative? There will be a place to opt in on your Federal, State, and Local tax returns. Being a representative is a serious and important public service that will require an established number of years of commitment. The terms will vary according to the position for which you have been selected. Federal congressional representatives will serve four years. Federal senators will serve six years. State, County, and Local representatives will serve according to the requirements of their location. Opting in is entirely voluntary. You will be notified via email or mail if your name has been selected in the first draft. You can select "Federal," "State," "County," or "Local," or all of the above.

The first round of elimination takes place when you opt in. This level screens out people who do not pay taxes, as well as those people who are not interested in serving as representatives, for whatever reason. You may want to be a representative, but are unable due to health reasons, family commitments, business obligations, or any of a host of justifications for choosing to opt out. Your circumstances can change from time to time; therefore, you may want to opt in on a future tax return.

A rough estimate of people who are inclined to opt in is about 5% of taxpayers; 95% would have little or no interest or have circumstances that make it impossible for them to devote years to a government position. However, the position doesn't have to be a full-time job, thereby allowing representatives to maintain a part-time commitment to a business, family,

'The Government Is Not Our Friend': Founder of True the Vote Discusses Being Targeted by FBI, IRS

"There was a time when citizens getting responsibly involved in supporting civic engagement would be a good thing. That would be a thing we should aspire to, and tell our kids they should do," Engelbrecht said. "Instead, it's being used as a weapon to silence people. It's government as a weapon, she says. "I have steeled myself with the acceptance that yes, everything we do is being watched–that privacy is an illusion–and that the government is not our friend."

Court Orders Release of True the Vote Leaders From Jail

Engelbrecht and Phillips were imprisoned on Oct. 31 after U.S. District Judge Kenneth Hoyt, a Reagan appointee, found them in contempt of court for not revealing the identities of people who allegedly accessed information from Konnech, a Michigan-based election management software company whose founder was recently arrested for allegedly stealing poll worker data and hosting it

CEO of election software firm Konnech charged with grand theft by embezzlement

The election software CEO who picked up more than a quarter-million dollars from Michigan Economic Development Corp. funding is facing theft and embezzlement charges in addition to accusations of putting poll worker personal information on a Chinese server. Eugene Yu, founder and CEO of Konnech, Inc., was arrested with extradition to Los Angeles County pending on Oct. 5.

Plaintiffs Ask Judge to Find Benson in Contempt of Court for Failing to Correct Election Guidance Manual

2020 Election Rigged 7 Months in Advance, Investigation Finds

Bombshell evidence has emerged to reveal that the 2020 election on was rigged with a sophisticated and well planned campaign that started 7 months in advance.

Censorship expert Mike Benz made a damning case on *Tucker Carlson Uncensored* that the **rig** was in for the 2020 election **seven months** ahead of time.

This involved, as Benz described, "**a government-coordinated mass censorship campaign** spanning every single social media platform on earth in order to **pre-censor** the ability to dispute the legitimacy of mail-in ballots."

"We should never forget that the Constitution wasn't written to restrain citizen's behavior it was written to restrain the government's behavior."
-Rand Paul

farm, or other natural obligation that citizens may not want to abandon. Much of the work of representatives can be done remotely.

Representatives won't be wasting any time trying to raise money for reelection. Instead, representatives will be devoting *all* of their time doing their job. They will receive government paychecks and benefits just like representatives receive today. Their terms will be automatically limited because there will be no elections. Representatives will be selected on a schedule. There can be no "career politicians" in such a legislative body.

At the federal level, 150 million tax returns are likely to be submitted annually, providing about 7.5 million (5%) potential volunteer candidates. This selection process is color blind, free of racism, ageism, sexism, and any other form of discrimination; is not related to any political party; is not influenced by money; does not require any candidate to run for office; eliminates campaign finance issues; eliminates voter machines, ballot stuffing, dead voters, senile voters, corrupt election workers, election malfeasance, election propaganda, election censorship, and the entire host of ills now infecting the American electoral process.

Out of the 7.5 million potential candidates at the federal level, a specified number are randomly selected for further consideration. For example, let's assume 0.1% are randomly selected, or 7,500 candidates. This is your randomly selected candidate base. The percentage selected must be enough to provide representatives and staff for every constituency and could vary depending on the government level and location.

This random selection would likely yield approximately half men and half women. Party affiliation, skin color, sexual orientation, physical disabilities, religious association, level of wealth, and all such things are irrelevant and would play no role in the selection process. Every tax-paying citizen who willfully volunteers is randomly selected according to his or her Social Security number. They all would have an equal opportunity.

Of the 7,500 candidates, additional elimination occurs when incarcerated persons, underage persons, persons not residing in the United States, non-citizens, and other limiting factors are applied. The remaining candidates are informed of their consideration, provided with a detailed outline of the responsibilities they will be required to assume, and are given an opportunity to opt out, no questions asked. It is quite likely

20% of Voters Admit to Mail-In Ballot Fraud in 2020 Election, Poll Shows

An eye-opening new poll has found roughly 20 percent of voters admit that they committed mail-in ballot fraud during the 2020 elections.

US And UK Military Contractors Created Sweeping Plan For Global Censorship In 2018, New Documents Show

Whistleblower makes trove of new documents available showing the birth of the Censorship Industrial Complex

New York Times Election Report Reveals 104,984 Stolen Votes in Ga, 347,768 in PA

5,000 Duplicate Ballots Sent to California Voters in Riverside County

Voter Fraud Convictions Challenge Narrative of Secure Elections

Criminal convictions of election fraud across America have called into question the narrative that cheating is rare and of little impact.

Mystery Swirls Over Batch of Thousands of 2020 Voter Registration Forms in Michigan

States reportedly run out of ballots

With several states turning out to vote in full force Tuesday, the Internet was abuzz with reports that some areas were running out of ballots before polls closed. With some calling it a conspiracy, people on Twitter wondered how it could be possible to run out of ballots on an election night.

that a significant proportion of the candidates will opt out at this time.

The remaining candidates must then undergo a testing procedure. Why would anyone be considered eligible for a role in government as a representative without any background, education, or knowledge in government operations? A comprehensive competency test must be administered to prospective representatives regarding government operations as well as basic language skills, civic knowledge, the U.S. Constitution, laws and statutes, the legislative process, computer skills, communication skills, the executive branch, the judicial branch, and other details relating to a potential role working in a legislative body.

This is the next round of elimination. Persons whose test results are in the top percentages remain eligible as candidates. Finally, there would be a random selection of these top candidates, with a percentage selected as backup candidates in the event a selected candidate would be unable to perform his or her duties, plus additional backup candidates to fill committee seats or for staff personnel.

Now we have truly democratic houses of representatives. All are randomly selected, approximately half are women, all have been tested and have exhibited a high level of competency, none have been selected based on financial backing, party affiliation, level of wealth, skin color, gender, or any other irrelevant factor.

These representatives are reflections of their constituents. The house of representatives would reflect the makeup of the population. It would not be mostly wealthy, white men, as has been customary. Nor would it be made up of people installed by special interests, billionaires, globalists, war mongers, or any industrial complex. We would have representation that would truly, and for the first time ever, let the people decide!

Representatives could not be bribed to vote one way or another, as is commonplace today. Why? Because representatives have only one vote. The constituency votes, then the representative reports *that* vote, with oversight from other, randomly selected assistants and co-workers. There would be very little wiggle room to insert fraud and corruption, and certainly any cracks, once identified, would be sealed up quickly!

Muskegon Voter Registration Probe: Michigan Election Integrity Group Wants to Know What Happened

Milwaukee DA Ignores 354 Referrals for Possible Registration Fraud From 2020 Election

"Campaign Finance Mules" UNEMPLOYED Missouri Donors Exposed Who Made Thousands of Donations Totaling Hundreds of Thousands of Dollars

Data analyst Chris Gleason came out with a new report on the millions of dollars in donations sent to Democrat candidates across the country in the most recent election cycle.

According to Chris, "Steven in Missouri" made **14,111 political donations** totaling **$180,727.97** in the last two years.

And Steven is UNEMPLOYED.

Chris said, "When I noticed this "generous donor" I was taken aback by the number of times that he donated. By far this was the most amount of "Times Donated" that I have found thus far in the states that I have looked into."

Steven from Missouri donated on average **19 times a day**.

Georgia Officials Sued Over Unsent Absentee Ballots

As hundreds waited to vote in Houston, a dozen -plus polling sites ran out of ballot sheets

Judge Orders Voting Machines to Be Opened Following Mistake by Poll Worker

A judge in Monmouth County, N.J., ordered two voting machines to be opened following the poll worker's error. The New Jersey Globe reported that the incident occurred in the town of Manalapan. Deputy Attorney General George Cohen noted on Thursday that the unnamed poll worker "inadvertently failed to get vote results" before sealing the machines, the Washington Examiner reported.

A major Arizona county ran out of ballots during primary voting. Republicans are now demanding the election director resign.

3

Let the People Decide

Democracy, described in a nutshell, means "let the people decide." Yet, democracy is dying a hasty death right before our eyes. Globalists want to rid the world of the U.S. Constitution, everything it represents, and all the rights it enshrines. They took a stab at it with a so-called "pandemic" in 2020, stripping societies around the world of the rights that Americans consider inalienable: freedom of speech, freedom of assembly, freedom of religion, freedom from unreasonable searches and seizures, replacing them with forced drug injections, home detention, forced face coverings, brutal police and military repression, censorship, propaganda, seizure of bank accounts, credit cards, property, and so on. And many people let them do it.

The Schwabites famously stated, *"You will own nothing, and you will be happy."* The rest of the statement can be assumed: *"We, on the other hand, will own everything, and we will be even happier."* Global elites represent a new world order where liberty and basic human rights, individualism, free speech, independent thought, "life, liberty, and the pursuit of happiness" are replaced with obedience and conformity. A handful of billionaires want to decide the fate of humanity. Their ability to hoard material wealth has given them the opinion that they know what's best for the rest of the world — the other 99.999% of the population.

Karl Marx and Friedrich Engels famously published *The Communist Manifesto* in 1848, a publication that had a massive effect on humanity worldwide for many generations. In the mid-1800s, people faced the same sort of challenges we are plagued with today, such as an incredible disparity of wealth, with most human wealth concentrated in the hands of a tiny number of people. That wealth concentration creates a massive power concentration. Wealthy people can have their own security forces, armies of lawyers, unlimited financial resources, sometimes coupled with the absence of a moral compass. Marx and Engels came up with a solution: eliminate private property. This would, they assumed, get rid of the tyrants and create equality among all people.

Communism's efforts to abolish private property proved to be its

Indicted Virginia Election Official 'Altered Election Results': Filing

Alteration caused false reporting of results, according to prosecutors.

Federal Budget Deficit Suddenly Doubles, Signaling Disaster

As a result, the government now faces an epic fiscal disaster with no solution. And the public is so angry at the government in general that appetites are very high just to let the whole thing default rather than go through another round of tax increases or inflation to deal with it.

Group Releases Analysis of Pinal County's 2022 Election, Finds 'Deliberate Malfeasance,' Concludes Election Should Not Have Been Certified

The CONELRAD Group **found "malfeasance, incompetence, and possible criminal activity" in their review of the 2022 election in Pinal County.** The team of mostly former intelligence and military officers located primarily in southern Arizona concluded in a new report sent to *The Arizona Sun Times* on Wednesday, "Evidence was clearly identified that should have led to an immediate halt to certifying the General Election."

"It is our opinion that the entire legal system in Arizona may be compromised. From the State Bar attacking the law license of Brian Blehm, to the entire judicial system of Arizona dismissing election integrity cases, **this appears to be a coordinated effort to intimidate and block any BOS [board of supervisor] elected official attempting to verify our election system via hand counts, or any election integrity transparency at all," he said.** "All cases being blocked and shut down via 'lawfare' in the courts and by county attorneys ... All avenues of redress are being shut down."

More than 100 Lancaster County mail-in ballots tossed after postal service delay

Several Lancaster County voters are trying to get answers from the U.S. Postal Service about why their mail-in ballots, all postmarked Oct. 30 in Harrisburg, did not arrive at the county elections office until two weeks later. Since the ballots were not received by the deadline – 8 p.m. on Election Day, Nov. 7 – they were tossed out.

Democracy Lost: A Report on the Fatally Flawed 2016 Democratic Primaries

Election Justice USA | ElectionJusticeUSA.org | ElectionJusticeUSA@gmail.com

Alba and Chloe's stories are just two of thousands of reports of voter registration tampering, purging, or obstruction recorded by Election Justice USA (EJUSA). Many cases in EJUSA's database are supported by registration records, emails to and from officials, phone records, or affidavit testimony. Available evidence from Arizona, New York, and California suggests more than 500,000 registrations were tampered with or improperly handled. While Ms. Guerrero was allowed to vote, hundreds of thousands of voters were denied the right to vote or were forced to vote provisionally. A quarter million or more provisional or affidavit Democratic ballots were not counted. Available evidence also suggests that the vast majority of suppressed voters would have voted or tried to vote for Senator Bernie Sanders.

downfall. Human nature must be taken into consideration. People want their own homes. They want private property — and they don't want it taken away from them, certainly not by the government. The government exists to serve the people. It is a tool *for* the people, not a weapon to be used *against* it.

Marx and Engels would have been better advised to demand a *limit* to private property, like a limit to driving speeds on a highway. If you drive too fast, you endanger other drivers. If you hoard too much material wealth, you endanger society, because you can easily bribe and/or threaten senators, congresspersons, judges, police officers, governors, mayors, universities, churches, medical institutions, government agencies, and anyone in a position of authority who can be persuaded with a big enough bribe, perhaps hidden as an endowment, campaign contribution, or grant.

A limit to wealth would have muted the power of the kings, queens, royalty, czars, sultans, and other obscenely wealthy individuals, families, and oligarchs. Hard-working commoners would better be able to reap the rewards of their hard work. Farmers don't need kings; they need shovels. When a king takes their shovels, thoughts of revolution will foment in the minds of the masses.

It was 100 years after the Communist Manifesto when George Orwell published a veiled condemnation of communism in his dystopian social science fiction novel and cautionary tale *1984*, published in 1949. Orwell focused on totalitarianism, mass surveillance, government repression, human regimentation, mass obedience, government-imposed censorship, government-controlled media with massive propaganda campaigns, and other ills spawned in an authoritarian state. His novel imagines what communism would become if it were allowed to be carried to fruition.

Fast forward to the 2020s. The global elites have come up with a new plan: eliminate private property for everyone, as Marx and Engels had suggested, but make an exception for the already rich. Then allow a tiny fraction of the population, the wealthy elite, to control the world through mandates, dictates, and edicts.

They would achieve this plan in a number of ways:

1. They would convince the populace that government-mandated drug injections are in the people's best interests. Those injections can in-

Georgia Investigating 17,000 Missing Ballot Images from 2020 Presidential Election

The Georgia State Board of Elections (SEB) is investigating the bombshell discovery of 17,000 missing ballot images from the 2020 presidential election in the state.
The investigation was launched after "2020 recount violations" were exposed.

Watchdog Groups Allege Election Violations in Florida's 2022 and 2020 Elections

A grassroots group presented evidence to Florida election officials and law enforcement last week showing that almost 1,100 mail-in ballots in one county were cast from undeliverable addresses in the state's Aug. 23 primary election.

Pennsylvania Settles Election Integrity Lawsuit, Deletes 178,000 Names From Voter Rolls

Pennsylvania has settled a federal election integrity lawsuit, saying that it has removed more than 178,000 ineligible voter registrations and promising greater transparency in its future housekeeping efforts.

Wisconsin Voter Roll Contains 350,000 Errors, Alleges Watchdog Group

More than 350,000 informational data points on Wisconsin's state voter roll are alleged to be inaccurate, according to a citizen activist.

D.C. Forced to Purge Over 100,000 Ineligible Names from Voter Rolls

Washington D.C. officials have been compelled to comply with legal threats from a judicial watchdog and is now purging its voter rolls of over 100,000 ineligible names.

"We sent notice letters to election officials in the District of Columbia, California, and Illinois, notifying them of evident violations of the National Voter Registration Act(NVRA) of 1993, based on their failure to remove inactive voters from their registration rolls," Judicial Watch announced on Friday.

"In response to our inquiries, Washington, DC, officials admitted that they had not complied with the NVRA, promptly removed 65,544 outdated names from the voting rolls, promised to remove 37,962 more, and designated another 73,522 registrations as 'inactive'," the announcement noted.

Missing Ballots Found in New Jersey County

Ballot paper shortage could cause problems on Election Day

PHOENIX -- A paper supply crunch is testing the preparedness of U.S. election officials and exposing a key vulnerability in America's democratic process as midterm voting gets underway. The 2022 election cycle will use an estimated 30 million pounds of paper, according to industry experts. Soaring demand and a shortage of manufacturers during the pandemic have pinched national stockpiles, leaving little room for error.

clude genetically altering drugs designed to change the DNA of humans, thereby allowing the elites to control the behavior of the masses, such as by making them more conforming and obedient, or by shortening their lives.

The drug injections could be designed to introduce specific nefarious factors into human bodies on a mass scale unlike anything ever envisioned in the history of the human species. Cancer-causing genes can be injected into human blood streams, as can biochemical factors that can cause sudden heart failure or other forms of "time-released death" for the purpose of thinning out the human population, thereby eliminating the "useless people" and anyone else deemed expendable by those in control.

2. The elite can eliminate free speech, arresting anyone who dares to counter their agenda, while blocking and censoring, even murdering anyone who promotes or provides an alternative viewpoint. The official narrative is broadcast constantly on "mainstream propaganda" outlets. Public protests against the crimes of the ruling class will be outlawed and the protestors arrested, charged, and imprisoned as "domestic terrorists," which is already happening just as Orwell had predicted.

3. The elites can block access to anyone's monetary property — bank accounts, credit cards, and so on, while imposing a digital currency that only they control, rendering cash obsolete and worthless.

4. The wealthy minority can and will confiscate private property, including family farmland owned and farmed for generations.

5. They can and will round up resisters and herd them into impoundments.

6. They will ban all forms of self-defense that could allow citizens to protect themselves against government tyranny, especially personal firearms.

7. They will attempt to eliminate the core and fundamental foundation of humanity — the family, by confusing the lines between genders, stripping mothers and fathers of their parental rights, and encouraging men to "identify" as girls and compete in women's sports, among other things.

8. The elites will justify their agenda as "saving the Earth." They will ban grandma from using her gas-fired kitchen stove to cook her holiday

Hacking the Vote: It's Easier Than You Think

Professor J. Alex Halderman made a career studying electronic voting security.

"I know America's voting machines are vulnerable. . . because my colleagues and I have hacked them — repeatedly — as part of a decade of research. We've created attacks that can spread from machine to machine like a computer virus and silently change election outcomes. We studied touch screens and optical scan systems. And in every single case, we found ways for attackers to sabotage machines and to steal votes. These capabilities are certainly within reach for America's enemies."

BREAKING: Yesterday in court, Michigan University professor & voting machine expert J. Alex Halderman hacked into a Dominion voting machine & changed vote totals while only using a pen IN FRONT OF THE JUDGE   George

@LauraLoomer. To get the endorsement of Yass' PAC for PA governor, I was asked to renounce Trump. I refused. After I won the primary, the Yass controlled PAC withheld $10 million from my gubernatorial and undercut my fundraising, ensuring a democrat victory. Doug Mastriano

Investigation Reveals How CCP Interfered in US Election

The Chinese regime interfered in the U.S. 2022 midterm elections through various means, according to a declassified intelligence report and multiple private-sector investigations.

A declassified assessment published by the director of national intelligence (DNI) in December 2023 found that the regime tried to "influence" U.S. congressional elections involving both Democrats and Republicans who espoused tough-on-China policy stances.

Government Suppressed, Censored Concerns Over Mail-In Voting in 2020

The Cybersecurity and Infrastructure Security Agency knew mail-in voting was less secure ahead of the 2020 election but worked to suppress that information

Multiple Errors Found in Virginia's 2022 Election Scanner and Pollbook Data

At Least Two Precincts Showed Different Physical Ballot Count Compared to Scanner Counts

Non-profit electoral process group calls for a full audit of precincts with discrepancies before Commonwealth of Virginia certifies local and statewide election results.

turkey while they fly around the world in private jets having meetings on how to further mold humanity to their liking.

9. The elites will promote wars, which are ultimate transgressions against planet Earth and against all of us. Wars are grievous, destructive, polluting attacks of insanity that gobble up and destroy natural resources while the rich get richer and everyone else pays for it with their tax money, with their health, or with their lives.

10. The elites will infiltrate governments at all levels. They will buy congressmen, senators, judges, governors, state prosecutors, assemblymen, "health" officials, military leaders, and members of parliament. They will rig elections, and when they count the "votes," they will win.

With their selected representatives in position, their mainstream propaganda apparatus well oiled, the population thoroughly intimidated, scared, obedient, and conforming, the success of their agenda will be virtually certain. We are seeing all of this occurring right before our eyes in the 2020s.

But there is a way out of this mess: Government representatives can be randomly selected; they don't have to be elected. This bears repeating: We no longer need to pick our representatives by election. It's not 1776. We have the technological ability to do better, much better. We can revolutionize humanity. We don't need to ban private property. We don't need to allow tyranny to fester among us like a cancer. We don't have to tolerate authoritarian rule. We can craft truly democratic representation.

Through random selection a number would be selected, not a person. A number has no skin color, no gender, no ethnicity, no age, no way to be considered racist, sexist, ageist, or discriminatory in any manner. A person's eligibility for random selection is by *voluntarily* checking a box on their income tax return. Citizens will be able to vote directly on legislation. Citizens will also be able to directly introduce legislation. Representatives will not vote on our behalf. They would, as esteemed, respected, well-paid public servants, coordinate and organize our votes and our legislation, while casting their own single vote as they see fit.

On matters of importance to the people, the people would decide. That's how it should be. That's how we eliminate tyranny. That's how we protect our freedoms. That's how we preserve all that is sacred to us.

That's how we cultivate a common set of values that we fiercely defend to our deaths. And we do this in the United States by building upon our existing foundation: the United States Constitution.

In 1776, the population of the entire United States was less than the population of Toledo, Ohio today. In 1776, without cars, electricity, Internet, or advanced technology, and with such a small population, a "Constitutional Republic" made sense. It was a revolutionary leap away from the rule of kings. It was a successful model that suited the times and it worked. But it has become obsolete. By clinging to an outdated, anachronistic mode of governing, we are creating a monster. And that monster will devour us if we don't get it under control.

But "true democracy" is the same thing as "mob rule." Such were the sentiments in the late 1700s when blacks were slaves and women were denied the right to vote. At that time, democracy posed a threat to the ruling white, male, property owners. Do "we the people" constitute a mob in the present time? Of course not.

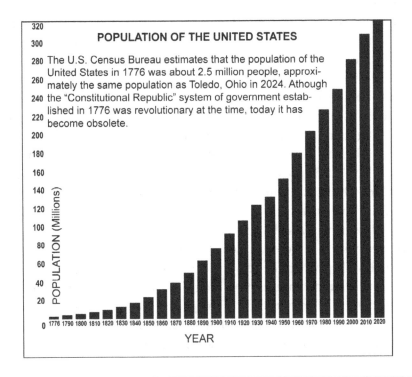

POPULATION OF THE UNITED STATES

The U.S. Census Bureau estimates that the population of the United States in 1776 was about 2.5 million people, approximately the same population as Toledo, Ohio in 2024. Athough the "Constitutional Republic" system of government established in 1776 was revolutionary at the time, today it has become obsolete.

4

The Mutants vs the Rest of Us

"If you shut up truth and bury it under the ground, it will but grow, and gather to itself such explosive power that the day it bursts through it will blow up everything in its way."
Émile Zola

Was it a genetic mutation or is it simply human nature to crave excess material wealth? Theoretically, a subset of humans, through a genetic mutation, developed a "greed gene," which made them dissatisfied with whatever number of possessions they had managed to hoard. Wealth is acquired by these humans in any way possible, often by force, robbery, pillaging, corruption, and violence. As their material wealth increases, so does their power. They share their wealth with others — soldiers, police, thugs, death squads, to help them engage in more pillaging, thereby increasing their wealth further and gaining even more power and influence.

In time, these genetically mutated people and their families become dynasties, kingdoms, rulers, oligarchs, and criminal kingpins, leeching off the common folk to enrich themselves. This is a complicated issue that has plagued humanity for eons, greatly simplified here for brevity.

The Declaration of the Rights of Man

Eventually, the common folk rebel. The French revolution in the late 1700s resulted in the massacre of nobles, the abolishment of the monarchy, and the establishment of a republic, leading to *The Declaration of the Rights of Man and of the Citizen* in 1789 by the National Assembly.

To summarize, this declaration states the following:

1. People are free and equal in respect of their rights.

2. Natural rights include liberty, property, security, and resistance of oppression.

What Did The W.E.F Mean By: "You Will Own Nothing And Be Happy, By 2030"

The collaboration between the World Health Organization (WHO) and the World Economic Forum (WEF) in shaping the global agenda for 2030 has sparked intense debates and speculation. This partnership, aimed at "addressing global health challenges" and "fostering economic development" has raised eyebrows due to the inclusion of controversial statements such as "You will own nothing and you will be happy."

'You'll Own Nothing'—and Like It. Or Will You?

The much-circulated slogan "You will own nothing, and you will be happy" was coined by Danish MP Ida Auken in 2016 and included in a 2016 essay published by the purveyors of the so-called "Great Reset" at the World Economic Forum (WEF) headquartered in Davos, Switzerland. It is, of course, only half true. Nonetheless, the phrase is certainly apt and should be taken seriously. For once the Great Reset has been put in place, we will indeed own nothing except our compelled compliance.

What the %!@- happend in Pennsylvania... AGAIN?

In the 2022 Gubernatorial Election, my amazing Director of Data and Analytics for Audit The Vote PA, Vico Bertogli, noticed an anomaly on the Department of State's website around 8:30pm. Democrat candidate, Josh Shapiro, had been awarded over 10M mail-in ballots while Republican candidate, Doug Mastriano, was given 2M mail-in ballots. The problem with those reported numbers is that Pennsylvania only has 9M registered voters statewide.

In Georgia, 19,000 ballots were counted from a single Zuckerberg dropbox over one weekend, but surveillance shows only 24 people dropping off ballots.

Is the Electoral Fix Already In?

*The malady now exposed is this: **the elites have lost faith in representative democracy**. To smash the nightmare image of themselves that Trump evokes, they are willing to twist and force our system until it breaks... The implications are clear. Not only Trump, but the nearly 75 million Americans who voted for him, must be silenced and crushed.*

Alachua County precincts ran out of Republican ballots on election day

Soros Vows to Focus on Defeating Trump in 2024, Warns 'MAGA-Style Victory' Will 'Undermine' Globalism

3. Liberty consists in the power of doing whatever does not injure another.

4. Law is an expression of the will of the community. All citizens have a right to concur, either personally, or by their representatives, in its formation. It should be the same to all, whether it protects or punishes.

5. No person should be accused, arrested, or held in confinement, except in cases determined by the law, and according to the forms which it has prescribed.

6. Every person is presumed innocent until he or she has been convicted.

7. No person should be molested on account of his or her opinions, even religious opinions.

8. Every citizen may speak, write, and publish freely, provided he or she is responsible for any abuse of this liberty.

9. A public security force is instituted for the benefit of the community.

10. Taxes are to be divided equally among the members of the community, according to their abilities.

11. Every citizen has a right to a free voice in determining the necessity of taxes, their appropriation, and their account, mode of assessment, and duration.

12. The right to property is inviolable and sacred.

The U.S. Bill of Rights

These basic rights and liberties are reflected in the Bill of Rights of the U.S. Constitution, ratified two years later, by three-fourths of the state legislatures on December 15, 1791. The U.S. Constitution has 27 Amendments, the first 10 of which constitute the Bill of Rights and relate to personal and individual rights. Over 11,000 other amendments have been proposed, but not ratified. Existing amendments are summarized here:

DOJ Conceals Records About Biden's Use Of Federal Agencies To Influence Elections

The Department of Justice (DOJ) is concealing key documents related to President Joe Biden's March 2021 order that directed executive agencies to develop plans for federal interference in state election administration.

Chicago Board of Elections 'Mistakenly' Left Out Over 9,000 Mail-In Ballots in Primary Election

An official at the Chicago Board of Elections said he mistakenly failed to count over 9,000 ballots in a state's attorney race in the primary election.

Judge Tosses Challenge, Upholds Law Allowing 'Noncitizens' to Vote in DC

The plaintiffs failed to demonstrate 'that they have personally been subjected to any sort of disadvantage as individual voters,' the judge said.

Court Strikes Down Law That Let Noncitizens Vote in New York Elections

An appeals court has declared a New York law that allowed noncitizens to vote in local elections as unconstitutional.

Citizens Urged to Prepare as 2024 Election Riot Season Draws Near

As the 2024 election draws near, many are expecting corporate media outlets to be dominated by reports of widespread rioting in Democrat-led cities across the country.

74 Harvesting and Mule Rings: Where They Were, How They Did It, And The Impact Our Work is Now Corroborated

The reader must understand that these organized crime cells, under cover of mask and darkness of night, harvested and trafficked ballots across county (and even country) and state lines with impunity, warping the electoral landscape to an unrecognizable state and permanently damaging the national attitude toward the electoral process.

Documentary Exposes Rise of the Unaccountable Fourth Branch of Government, Rule by Experts

A new documentary film attempting to throw light on the rise of government power wielded by unelected experts--known today as the fourth branch of government or the administrative state--launched online on Jan. 27. This unaccountable administrative state, which is reined in at the margins by the courts from time to time, is why laws today largely come from administrative agencies, not from elected lawmakers responsible to voters.

1st: Congress shall make no law respecting an establishment of religion or prohibiting the free exercise thereof; or abridging the freedom of speech, or of the press; or the right of the people peaceably to assemble, and to petition the Government for a redress of grievances.

2nd: A well-regulated Militia, being necessary to the security of a free State, the right of the people to keep and bear Arms, shall not be infringed.

3rd: No Soldier shall, in time of peace be quartered in any house, without the consent of the Owner, nor in time of war, but in a manner to be prescribed by law.

4th: The right of the people to be secure in their persons, houses, papers, and effects, against unreasonable searches and seizures, shall not be violated, and no Warrants shall issue, but upon probable cause, supported by Oath or affirmation, and particularly describing the place to be searched, and the persons or things to be seized.

5th: No person shall be held to answer for a capital, or otherwise infamous crime, unless on a presentment or indictment of a Grand Jury, except in cases arising in the land or naval forces, or in the Militia, when in actual service in time of War or public danger; nor shall any person be subject for the same offence to be twice put in jeopardy of life or limb; nor shall be compelled in any criminal case to be a witness against himself, nor be deprived of life, liberty, or property, without due process of law; nor shall private property be taken for public use, without just compensation.

6th: In all criminal prosecutions, the accused shall enjoy the right to a speedy and public trial, by an impartial jury of the State and district wherein the alleged crime has been committed, which district shall have been previously ascertained by law, and to be informed of the nature and cause of the accusation; to be confronted with the witnesses against him; to have compulsory process for obtaining witnesses in his favor, and to have the Assistance of Counsel for his defense.

7th: In Suits at common law, where the value in controversy shall exceed twenty dollars, the right of trial by jury shall be preserved, and no fact tried by a jury,

Bill Gates Says He Needs to Own 4 Private Jets Because He's 'The Solution' to 'Climate Change'

Billionaire globalist Bill Gates has defended his jet-setting lifestyle by arguing that he needs to own four private jets because he's "the solution" to "saving the planet" from "climate change."

Ex-Wikipedia Co-Founder Says Site Hijacked by US Intelligence for 'Info Warfare'

Wikipedia co-founder, Lawrence Mark Sanger, has accused U.S. intelligence agencies of manipulating the online encyclopedia for nearly two decades. In an interview with Pulitzer Prize-winning investigative journalist Glenn Greenwald, Sanger claimed that Wikipedia had become a tool of "control" in the hands of the U.S. establishment, which includes the CIA, FBI, and other intelligence agencies. "We do have evidence that ... even as early as ... 2008 ... that CIA and FBI computers were used to edit Wikipedia," Sanger stated during the interview.

Arizona County Refuses To Certify Election Results, Threatening A GOP House Win

A Turning Point for the World's Elite?

The annual conference of the World Economic Forum in Davos has always been a high-profile event, bringing together the so-called 'Communist Elite' of the global economic scene. This year, however, the atmosphere was markedly different. Amidst the usual planning and discussions, there was a palpable sense of fear among the elite - a fear that their grip on global affairs might be loosening.

1. The Elite's Fear of Losing Control
Recent developments have suggested that the global elite is concerned about losing power.
2. The Backlash Against Davos Ideologies
The ideologies championed at Davos have faced pushback, particularly in America and Europe.
3. The Evaporating Consensus and Voter Sentiment
Despite attempts to maintain control through institutional capture, especially in the financial sector, the elite's influence seems to be waning.
4. Signs of a Shift in Elite Perspectives
Interestingly, some key figures within the elite circle appear to be reevaluating their stance.

Milwaukee Officials Sued in Zuckerberg Related Election Bribery Case

Facebook 'Fact Checker' Caught Running Political Censorship Operation to Manipulate Voters

shall be otherwise re-examined in any Court of the United States, than according to the rules of the common law.

8th: Excessive bail shall not be required, nor excessive fines imposed, nor cruel and unusual punishments inflicted.

9th: The enumeration in the Constitution of certain rights, shall not be construed to deny or disparage others retained by the people.

10th: The powers not delegated to the United States by the Constitution, nor prohibited by it to the States, are reserved to the States respectively, or to the people.

11th (1795): The Judicial power of the U.S. shall not be construed to extend to any suit in law or equity, commenced or prosecuted against one of the States by Citizens of another State, or by Citizens or Subjects of any Foreign State.

12th (1804): The Electors shall meet in their respective states and vote by ballot for President and Vice-President…

13th (1865): Neither slavery nor involuntary servitude, except as a punishment for crime whereof the party shall have been duly convicted, shall exist within the United States, or any place subject to their jurisdiction.

14th (1868): All persons born or naturalized in the United States, and subject to the jurisdiction thereof, are citizens of the United States and of the State wherein they reside…

15th (1870): The right of citizens of the United States to vote shall not be denied or abridged by the United States or by any State on account of race, color, or previous condition of servitude.

16th (1913): The Congress shall have power to lay and collect taxes on incomes, from whatever source derived, without apportionment among the several States, and without regard to any census or enumeration.

Sen Johnson: FBI's Sabotage of Hunter Biden Laptop Story Was 'Preplanned'

Republican Senator Ron Johnson (R-WI) has revealed that the FBI was aware of the Hunter Biden laptop story way before it first emerged and had "preplanned" a sabotage effort for when it surfaced.

Speaking during a Monday interview with Newsmax, Sen. Johnson said the FBI illegally colluded with the Democrats in the run-up to the 2020 election to help Joe Biden's campaign.

Johnson said agents had a sabotage plan in place so they could quickly bury reports on Hunter's "Laptop from Hell" should they emerge before election day.

> "YOU NEVER CHANGE THINGS BY FIGHTING THE EXISTING REALITY. TO CHANGE SOMETHING, BUILD A NEW MODEL THAT MAKES THE EXISTING MODEL OBSOLETE."
>
> Buckminster Fuller

Legal Foundation Sues New York City to Keep Non-Citizens from Voting in Municipal Elections

Box of 2020 Election Absentee Ballots Found Stashed in Michigan Storage Unit

Fate of Wisconsin's Use of Private Vendor to Maintain Voter Roll on the Line After Citizens File Complaint

17th (1913): The Senate of the United States shall be composed of two Senators from each State, elected by the people thereof, for six years; and each Senator shall have one vote.

18th (1919): The manufacture, sale, or transportation of intoxicating liquors within, the importation thereof into, or the exportation thereof from the United States and all territory subject to the jurisdiction thereof for beverage purposes is hereby prohibited.

19th (1920): The right of citizens of the United States to vote shall not be denied or abridged by the United States or by any State on account of sex. Women gain the right to vote in America.

20th (1933):

> *Section 1: The terms of the President and the Vice President shall end at noon on the 20th day of January, and the terms of Senators and Representatives at noon on the 3d day of January, of the years in which such terms would have ended if this article had not been ratified; and the terms of their successors shall then begin.*

> *Section 2: The Congress shall assemble at least once in every year, and such meeting shall begin at noon on the 3d day of January, unless they shall by law appoint a different day...*

21st (1933): The eighteenth article of amendment to the Constitution of the United States (prohibition) is hereby repealed.

22nd (1951): No person shall be elected to the office of the President more than twice...

23rd (1961): The District constituting the seat of Government of the U.S. shall appoint in such manner as the Congress may direct: A number of electors of President and Vice President equal to the whole number of Senators and Representatives in Congress to which the District would be entitled if it were a State...

24th (1964): The right of citizens of the U.S. to vote in any primary or other election for President or Vice President, for electors for President or Vice President,

DOUGLASS MACKEY PRISON SENTENCE POSTPONED BY APPEALS COURT IN MEME CASE

MACKEY WAS SENTENCED TO 7 MONTHS IN FEDERAL PRISON FOR 2016 MEME INSTRUCTING HILLARY CLINTON SUPPORTERS TO VOTE VIA TEXT

Mackey, who shared a meme encouraging Hillary Clinton supporters to vote via text message in 2016, was convicted of the charge of Conspiracy Against Rights in March of 2023. In October, he was sentenced to seven months in federal prison.

Mackey's fundraising site, Meme Defense Fund, provides several details that preceded his conviction.

"On January 26, 2021–six days after Joe Biden was inaugurated– eight FBI and other law enforcement agents showed up at Douglass Mackey's home and arrested him on felony charges with a ten-year maximum sentence," the site states. "Despite living in Florida, Mackey was prosecuted in the Eastern District of New York before two liberal judges and was convicted."

Voters Appeal Dismissal of Lawsuit Over Use of Zuckerberg Millions in Michigan Elections

A years-long legal battle alleging dereliction of duty on the part of Michigan Secretary of State Jocelyn Benson has moved to the Michigan Court of Appeals.

In the early fall of 2020, four Michigan voters said they had discovered that some local election officials were allegedly using millions of dollars of private donations from the Center for Technology and Civic Life (CTCL) to pay for what they call "get-out-the-vote efforts" in urban Democrat strongholds around the state.

CTCL is a non-profit organization heavily funded by the Mark Zuckerburg family.

Report Critical of Group Managing Voter Rolls in 33 States
Personal information of 56 million voters shared

Your voter registration shouldn't be used by another person to cast a ballot. When someone moves or dies, their name should be removed from the registered voters' roll so it can't be used to vote. The National Voter Registration Act (NVRA) of 1993 requires states to make a reasonable effort to remove ineligible people from voter rolls.

Robert F. Kennedy Jr. to Tucker Carlson: I've Talked to CIA and Mob Hitmen Who Were Assigned to JFK Assassination

"Almost all of the people associated with (JFK's assassination) were involved with the Miami Station, which was the largest CIA Station at the time and was basically the Cuban Station", Robert F. Kennedy Jr. said.

"The JFK Assassinations Law required that all documents be released by 2017. Yet they refused. There are about 4000 (classified documents) left," RFK said.

"That suggests that there's something big", Tucker said.

or for Senator or Representative in Congress, shall not be denied or abridged by the United States or any State by reason of failure to pay any poll tax or other tax.

25th (1967): In case of the removal of the President from office or of his death or resignation, the Vice President shall become President...

26th (1971): The right of citizens of the United States, who are eighteen years of age or older, to vote shall not be denied or abridged by the United States or by any State on account of age.

27th (1992): No law, varying the compensation for the services of the Senators and Representatives, shall take effect, until an election of Representatives shall have intervened.

The Universal Declaration of Human Rights

The Universal Declaration of Human Rights (UDHR) is a document proclaimed by the United Nations General Assembly in Paris on December 10, 1948, which lists fundamental human rights that must be universally protected, and recognizes the dignity, equality, and inalienable rights of all humans. To summarize:

1. All human beings are born free and equal in dignity and rights.

2. Everyone is entitled to these rights and freedoms regardless of race, skin color, sex, language, religion, political or other opinion, national or social origin, property, birth, or other status.

3. All people have the right to life, liberty, and the security of person.

4. Slavery and the slave trade is prohibited.

5. Torture, or cruel, inhuman, or degrading treatment or punishment is prohibited.

Fed-backed censorship machine targeted 20 news sites

"No news organization should be subjected to an enemies/censorship list for reporting newsworthy facts" Just the News Editor in Chief John Solomon said in a statement. "It's even more egregious that this censorship machinery was prodded, aided and sanctioned by the federal government."

NYT 'Right Wing Conspiracy Theory' Comes True In Less Than 24 Hours

In it, the *Times* wrote that "right-wing" election deniers in Arizona had fabricated a conspiracy theory that election software company Konnech had secret ties to the CCP, and was passing them information on around two million US poll workers.

The next morning, Konnech executive Eugene Yu was arrested for the alleged theft of poll workers' personal information.

Universal Mail-In Voting Violates Delaware Constitution: Delaware Supreme Court

A 'Cabal' Influenced the 2020 Election

To force these changes, they [DNC] ended up filing more election-related lawsuits than had ever been filed in an election year in U.S. history.

John Fund and Hans von Spakovsky, authors, "Our Broken Elections"

Wisconsin Judge Rules Use of Mobile Vans in Absentee Voting Violates State Election Law

Judge says use of a mobile van for absentee voting also unfairly benefited Democrats in August 2022 primary election.

Citing 'Orwellian' Tactics, Federal Judge Orders White House to Stop Censoring Americans' Social Media Posts

In his 155-page ruling, Judge Terry Doughty said there is "substantial evidence" the government violated the First Amendment by engaging in a large-scale censorship campaign targeting content that questioned or countered establishment narratives on COVID-19.

6. Everyone is equal under the law and is entitled to equal protection of the law.

7. No one shall be subjected to arbitrary arrest, detention, or exile.

8. Everyone is entitled to a fair trial.

9. Everyone is presumed innocent until proved guilty.

10. No one should be subjected to arbitrary interference with his privacy, family, home, or correspondence, nor to attacks upon his honor and reputation.

11. Everyone has the right to freedom of movement and residence within the borders of each State, and the right to leave any country, including his or her own, and to return to his or her country.

12. People have the right to seek asylum in other countries.

13. Everyone has the right to a nationality.

14. All adults have the right to engage in consensual marriage and to create a family.

15. The family is the basic natural unit of society and is entitled to protection by society and by the government.

16. Everyone has the right to own property, and no one shall be arbitrarily deprived of his or her property.

17. Everyone has the right to freedom of thought, conscience, and religion.

18. Everyone has the right to freedom of opinion and expression.

19. Everyone has the right to peaceful assembly and association, although no one may be compelled to belong to an association.

Brunson v. Alma S. Adams; et al.,
(Biden, Harris, Pence & 385 Members of Congress)

BACKGROUND

Loy, Raland, Deron and Gaynor Brunson (the brothers) witnessed the 2020 election along with claims from members of congress that the election was rigged. What got their attention was when the proposition to investigate those claims was presented to Congress and put to a vote. What came as a shock to the four brothers is when they discovered that 387 members of Congress along with VP Mike Pence actually voted against the proposed investigation, thus thwarting the investigation. Whether the election was rigged or not was no longer their main concern. What now became the concern was when those members of Congress violated their sworn oath by voting to thwart the investigation.

Brnovich Ignoring Credible Concerns About Ballots Cast Through Arizona's Overseas Internet Portal

The federal Uniformed and Overseas Citizens Absentee Voting Act (UOCAVA) outlines procedures and requirements for citizens voting from overseas, a substantial number of which are service members and their families.

The 68% increase in overseas ballots is even more concerning considering there was no corresponding increase in Arizona service members deployed overseas during that same time period. Moreover, the population of all U.S. citizens overseas is estimated to have only increased by around 11-12% between 2016 and 2020. The Federal Voting Assistance Program estimates that overseas voting rates remained steady in 2020. Considering these data points, the 68% increase in Maricopa County UOCAVA ballots simply doesn't add up and is deserving of the Attorney General's attention.

Further highlighting election integrity concerns, Mr. Harris testified that of the purported UOCAVA ballots accepted by Maricopa County, approximately 95% of those 10,396 ballots were cast for a single candidate. According to Mr. Harris, that candidate was Joe Biden.

Wisconsin Election Chief Hit with Articles of Impeachment

Did data from Georgia voting machine breach play role in alleged Michigan election plot?

Arizona's Law to Confirm Who Mails in Election Ballots (Signature Verification) Is Ignored to Steal Elections

20. Everyone has the right to take part in the government, directly or through representatives.

21. The will of the people shall be the basis of the authority of government.

22. Everyone has the right to Social Security.

23. Everyone has the right to free choice of employment, to receive fair pay, to join trade unions, including reasonable limitation of working hours and periodic holidays with pay.

24. Everyone has the right to a standard of living adequate for his or her health and well-being.

25. Everyone has the right to education. Parents have the right to choose the kind of education given to their children.

26. No state, group, or person may engage in any activity or perform any act intended to destroy any of the rights and freedoms set forth herein.

The Magna Carta

The *Magna Carta* is considered a forerunner of the *U.S. Declaration of Independence*, the *French Declaration of the Rights of Man and of the Citizen*, the *U.S. Constitution* and *Bill of Rights*, and the *UN Universal Declaration of Human Rights*. It was created as a response to the tyranny, cruelty, and greed of King John of England, who, among other things, continued to raise taxes to pay for war.

The Magna Carta stated that the king must follow the law and could not simply rule as he wished. It limited taxes and assessments, reformed laws and judicial procedures, and included protections for the rights of the church, businesspeople, and townspeople. It stated that people could not be punished for crimes unless they were lawfully convicted, and it reserved the right of the people to declare war against the king if he did not follow its provisions. In short, people organized and banded together

The 2020 Presidential Election - Comments on Twitter:

Why did 7-8 swing states stop counting votes at 10pm on election night when Trump was winning by a landslide in those states? Did that ever happen in any prior Presidential election?

Why did they cover and block the windows in Detroit's Cobo Hall Arena so observers could not see what was going on inside the arena where votes were being tabulated?

Why did Fulton County Georgia election officials say there was a massive water leak at the place where votes were being tabulated and then send everyone home? Later, it was discovered to be a minor leak in one bathroom.

Why did Fox News call Arizona for Biden at 9pm election night when the race was too close to call two weeks later?

Why did a white truck/van bring thousands of ballots into Detroit's Cobo Hall Arena at 3am?

Why did Ruby Freeman and her team tell Republican observers that counting had stopped for the night and as soon as observers leave, they pull out suitcases of ballots and scanned ballots for two hours without observers?

Why did Mark Zuckerberg give 400+ million dollars to Democrat strong districts to make drop boxes more available?

Why did Donald Trump have rallies with over 30,000+ supporters and Joe Biden get only 10 people at his rallies?

Why did they tell us that the 2020 Presidential Election was the safest and most secure in US history?

Why did the majority of Congress refuse to investigate the allegations of election fraud and instead rush to certify the electors?

Why did the courts refuse to consider the election fraud lawsuits on their merits and instead reject them because "the plaintiffs lacked standing"?

Why did the District Attorney of Fulton County Georgia, Fani Willis, charge President Donald Trump and 18 others with 41 RICO racketeering charges for insisting that the Georgia election fraud allegations be investigated?

to assert their rights and to curtail the abuses of a tyrannical government.

In the 2020s, tyranny once again threatens humanity. A charter of rights must be accepted that serves everyone. In a democracy, governments exist for the sole purpose of serving the people. The purpose of government is to protect and preserve the rights of human beings and to support the provisions of goods and services for that purpose. When a government degrades into tyranny, it must undergo a correction.

The various charters and declarations outlined in this chapter all exist for the purpose of declaring, protecting, and preserving basic human rights. Their details differ based on location and era in which they were created. However, their commonalities can be listed and should be agreed upon by all peoples. Let's call these "fundamental human rights."

The Declaration of Fundamental Human Rights

1. Governments exist to serve the people, regardless of race, skin color, sex, language, religion, political or other opinion, national or social origin, property, birth, or other status.

2. The will of the people shall be the basis of government authority.

3. The intentional killing or wounding of innocent people, whether by individuals, groups, or by government actors, is a crime and is prohibited.

4. Every person has the right to a place on this Earth.

5. Every person has the right to freedom of speech.

6. Every person has the right to freedom of religion.

7. Every person has the right to freedom of peaceful assembly.

8. Every person has the right to freedom to publish.

9. Every person has the right to own property, and no one can be arbitrarily de-

Angry Maricopa Residents Deliver Blunt Election Comments During Board of Supervisors Meeting

Heated reactions come after thousands of votes set aside for later counting after glitches in ballot tabulation process

RNC Files Election Integrity Lawsuit Targeting Michigan's Handling of Absentee Ballots

'Election officials have to verify the identity of voters casting absentee ballots,' RNC Chair said in a statement.

Woman Found Guilty of 52 Counts of Voter Fraud, Sentenced to Prison

Enforcement Win: Arizona Court Backs RITE

Superior Court for the County of Yavapai agreed with RITE that the state is conducting signature matching in an unlawful manner. The court said that the "statute is clear and unambiguous" and that *"the legislature intended for the recorder to attempt to match the signature on the outside of the envelope to the signature on the documents the putative voter used to register."* The court found that the Secretary's signature-match process unlawfully *"contradicts the plain language"* of the statute by permitting signature comparison with documents that have *"nothing to do with the act of registering."* Restoring Integrity and Trust in Elections

Elon Musk: FTX CEO Funneled 'Over $1B' to Democrats

Twitter boss Elon Musk has demanded to know where "the money went" after declaring that Sam Bankman-Fried, the disgraced former CEO of cryptocurrency exchange FTX, funneled "over $1B" to Democrats. If the number is accurate, Musk's allegation would mean Sam Bankman-Fried (SBF) donated significantly more than the initially reported $40 million figure to Democratic politicians.

prived of his or her property.

10. The Family is the basic unit of humanity and is entitled to protection by society and by the government.

11. Parents have the right to choose the education given to their children, the religious participation their children may have, and the kind of health care their children receive.

12. Every person has the right to medical informed consent, the right to protect the sanctity of their bodies from forced drugs or pharmaceuticals, and the right to choose what drugs, if any, are injected into their bodies.

13. Every person has the right to the health care of their choice, whether it be medical or natural or a combination thereof.

14. No person should be subjected to arbitrary interference with his or her privacy, family, home, or correspondence.

15. Every person has the right to be safe and secure in their homes, without unwarranted intrusions, searches, or seizures.

16. Every person has the right to life and to liberty. No one shall be subjected to arbitrary arrest, detention, or exile.

17. Every person is entitled to a fair trial, and everyone is presumed innocent until proved guilty.

18. Every person has the right to self-defense, including the bearing of arms.

It should be clear that, for a tyrannical government to undergo a Great Reset, placing power and authority in the hands of the people, and removing it from authoritarians, corrupt politicians, fascists, and dictators, a struggle of some sort will likely be necessary. Thomas Jefferson, in 1787, once famously wrote in a letter that *"The tree of liberty must be re-*

Here's the numbers for an 86 year old man from Oak Park, Illinois. He made 11,285 donations to Democrats between April 11, 2019 and December 31, 2023. That's roughly 6.5 donations/day, every day, for 1,725 days straight. He's 86 years old. Now ask yourself this... who donates 659 times to a congresswoman in another state but never gives a dime to any candidates running in their state? Answer? Bots. Specifically, bots being ran by dark money groups who are using campaign funds to control their puppets in DC. Think it's just Republicans? HA! Democrats were the master minds of this scam.

committee_id committee_name	report_year	contribution_receipt_amount
committee_name:	Count (All):	Sum:
▶ ACTBLUE	8186	72024.60
▶ DNC SERVICES CORP / DEMOCRATIC NATIONAL CON	340	5102.00
▶ CONGRESSIONAL PROGRESSIVE CAUCUS PAC	309	6161.00
▶ DEMOCRACY FOR AMERICA	180	1994.00
▶ DEMOCRATIC ACTION	180	3625.00
▶ WARNOCK FOR GEORGIA	162	3697.79
▶ WARREN DEMOCRATS, INC.	159	1976.00
▶ CHC BOLD PAC	152	2338.50
▶ CONGRESSIONAL BLACK CAUCUS PAC	150	2653.50
▶ INDIVISIBLE ACTION	138	3610.00
▶ MARCH ON PAC	121	2109.00
▶ MARK KELLY FOR SENATE	100	1509.00
▶ 21ST CENTURY DEMOCRATS	69	2300.00
▶ NATIONAL DEMOCRATIC TRAINING COMMITTEE PAC	70	995.00
▶ MOVEON.ORG POLITICAL ACTION	70	1313.50
▶ VOTEVETS	69	1275.00
▶ JUSTICE DEMOCRATS PAC	65	1625.00
▶ ALEXANDRIA OCASIO-CORTEZ FOR CONGRESS	63	339.99
▶ WARREN FOR SENATE, INC.	61	533.00
▶ GRASSROOTS VICTORY PAC	41	537.00
▶ MANDELA BARNES FOR WISCONSIN	39	459.43
▶ FRIENDS OF SCHUMER	38	2375.00
▶ TRUTH TO POWER	38	790.00
▶ JON OSSOFF FOR SENATE	35	1775.52
▶ BLUE STATES PAC	34	2165.00
▶ WARREN FOR PRESIDENT, INC.	31	1482.94
▶ FETTERMAN FOR PA	29	1130.00
▶ BIDEN FOR PRESIDENT	27	807.00

freshed from time to time with the blood of patriots and tyrants."

Nearly 250 years ago, rifles, bayonets, and guillotines may have been the tools of choice to rid society of tyranny. Today, we have the capability, through the use of technology, creativity, cooperation, and intelligence, to return the legislative branch of government to the control of the people without the need for violence, war, or insurrection. How? By introducing the random intelligent selection of representatives and by establishing direct citizen vote on legislation.

Milking the Citizens

Median annual income in the United States in the early 2020s was about $75,000. With that in mind, it's hard to imagine being able to generate $100 billion of income in one year. Where would all that money come from? One pharmaceutical company generated that amount in 2022. It came primarily from the U.S. treasury. Nobody is "minding the store," our national bank account, and it is being repeatedly robbed. The criminals have masterminded the crime of tapping into the U.S. treasury by using mainstream propaganda, brainwashing machines, censorship, scare tactics, and threats, all in contradiction to our basic constitutional rights. They are milking U.S. citizens like dairy goats, and we are allowing them to do it.

In 2022, when the median income in the U.S. was $74,580, Mark Zuckerberg made $27 million. The 10 richest people on the planet were worth nearly $1.47 trillion. Worldwide, there were 2,640 billionaires collectively worth $12.2 trillion. This is 0.00000033% of the world's population.

Although the average person earns about $2.7 million in their lifetime, Bill Gates gains three to four times that in one day. Some sources estimate Gates' daily income at around $10.95 million, or about $117 per second. Another source suggests a lower amount of approximately $7.6 million per day or $319,635 per hour. In one hour, Bill Gates earns over four times as much as the median annual income in the United States.

When the Founding Fathers enshrined "freedom of speech" in the Bill of Rights, there were no billionaires, no electricity, no television, no computers, no social media, or any other means of amplifying one's "speech." In the 2020s, freedom of speech doesn't mean much. You are free to speak, but not free to be heard. How can anyone hear you over the magnified speech of the very wealthy, those who control radio, TV, newspapers, magazines, social media, the Internet, and search engines?

One way to counter authoritarianism is by creating more democracy. Instead, we are being plundered by a corrupt shadow government that has built a legal system that allows the plunder to take place, year after year, generation after generation. The Chinese military strategist Sun Tzu once wrote: *"The supreme art of war is to subdue the enemy without fighting."* We live in an age when battles are not solely fought with guns and bombs. The new battlefield is in the minds of every citizen. Let's use our intelligence to create the future that we want, while leaving the bombs behind.

"The real cost of the State is the prosperity we do not see, the jobs that don't exist, the technologies to which we do not have access, the businesses that do not come into existence, and the bright future that is stolen from us. The State has looted us just as surely as a robber who enters our home at night and steals all that we love." ~ Frederic Bastiat

ˈ5

The Curse of the Boiled Frogs

Mass hysteria is a phenomenon that has plagued humanity for millennia. Humans are herd animals — large groups of them can be readily influenced by outside controlling factors. A notable example: the legal tradition of prosecuting people suspected of practicing witchcraft, which was well-established in Europe from the fifteenth through seventeenth centuries.

Estimates are that 10,000 to upwards of 9 million people were accused of, and persecuted for, practicing "witchcraft," mostly in what is now central Europe, where Germany, France, the Netherlands, and Switzerland exist today. Most of the "witch" executions occurred between 1580–1650. Perhaps the most famous American witch trials occurred in Salem Massachusetts in the late 1600s, at the tail end of the European witch persecutions.

English colonists brought the concept of a "witch" to colonial New England where belief in the devil was widespread. The Salem witch trials were fueled by people's suspicions of and resentments toward their neighbors, as well as their fear of outsiders.

The ergot fungus found in rye, wheat, and other cereal grains, when eaten, can cause symptoms such as delusions, vomiting, and muscle spasms. Two girls in Salem, in early 1692 (ages 9 and 11), came down with a mysterious illness not unlike ergot poisoning. However, a medical doctor concluded that it looked like witchcraft. Hard to believe these days that a doctor declared that witchcraft was the cause of an illness, but it was considered a legitimate diagnosis at that time.

Not only did the Salem Witch Trials wrongfully accuse and convict many women during this era, but men and even dogs were declared possessed by the devil, convicted, and executed. When accused witches were brought before magistrates and questioned, their accusers appeared in the courtroom engaging in spasms, contortions, screaming, and writhing. Some who were accused became informers and confessed to save themselves, then claimed knowledge of other witches, who were pointed out and subsequently rounded up, some as young as four years old.

Robert F. Kennedy Jr. to Run as an Independent

Democrat presidential candidate Robert F. Kennedy Jr discussed the latest dirty tricks that the Democrat National Committee is attempting to use against him. "It's pretty clear that the DNC does not want a primary. I don't want to say that they want a coronation, but I think that's a fair way to put it. Essentially, they're fixing the process. They're disenfranchising the Democratic voters from having any choice in who becomes president. Things they've done today is moved the Iowa primary and made rules that if anybody campaigns in Iowa, or any candidate sets foot in the state of Iowa, or sets foot in the state of New Hampshire, then none of the votes that are cast for that candidate will be counted. They're rigging it so that if you add up all the super delegates they control and all the automatic delegates that just go to the party and to the president, I will have to win almost 80 percent of all of the states in order to beat President Biden even if he only wins 20 percent."

History of Influence, Scandal, and Denial

In December 1953, America's leading tobacco companies gathered to confront a menace to their incredibly profitable industry. Science published in medical journals had cast doubt on the safety of cigarettes and had threatened to destroy a half-century of corporate profiteering. Joining them was John W. Hill, president of America's top public relations firm, Hill & Knowlton. Hill had closely studied Edward Bernays, whose work on propaganda in the 1920s and 1930s defined techniques to manipulate popular opinion. Effective public relations at its best left no fingerprints. Instead of ignoring or denigrating new data that found tobacco dangerous, Hill proposed the opposite: embrace science, trumpet new data, and demand more, not less research. They would then fund scientists, thereby corrupting science and medicine for decades to follow.

The Epidemic Eating Americans' Minds

Americans spend seven hours a day behind screens on average, excluding time spent at school or work.

The initial link between screen time and poor mental health was spotted through generational studies by Jean Twenge, who has a doctorate in psychology and is a professor of psychology at San Diego State University.

Witch trials began to overwhelm the local justice system. In May 1692, the newly appointed governor of Massachusetts, William Phips, ordered the establishment of a special court to try these cases. Witchcraft then became the second capital crime, punishable by death, listed in the Massachusetts Bay Colony's criminal code.

Presided over by seven judges, the court handed down its first conviction, against Bridget Bishop, on June 2, 1692; she was hanged eight days later. The trial lasted one day. The accused had no counsel, and was doomed by sensational stories involving flying monkeys, black pigs, and the devil, potentiated by popular opinion and prejudice.

Five more people were hanged that July; five in August, and eight more in September. In addition, seven other accused witches died in jail, while an 81-year-old man who refused to admit innocence or guilt when accused of witchcraft was wedged between two heavy stones until he died, days later. Many of these victims were found guilty based on "spectral evidence," i.e., witness testimony based on dreams and visions.

Support eventually waned for the sensational witch trials, perhaps because of the many innocent people put to gruesome deaths because of flimsy and foolish accusations. Governor Phips dissolved the Witch Court and mandated that its successor disregard spectral evidence. Trials continued with dwindling intensity until early 1693, when Phips had pardoned and released all those in prison on witchcraft charges.

It is still not clear why girls began having fits in early 1692, or why their condition seemed to spread to others. Whatever the cause, mass hysteria — a collective phenomenon in which a group of people experience delusions, fear, and perceived threats — seems to have played an important role. How does this happen?

Two primary factors are required to conjure up mass hysteria: 1) powerful people with vested interests in eliminating their competitors or detractors; and 2) a form of mass communication that can provoke large numbers of people to the extent that they lose touch with reality.

Imagine a century during which people were charged with witchcraft, tied to poles, and burned alive or hung by the neck to die in front of large crowds of cheering people who had been brainwashed to believe this was righteous and necessary or were too frightened to speak out for fear of

Sean Davis

According to a new investigative report by @JudiciaryGOP, we know for a fact that DHS/CISA and its censorship regime, in concert with corrupt third-parties and Big Tech apparatchiks conspired to target and censor me specifically.

Just days before the 2020 election, I reported on a Pennsylvania Supreme Court decision that allowed late ballots without a postmark to be counted as valid ballots. I took a screenshot of the opinion, quoted it, and provided a link to the court decision. Twitter censored my post at the time and falsely claimed I was "misleading about an election or civic event."

We noticed it when it happened and called it out immediately. Now we know why it happened: DHS/CISA specifically targeted me, complained that the reach of my tweet was "viral" and "growing exponentially" and then demanded that it be censored by Twitter. You read that correctly: our own government had a temper tantrum that my indisputably accurate tweet was gaining traction and calling into question the integrity of the officials who defied state law and allowed late, un-postmarked ballots to be counted. Our own government demanded that Twitter violate 1st Amendment right to speak and to report the news, and they demanded that Twitter violate your right to consume news in the middle of an election.

CISA Was Behind the Attempt to Control Your Thoughts, Speech, and Life

On Monday, the House Judiciary Committee released a report on how the Cybersecurity and Infrastructure Security Agency (CISA) "colluded with Big Tech and 'disinformation' partners to censor Americans."

The 36-page report raises three familiar issues: first, government actors worked with third parties to overturn the First Amendment; second, censors prioritized political narratives over truthfulness; and third, an unaccountable bureaucracy hijacked American society.

The House Report reveals that CISA, **a branch of the Department of Homeland Security,** worked with social media platforms to censor posts it considered dis-, mis-, or malinformation.

Additionally, **CISA funded the nonprofit EI-ISAC in 2020 to bolster its censorship operations.** EI-ISAC worked to report and track "misinformation across all channels and platforms." In launching the nonprofit, the government boasted that it "leverage[d] DHS CISA's relationship with social media organizations to ensure priority treatment of misinformation reports."

being accused of being a witch themselves and thereby meeting a similar fate.

Who were the powerful people behind these crimes against humanity? Was it the church and the scientists, doctors, and politicians who may have been in the pockets of the clergy? How did they amplify their propaganda? Was it from the pulpit? There is no doubt that mass hysteria was fortified by judges and courts, amplified by social influencers, and confirmed by doctors and scientists, while soldiers and police meted out punishments to innocent victims, leading to horrible crimes against humanity and indelible stains on human civilization.

The persecution of accused witches and other relatively defenseless targeted minorities has occurred repeatedly throughout human history. People who spoke out against the persecutions were themselves accused, then imprisoned, tortured, then had their homes, businesses, reputations, and families, either damaged, taken away, or destroyed altogether. The deranged actors behind the mass crimes included people who controlled the public purse and therefore the police and military. These armed forces made sure that the dissenters were kept out of the way, in line, intimidated, or eliminated.

Arguably, other examples can be attributed to mass hysteria, such as the slave trade, during which basic human rights were ignored on a massive scale on behalf of commerce and profit, for hundreds of years. Or the mass destruction of the Native Americans by European immigrants determined to steal the land belonging to the native people, and the resources upon it. These were certainly grave crimes against humanity if you were the native residents, although the moral implications of such behavior seemed to be largely ignored by the perpetrators.

Jump ahead to the twentieth century. A notable mass hysteria occurred when the Nazis provoked the German population into believing Jewish people had to be eliminated by any means necessary. This is a complicated issue. Nazi Fascists promoted a government system led by a dictator, Hitler, who had complete power. He used it to forcibly suppress opposition and criticism. The Nazis used an aggressive nationalism to regiment industry and commerce.

At the same time, a number of vocal Jews advocated socialism. They

THE WEAPONIZATION OF "DISINFORMATION" PSEUDO-EXPERTS AND
BUREAUCRATS: HOW THE FEDERAL GOVERNMENT PARTNERED
WITH UNIVERSITIES TO CENSOR AMERICANS' POLITICAL SPEECH
Interim Staff Report of the Committee on the Judiciary and the
Select Subcommittee on the Weaponization of the Federal Government
U.S. House of Representatives

Box of 2020 Election Absentee Ballots Found Stashed in Michigan Storage Unit

Censorship Not Easy, Journalists Tell Congress

During last week's hearing of the U.S. House of Representatives Select Subcommittee on the Weaponization of the Federal Government, investigative journalists Michael Shellenberger and Matt Taibbi said they were "obstructed at every turn" in their efforts to uncover the scope of the government's censorship of narratives it wanted to suppress.

The First Black Man Elected to Congress

Hiram Rhodes Revels arrived on Capitol Hill to take his seat as the first Black member of the U.S. Congress in 1870. But first, the Mississippi Republican faced Democrats determined to block him.

The Constitution requires senators to hold citizenship for at least nine years, and they argued Revels had only recently become a citizen with the 1866 Civil Rights Act and the 14th Amendment. Before that, the Supreme Court had ruled in its 1857 *Dred Scott* decision that Black people weren't U.S. citizens.

This technicality wasn't actually their main issue with Revels. At the time, the Democrats were the party of white southern men, and they simply didn't want any Black men in Congress.

In any case, their bad faith legal argument didn't hold up. Revel's fellow Republicans argued he was born a free man in the United States and had lived there all his life.

Revels took his oath only five years after the Civil War. Over the next decade, 15 more Black men took their seats in the House and Senate.

Voting Machine Company That 'Flipped' Votes in Pennsylvania Admits 'Someone Programmed the Election'

A top executive from the company behind the voting machines that "flipped votes" in Pennsylvania on Tuesday has admitted that "someone from our team programmed the election."

The voting machine issued caused votes in an eastern Pennsylvania county to appear to be "flipped" on a ballot question, officials said Tuesday.

Zuckerberg Ends Controversial Grants to Election Offices

wanted the ownership and control of production, distribution, capital, and land to be in the hands of the community as a whole. Their system was directly contradictory to that of a fascist government.

Nazi leaders and their fascist supporters officially encouraged the massacre and persecution of Germany's Jewish population. They disseminated propaganda using amplified public speeches and a new technology — radio.

To be clear, propaganda is based on emotion, and *it affects people regardless of their level of intelligence.* Extremely smart people can quickly fall under the influence of propaganda just the same as dumb ones. Many of the German population were quite intelligent, but they nevertheless supported the Nazis as they engaged in the mass murder of Jews and others. Why would they do this? Either because they were brainwashed, or because they were afraid to speak out for fear of retribution. Those who spoke out could be imprisoned, tortured, lose their livelihood, their homes, their families, their reputation. Or be murdered.

Communists

Mass hysteria reared its ugly head again during the "anticommunist" era in the United States after World War II, an era which is ongoing. It wasn't "witches" or slaves or native peoples or minorities who were the target of deranged people in power; it was "communists." What was or is a communist? A dictionary definition of communism is: "a system in which goods are owned in common and are available to all as needed; a theory advocating elimination of private property."

Here, we circle back to Marx and Engels and *The Communist Manifesto* of the mid-1800s, describing a philosophy that began to flourish in the early 1900s with the Russian Revolution in 1917, followed by the formation of the Soviet Union in 1922. The Soviet Union, or the Union of Soviet Socialist Republics, as it was formally called (the USSR), eventually included 15 republics and nearly 130 ethnic groups spanning 11 time zones.

The philosophy of Communists can be summed up in one sentence: Abolish private property. *The Communist Manifesto* states,

Republicans Score Win in Court Battle Over Pennsylvania Ballot Requirements

Mail-in ballots without dates, or with incorrect dates, should not be counted, federal appeals court rules.

Deep State Censorship Exposed.

A bombshell new report has been published, titled: "WEAPONIZATION OF 'DISINFORMATION' PSEUDO-EXPERTS AND BUREAUCRATS: HOW THE FEDERAL GOVERNMENT PARTNERED WITH UNIVERSITIES TO CENSOR AMERICANS' POLITICAL SPEECH," Interim Staff Report by the Committee on the Judiciary and the Select Subcommittee on the Weaponization of the Federal Government U.S. House of Representatives was released on November 6, 2023.

As this new information reveals, and this report outlines, the federal government and universities pressured social media companies to censor true information, jokes, and political opinions. This pressure was largely directed in a way that benefitted one side of the political aisle: true information posted by Republicans and conservatives was labeled as "misinformation" while false information posted by Democrats and liberals was largely unreported and untouched by the censors.

DETROIT ELECTION UPDATE: GOP and Independent Poll Challengers Claim "At least 50 percent of absentee ballot envelopes missing signature verification check mark"

6 Minnesota Counties Have 515 Duplicate Registrations on Voter Rolls, Watchdog Alleges

Illinois Illegally Denied Elections Group Access to Voter Records, Federal Court Rules

Texas GOP launches probe into 23 precincts that ran out of paper ballots... ALL Republican strongholds

Watchdog Group Finds 24,896 Questionable Names on North Carolina Voter Rolls

"You are horrified at our intending to do away with private property. But in your existing society, private property is already done away with for nine-tenths of the population, its existence for the few is solely due to the non-existence in the hands of those nine-tenths . . . In a word, you reproach us with intending to do away with your property. Precisely so, that is just what we intend."

The Manifesto, sightly paraphrased, also states:

"Above all, the control of industry and of all branches of production must be taken out of the hands of individuals, and instead a system must be instituted in which all of these branches of production are operated by society as a whole. Private property must be abolished and in its place must come the common utilization of all instruments of production and distribution of all products according to common agreement — in a word, what is called the communal ownership of goods. In fact, the abolition of private property . . . is rightly advanced by communists as their main demand."

Additionally, from *The Manifesto*:

"Finally, when all capital, all production, all exchange have been brought together in the hands of the nation, private property will disappear of its own accord . . . It follows that the communist revolution will be not merely a national phenomenon but must take place simultaneously in all civilized countries . . ."

"Society will take all forces of production and means of commerce, as well as the exchange and distribution of products, out of the hands of private capitalists and will manage them in accordance with a plan based on the availability of resources and the needs of the whole society. In this way, most important of all, the evil consequences which are now associated with the conduct of big industry will be abolished."

The Manifesto also insists that children's education be controlled by

Democrats Exploit Automatic Voter Registration Systems to Register Non-Citizens

Investigation finds printers and ballot size responsible for 2022 election troubles in Arizona

Angry Maricopa Residents Deliver Blunt Election Comments During Board of Supervisors Meeting

Heated reactions come after thousands of votes set aside for later counting after glitches in ballot tabulation process

'Never Trump' Billionaires Lead Nikki Haley's 2023 Fundraising

Nikki Haley's presidential campaign is fueled in large part by cash from anti-Trump billionaires, according to new federal disclosures.

RNC Files Election Integrity Lawsuit Against Nevada Secretary of State

The Nevada Secretary of State is facing a lawsuit over an alleged failure to maintain accurate and up-to-date voter rolls, undermining voter confidence.

New Evidence Shows Crooked Electronic Voter Registration System ERIC Is Politically Compromised
STUNNING 104% of Voting Aged Population In MI Is Registered To Vote!

More Than 8,000 Double-Registered Voters Found on New Jersey Rolls

the state, and that the basis of traditional marriage must be eliminated, namely *"the dependence of women on the man and the children on the parents."*

The establishment of a large bloc of humanity, which espoused a political philosophy that eliminated private property, terrified the wealthy elite. The Kings, Queens, and other Royalty, the Tsars and Emperors, Lords, magnates, tycoons, aristocracy, capitalists, autocrats, despots, oligarchs, and other hoarders of material wealth had a lot of property. They also had a lot of power and influence.

The Anticommunists

By the 1950s, a new invention enabled the amplification of communication. It was called *television*. Broadcast networks, TV stations, their owners, managers, and employees, were controlled by wealthy private individuals. This allowed immense media power to be concentrated in the hands of a small minority of people, allowing the science of propaganda to evolve from the crude but effective rantings of the clergy from pulpits in medieval times, to a fine science that would be used to control the minds of millions of people in the modern world.

President Harry S. Truman, who had ordered the bombing of civilian cities in Japan with the Atom Bomb at the end of World War II, issued an Executive Order after the war requiring that all federal civil-service employees be screened for affiliation with any organization determined to be communist, despite the fact that the United States had recently fought side-by-side with the communist Soviet Union during World War II. In March of 1947, Truman announced a new foreign policy requiring the United States to oppose communist expansion. This came to be known as the Truman Doctrine, and it forced the United States to support anticommunist forces around the world.

McCarthyism, an extreme American anticommunist movement, was sparked by communism's emergence as a political force in the United States. American communists organized labor unions, opposed fascism, and offered an alternative to capitalism during the Great Depression. The U.S. Communist Party increased its membership to about 75,000 people in the early 1940s.

Office of the Special Counsel Second Interim Investigative Report
On the Apparatus & Procedures of the Wisconsin Elections System
Delivered to the Wisconsin State Assembly on March 1, 2022

Introduction

The Office of the Special Counsel files this Investigative Report on Wisconsin's administration of the 2020 elections as a first step to begin restoring faith in America's elections. This effort is undertaken because Americans' faith in its election system was shaken by events both before and after the November 2020 Presidential election. For example, a January 2022 ABC/Ipsos poll revealed that only 20% of the public is very confident about the integrity of our national election system. This 20% number is a significant drop from 37% from a similar ABC poll conducted one year earlier. America's doubts about its election system crosses partisan lines. Among Democrats, only 30% say they are "very confident" in the U.S. election systems overall. Among independents, only 20% consider themselves "very confident" in the nation's elections. Among Republicans, only 13% are "very confident" with America's elections.

Some unlawful conduct and irregularities outlined in this Report include:

1. Election officials' use of absentee ballot drop boxes
2. The Center for Tech and Civic Life's $8,800,000 Zuckerberg Grants
3. Failure to maintain an accurate voter database
4. Engaging private companies in election administration in unprecedented ways
5. Directing clerks not to send out legal voting deputies to nursing homes
6. Unlawful voting by wards-under-guardianship
7. Failure to record non-citizens in the voter database
8. Violation of Federal and Wisconsin Equal Protection Clauses

Anticommunist fervor enabled the wealthy elite to influence the American population to attack small nations and slaughter their inhabitants by the millions — to put it bluntly. There was little discussion on the merits or foundation of communism or on the dangers of wealth and power being concentrated in the hands of a small number of elite individuals. Instead, Americans were thoroughly brainwashed by radio and TV broadcasts, magazines, and newspapers, into believing that communism represented the pinnacle of evil and had to be stopped at all costs, even if it meant mass murder on a large scale while engaging in repeated and grotesque crimes against humanity.

Government-controlled schools amplified the anti-communist message, indoctrinating children to become obedient conformists, willing to kill or be killed in the name of "democracy" and "freedom."

Every day, children in U.S. government schools were forced to recite a pledge of obedience to the government in which they repeated Stepford-like, "with liberty and justice for all," as black Americans clogged the prisons, and high-school graduates were given the choice to be shipped overseas to slaughter foreigners or spend two years languishing in a federal penitentiary with murderers and rapists.

On TV in the 1960s the regular program *Superman* began with an intonation about Superman fighting for "truth, justice, and the American way." Turn the channel and the news showed American B52 bombers carpet bombing civilian villages in Vietnam.

Was there no middle ground between communism and capitalism? Could there be no compromise? Was there no way to resolve these issues without mass violence and bloodshed? What about "social capitalism" or something like that — an intelligent and reasonable combination of the two opposing perspectives? No, nothing like that existed at that time.

The personal accumulation of massive wealth is not necessarily an indication of intelligence and certainly not of wisdom. Extremely wealthy individuals' knee jerk reaction to communism was to stop it completely, stamp it out at any cost. "The end justifies the means" as the saying goes. There was no interest in compromise, no point in discussing limits to wealth, or a more equitable distribution of natural resources so that everyone could have their piece of earth, with liberty and justice, free of en-

ARIZONA

2022 Midterm Election Survey Report

Based on your participation/ experience this year, how confident are you that the election results in your state are completely accurate and honest?

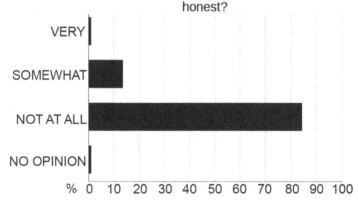

Based on what you observed, what is your level of confidence in the accuracy and reliability of the voting machines and other technology used by your county?

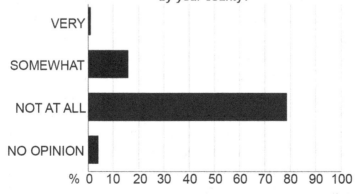

slavement and oppression. In the United States, capitalists controlled the government, and the government's intent was simply to wipe out communism at any cost.

The Korean War, or the "forgotten war," as some called it, followed. The United States military was engaged in this war from 1950 until 1953. It started as a civil war between communist forces of Northern Korea (supported by the Soviet Union and People's Republic of China), and primarily American forces in Southern Korea.

Today the names of 54,000 American soldiers killed in the Korean War are engraved on the Korean War Veterans Memorial in Washington DC. It is estimated that two million Koreans (North and South), mostly civilians, were also killed in the war, which ended in a stalemate, creating a seemingly permanent division between what is now known as North Korea and South Korea.

The struggle between those who believe in unlimited personal wealth and those who believe in limiting private property is rooted in the abuse of the common people, the "working class," by wealthy elites — abuse that has spanned centuries. The solution that all private property should be abolished, espoused by the communists, was obviously faulty. It is contradictory to human nature and violates basic human rights, as outlined earlier. On the other hand, the perspective is based on a valid point: wealth and power, in excess, is inclined to be readily abused by wealthy elites who may lack morals, ethics, intelligence, judgement, and/or conscience. How will this dilemma ever be resolved?

Shortly after the Korean war, U.S. anticommunism turned to a different Asian nation: Vietnam. The 1960s ushered in a new era of heightened propaganda, especially effective against the TV generation. The "Red Scare" (red meaning communist) had infected much of the TV-watching population of the United States like a mental illness.

Children in grade schools were being taught to "duck and cover" by bending over at their desks, in their seats, and putting their heads between their legs in the event of an impending nuclear attack by the USSR. School classrooms were swiftly ushered into hallways to conduct drills where the kids sat on the floor with their backs against the walls, covered their heads with their hands, and bent over so their heads were between

AMERICANS......
DON'T PATRONIZE REDS!!!!

———•———

YOU CAN DRIVE THE REDS OUT OF TELEVISION, RADIO AND HOLLYWOOD.....

THIS TRACT WILL TELL YOU HOW.

WHY WE MUST DRIVE THEM OUT:

1) The REDS have made our Screen, Radio and TV Moscow's most effective Fifth Column in America ... 2) The REDS of Hollywood and Broadway have always been the chief financial support of Communist propaganda in America . . . 3) OUR OWN FILMS, made by RED Producers, Directors, Writers and STARS, are being used by Moscow in ASIA, Africa, the Balkans and throughout Europe to create hatred of America . . . 4) RIGHT NOW films are being made to craftily glorify MARXISM, UNESCO and ONE-WORLDISM . . . and via your TV Set they are being piped into your Living Room—and are poisoning the minds of your children under your very eyes ! ! !

So REMEMBER — If you patronize a Film made by RED Producers, Writers, Stars and STUDIOS you are aiding and abetting COMMUNISM .. . . . every time you permit REDS to come into your Living Room VIA YOUR TV SET you are helping MOSCOW and the INTERNATIONALISTS to destroy America ! ! !

their legs. Some considered this a drill on "how to kiss your ass goodbye," since nuclear bombs can simply vaporize entire buildings, schools included. The drills, if not protective, played a substantial role in the frightening of children as well as their parents.

It appeared that the country of Vietnam, once controlled by the French, was aligning itself with Communist China. It had to be stopped at all costs; otherwise, it would create a "domino effect," meaning once it adopted a communist government, all the other nations around it would do so as well, eventually spreading over the world, including the United States. TV stations, along with magazines, newspapers, and radio broadcasts, primarily owned by wealthy individuals, warned that "our way of life" in the United States would be destroyed by the Red Wave that would engulf our country should Vietnam be allowed to align with China, or "fall to the communists," as they put it.

Television technology had improved to the extent that stations were now starting to broadcast in color. The earliest color TVs entered private homes in the 1960s. People became glued to their TVs day and night to the delight of the government and the people who controlled it. TVs were becoming formidable propaganda machines, "brainwashing machines" so to speak. The art of propaganda had entered an entirely new, very advanced, and dangerous era.

The popular U.S. president at the time, John F. Kennedy, a Democrat and a Catholic, was not convinced that a war against Vietnam was a good idea. To make a long story short, behind-the-scenes actors in the U.S. government had him murdered, assassinated in broad daylight, in front of the nation, for everyone to watch on television. Kennedy's alleged assassin, Lee Harvey Oswald, a man with ties to the CIA and who claimed he was being set up, was also assassinated, shot by Jack Ruby, while everyone watched on television.

JFK's brother, Robert F. Kennedy, another democrat against expanding a war in Southeast Asia, then campaigned for the U.S. presidency. He was also assassinated. This was also broadcast on TV.

Government records relating to the investigation of the JFK assassination, which absolved the CIA of any responsibility in the crime, were sealed from public scrutiny. Sixty-two years later, as this book is being

Rachel Alexander

Yes, because I have reported numerous times on 300,000 misdemeanors being committed due to 300,000 ballots lacking chain of custody in the MaRICOpa County election, just to name one of many criminal laws broken in the 2020 or 2022 elections (and I am THE former Maricopa County Elections attorney and a former Maricopa County prosecutor) and no judge will do a d*** thing about it!

> **Love will keep us together.** @BlueIceAngels · Dec 30, 2023
> Replying to @Rach_IC @Ryan_L_Heath and @MaricopaGOP
> Am I to just accept the term "Election illegalities" as just being a normal thing.

MULTIPLE REPORTS of "Votes Getting Flipped" In Key Swing State, Voting Machines Shut Down

Trump: Colorado Supreme Court Decision 'Shame for Our Country'

The Colorado Supreme Court issued an order to disqualify former President Donald Trump from its primary ballot in 2024. The ruling passed by a narrow vote with three out of seven judges dissenting. It made Colorado the first in the nation to bar President Trump from the ballot.

The Colorado high court, composed entirely of Democrat appointees, said President Trump had engaged in "insurrection" during the Jan. 6, 2021, breach of the U.S. Capitol.

[This decision was reversed by a uninamous vote of the US Supreme Court.]

Colorado secretary of state calls Trump a 'liar,' vows to see ballot lawsuit through

Colorado Secretary of State Jena Griswold (D) called former President Trump a "liar," after he suggested a recent push to use the 14th Amendment to keep him off the ballot in the state was "election interference."

"Trump is a liar with no respect for the Constitution," Griswold said in an interview on MSNBC on Saturday.

written, the records have still not been fully released. What are they hiding? Who are "they"?

Credible rumors pin the blame for the assassination on the U.S. government, particularly the CIA. Robert F. Kennedy Jr., son of JFK's brother, has publicly stated that evidence shows that his father was murdered by one of his father's Secret Service agents, a man who was a federal government employee. It appeared that the assassin was carrying out an organized plot to eliminate an obstacle to America's expanding militarism. Kennedy was also threatening the anti-communist psychopathy that had deeply infected the U.S. government.

Lyndon Johnson, vice president under John Kennedy, assumed the role of president after the murder of JFK. His decision was to go to war against Vietnam, a nation of mostly agrarian peasants dating back at least 2,000 years and historically aligned with China. Maybe he didn't want to be assassinated by clandestine government actors, either.

Although this dark time in U.S. history was openly exposing the criminal side of the American government to anyone who was paying attention, a combination of censorship, propaganda, and persecution of dissenters managed to keep a lid on the opposition. Talk of the "Deep State" and a "Shadow Government" controlling the United States using the CIA and "Black Ops" was replaced in the public mind with TV broadcasts about Gilligan's Island, Superman, and other vacuous, inane entertainment shows, along with news broadcasts emphasizing the horrors of communism and the need to stop it at all costs.

To aid in this goal, the U.S. government instituted the "military draft," a system in which 18-year-old boys fresh out of high school, were forced into the military by being involuntarily selected at random using their birth dates. Registration for the draft was required by law for all males when they turned 18. If they refused to register, it was an automatic two-year sentence in a federal penitentiary. The boys were forced into the army, against their will, to "protect their freedom" and "preserve the American way of life." At age 18, they were not allowed to vote or to drink alcohol, yet they were *forced* to kill strangers in a strange land.

Those who went to prison could be raped by other inmates because they were considered cowards and traitors by the murderers and rapists

The Assassination of President John F. Kennedy

The Assassination of President John F. Kennedy: The Final Analysis presents indisputable forensic evidence that two shots fired from the front and one shot fired from the rear killed the president in a Dealey Plaza crossfire—exposing a sixty-year coverup by the CIA, the FBI, the Pentagon, and the Secret Service.

Mantik and Corsi present overwhelming testimonial and documentary evidence that proves the Bethesda surgeons performed pre-autopsy surgery on JFK's head to remove evidence of the forehead bullet, as well as to gain access to his brain and thus "sanitize the crime scene" by removing bullet fragments and bullet tracks in the brain tissue.

Insurrection Barbie

This is Stephanie Lambert, an election integrity attorney who is representing Patrick Byrne in a defamation lawsuit brought by Dominion. It is because of that lawsuit that she has access to internal company emails from Dominion which prove that the voting machines were in fact online during the 2020 election and that said voting machines were accessed by Serbian nationals.

She was indicted in MI, home of Dana Nessel lover of dr*g queen story hour and hater of election integrity, for accessing the voting machines.

Even though she signed a nondisclosure agreement with dominion, she released these documents to law-enforcement, because she believes that she had a duty to report a crime that has been committed. Pretty sure all lawyers have to report ongoing crimes when they discover them.

Instead of looking into the election fraud claim, DC marshals arrested her today. This should be the number one story in America right now, but our media is a joke. The only way that ever sees the light of day is if people on social media share it.

Supreme Court Denies Bid to Expand No-Excuse Mail-In Ballots in Texas

The Supreme Court's refusal to hear the appeal means that the Texas law stays in place, delivering a win to election integrity advocates.

Twitter Suspends 2020 Maricopa County Election Audit Accounts

Twitter on Tuesday appeared to suspend several accounts dedicated to 2020 election audits, including a prominent one that made announcements regarding the audit of Maricopa County. When trying to access the Maricopa County Audit, and various accounts, Twitter wrote: "Account suspended."

doing time in the penitentiary. Some of the "draft-dodgers" committed suicide after they were released from prison. Thousands fled the United States and sought refuge in Canada. The draft-dodgers were all eventually pardoned by Democrat President Jimmy Carter upon his election in 1977 (Carter was pushed out of office by the Republicans four years later). But the damage had been done. Many of the draft-dodging citizens never returned to the United States.

More Vietnam Vets committed suicide after the war than died in the war itself. One teenage boy who was thrown in prison for refusing to register for the draft, and was brutally raped there, committed suicide after his release from the penitentiary. His explanation: He could not justify living in a world where the government was so deranged and corrupt that it treated teenage boys with brutal repression and with absolutely no human respect whatsoever. This was not a world that he could justify living in. According to the TV, he lived in the land of "truth and justice." According to the pledge of obedience children were required to recite daily in the government schools, there was "liberty and justice for all." But this was propaganda, and he could not bear living in a world of lies.

To make a long story short, the Vietnamese won the war. The United States lost. No Red Wave followed. The American way of life was not destroyed. The heavily broadcast threats were all lies to the American people from the U.S. government and from the anti-communists who controlled both the government and the media.

In the meantime, American taxpayers had funded the slaughter of millions of people in Southeast Asia. American workers had paid for the destruction of Vietnamese roads, bridges, factories, dams, crops, herds, orchards, villages, homes, families, the natural environment, and so on. This was money that could have been spent on things that benefited the American taxpayer but was instead squandered on needless warfare. American capitalists raked in the profits. The expense of the war meant that a lot of money was draining from the U.S. treasury and was being funneled into the pockets of the people who were beating the war drums.

Anti-communists were orchestrating a modern-day witch hunt on a global scale. The public was driven into mass hysteria by the media, to the extent that they were *willing to sacrifice their own children* when their

Wisconsin Judge Orders Officials to Stop Allowing Voters to 'Spoil' Ballots and Cast New Ones

Voters in Wisconsin cannot cancel their ballot and cast a new one once a vote has been cast, a judge in the state has ruled.

David Shafer
Let me repeat. Fulton County elections officials told the media and our observers that they were shutting down the tabulation center at State Farm Arena at 10:30 p.m. on election night only to continue counting ballots in secret until 1:00 a.m. November 10th 2020

10,000 Uncounted Ballots Found in Texas County: Officials

San Antonio woman arrested on election fraud charges based on Project Veritas video

Iowa Officials Coordinated With Big Tech to Censor Election Posts

Polling places run out of ballots in Pennsylvania primary

Former Louisiana Police Chief, City Councilmember Plead Guilty in Federal Vote-Buying Case

Former Philly Democrat Sentenced to Prison for Election Fraud Scheme

Election Watchdog Finds 137,500 Ballots Unlawfully Trafficked in Wisconsin

government commanded it. Brainwashed fathers spit on their sons if they resisted the military draft. Over 58,000 American soldiers were killed during the Vietnam War (referred to as the "American War" by the Vietnamese). Ten times more were wounded. Many of the soldiers killed or wounded were young men just out of high school.

It's estimated that upward of five-million Vietnamese men, women, and children were killed, and many more wounded. Grotesque crimes against not only humanity, but also the environment, were committed during the 10 years when the United States was involved in the Vietnam War. Chemical defoliants, Agent Orange for example, were sprayed over the countryside of South Vietnam, killing the vegetation, polluting the water, and causing birth defects for generations to come.

This is where the saying "We must destroy the village to save it" was born. A communist government was considered so unacceptable by the anti-communists that mass murder was preferable. Entire villages in Vietnam were wiped out, men women and children, bombed and/or incinerated with napalm, a chemical firebomb that stuck to targets, including humans of all ages. Napalm explodes and ignites upon impact, burning at more than 5,000° Fahrenheit.

This sort of violent, horrible destruction was how innocent people around the world were being "saved" from communism. Of course, if you were a napalm manufacturer, you were making very good money, as were the manufacturers of all implements of warfare. The "military industrial complex" was profiting handsomely, while the national debt increased, and our tax dollars disappeared.

The Vietnam War, along with the other subjects mentioned in this book, have been greatly simplified herein. The point to focus on is the power of propaganda and the atrocities that have been committed against humanity when mass communication and mass media tools and techniques are used against the public for brainwashing purposes.

Brainwashing Machines

Let's use an analogy. It is obvious to anyone who pays attention that what you eat affects your physical health. Stand next to a checkout

Trouble in Fulton County? High-Powered Defense Attorneys Move to Withdraw Amid Questions About 2020 Ballots

There's trouble in Fulton County, Georgia as two high-powered criminal defense attorneys have suddenly filed a motion to withdraw from a 2020 election case.

Rasmussen speculated that the lawyers reportedly motioning to withdraw may have something to do with "missing" mail ballots.

"These 150,000 still secret 2020 unfolded mail ballots with the perfect ovals protected by court order for 3 years may have gone missing, and the county's lawyers have just quit," Rasmussen posted on X.

Human Events, however, had earlier reported on the 147,000 mail-in ballots controversy:

Fulton County poll manager Suzi Voyles was sorting through a large stack of mail-in ballots last November when she noticed something odd: several ballots marked for Joe Biden were extremely similar.

One after another, the votes contained perfectly filled ovals for Biden. What's more, each of the bubbles boasted an identical white void inside them in the shape of a tiny crescent, indicating they'd been marked with toner ink instead of a pen or pencil.

Voyles also noticed that all of the ballots were printed on different paper than the others she'd counted and none were folded or creased, which is standard for mail-in ballots as they come from envelopes.

"All of them were strangely pristine," Voyles said. She noted that she'd never seen anything like it in her 20 years monitoring elections in Fulton County.

All but three of the 110 ballots in the stack – which had been labeled "State Farm Arena" – were marked for Biden and appeared to be "identical ballots."

After Voyles came forward, she was fired as a poll manager by the Fulton County Department of Elections.

True the Vote Defeats Fair Fight, Stacy Abrams, Marc Elias, and the Biden Department of Justice in Landmark Election Case in Georgia Federal Court

In a resounding vindication, TTV successfully defended its actions of December 2020, aiding Georgia citizens in filing elector challenges based on data showing over 364,000 voters appeared to be ineligible to vote due to change in residency.

Courtroom Victory, Clean Rolls, and You

What a week it has been! In case you missed it, on Tuesday, we won our lawsuit against Stacey Abrams, Marc Elias, Fair Fight, and the DOJ. This lawsuit had been ongoing since 2020. The main issue was whether citizens have the right to lawfully petition their government in support of election integrity without facing persecution or prosecution. In a resounding victory, we successfully defended our actions from December 2020, where we assisted Georgia citizens in filing challenges to electors based on data that revealed over 364,000 ineligible records in the voter rolls.

The federal court's ruling sent a clear message to those who would attempt to control the course of our nation through lawfare and intimidation. American citizens will not be silenced.

counter at any grocery store and watch the contents of the shopping carts and the physical characteristics of the customers pushing them. Obese and overweight people will be loading up on sugary "foods." Unhealthy-looking customers will have their pop, their cigarettes, their processed food. Healthier, more slender customers will have more fresh, natural, and unprocessed foods. Put simply, if you live on a diet of donuts, your body will become physically unhealthy, even diseased.

Your mind works the same way. If you feed your mind "brain donuts" continually, your mind will become unhealthy, and it won't work correctly. Brain donuts are constantly served by commercial media, especially television, in the form of propaganda. Sit in front of commercial TV daily and you will become weak-minded and ultimately "brainwashed" and you won't know it because you will have become a "boiled frog," easily controlled, manipulated, incapable of independent thought, critical thinking, or even independent research.

Like a sugar addict who must taste sugar in everything they eat (spaghetti, cereal, bread, pastries, pickles, relish, even meat, breakfast, lunch, and dinner), or like a cigarette addict who must have just one more puff of his or her addictive chemical nicotine, so does the weak-minded TV watcher need to have their daily fix of propaganda.

You know the old story. If you put a frog in a pot of cold water on a stove, then turn the heat on low, the frog won't notice that the water is becoming hot enough to cook it until it is too late. On the other hand, if you throw a frog into a pot of hot water, it immediately tries desperately to escape. Commercial television is the pot on the stove and the people who watch it are the frogs.

Over the past 60 years, TV propaganda has developed into a formidable tool to influence the TV-watching public. People who don't watch commercial television notice this right away when they see commercial broadcasts, such as in a hotel room, or at an airport. They also notice it in the behavior of the boiled frogs (habitual TV watchers), and in what they think and what they say, which is often just a parroting of what they heard or saw on their brainwashing machines.

The boiled frogs don't see the propaganda; they see entertainment. Like the Germans who supported the Nazis, or the crowds cheering the torture and murder of witches, or the Americans who, to this day, lament that the United States hadn't killed enough people in Vietnam, boiled frogs wallow in the belief that their behavior is righteous and good, even necessary, for the benefit of humankind. And it can be very difficult to reach them through intelligent discourse or reasoning.

Let's use another analogy. Suppose you work in a plastics factory. When you started working there, you noticed a slight but foul chemical odor in the air. Before long, that odor had disappeared, and you paid no attention to it after that. However, one day a friend dropped by the factory to pick you up because you needed a ride. As soon as the friend walked in the door, she said, "Whew! What's that smell?" Your reply, of course, was "What smell? I don't smell anything."

A person who doesn't watch commercial TV drops by your house to visit and notices that you have a big-screen TV turned on with talking heads on a propaganda channel. She asks, "Why do you watch this propaganda?" You respond, "What propaganda?" You're a boiled frog. You own a brainwashing machine, and you feed your brain a constant diet of brain donuts. Your mind is unhealthy. A nation of weak-minded TV watchers is a nation where democracy cannot thrive.

We have a fake democracy in the United States. In a real democracy, citizens would vote directly on legislation and representatives would only have one vote, no matter how much money they have — one vote the same as everyone else. If we the people, the working class, were able to vote on legislation, there's a pretty good chance that we could craft national policies developed through sane, common sense, responsible, intelligent, practical, and purposeful procedures where any qualified citizen, who wants to, can participate in the process.

Want to start another useless war? Let's vote on that. Want to squander our tax dollars on handouts to the already wealthy? Let's take a vote. How should our tax dollars be spent? It would be up to us, not to the deranged criminals who continue to rob our treasury. But what if those deranged criminals are the same people who are feeding you the brain donuts? That might be humanity's Achilles' heel. Therein lies the dilemma. That's the *Curse of the Boiled Frogs*.

6
Milking the Cash Cow

The government milks us like cows. Instead of milk, they squeeze tax dollars out of us. Our tax dollars go into a central repository known as the national treasury. From this treasury our money continually disappears. If there isn't enough money to cover expenses, the government prints more. Then it spends that money, too. Our national debt was over $35 trillion in 2024 and climbing fast. That debt amounts to over $264,000 per taxpayer. With annual interest approaching one trillion dollars a year, servicing the debt is our second-largest budgetary item, second only to Social Security and topping mililtary spending.

Sound like a scam? Who is getting all this money? Not you or your co-workers. Instead, it's coming out of your pockets — out of your paychecks. As long as your "representatives" decide how much tax money to spend and where it's going to go, you have no say about it. And if you do have something to say and manage to get anyone to listen to you, you're largely, if not completely, ignored.

Milking this cash cow is a criminal's dream come true. Bought-and-paid-for politicians who call themselves senators and congresspersons are getting a piece of the pie. Granted, there are principled and honest representatives in Congress, but they are in the minority. How many thousands of dollars must representatives raise every single day during their entire term of office to be able to run for reelection? Hopefully, you're getting the picture. The thieves don't care if they run the country into the ground financially. They don't care if they bankrupt the United States. They don't care how hard you worked for your money or what the average American needs to have their tax dollars spent on. They have their fingers in the pie, and it's a really big pie, overflowing with your tax dollars and stuffed with mountains of debt that you and your descendants will be expected to pay off.

If only we could vote directly on legislation and cut out the middleman. You know, have a democracy. Just think, on your tax return there could be a list of expense items, and you could select the ones you want to fund and the ones you don't. Listed would be the top 10 expense items

Congress Guts Budget Rules and Misses Chance to Cut Spending

The most important solution lawmakers could advance to address the country's largest problem, inflation, is reducing government spending. The massive omnibus spending bill introduced by the leadership of both parties in the Senate included a provision that simply turned off enforcement of the Statutory PAYGO rules not just this year, but next year as well. This would result in a $260 billion deficit-fueled spending hike. 16 Senate Republicans and all Democrats voted to "waive all applicable budgetary discipline."

Uncounted Votes on Overlooked Memory Card Flip Election in Georgia

America's Runaway Debt Scenario: $1 Trillion in Interest per Year

The U.S. federal government has borrowed so much money that, over the past year, it has had to spend one-fifth of all the money it collected just on debt interest—which came to almost $880 billion. This fiscal year, interest is expected to reach over $1 trillion. The country teeters on the brink of a debt spiral that could devolve into a fiscal crisis or hyperinflation. "The problem is serious because, any way you cut it, taxpayers are paying interest on the mountain of debt that has been accumulated," said Steve Hanke, a professor of applied economics at Johns Hopkins University. "In short, they are paying something for nothing."

Goldman CEO Issues Warning as Interest Costs on America's Ballooning Debt Exceed Spending on Defense, Medicare

FedEx Founder Issues Dire Warning About 'Unsustainable' Government Debt

The founder of FedEx has added his voice to the chorus of views expressing concern about out-of-control spending in Washington.

in the U.S. government, which you would rank on a 1—10 basis: number one having the highest priority for funding, and number 10 having the lowest. Social Security, infrastructure, military spending, foreign aid, education, environment, agriculture, veterans, homeland security, and so on, would be listed. Then, underneath each category would be subcategories. Under military spending of example, would be "defense spending," and "offense spending." How much do we want to allocate for defense, and how much do we want to allocate for attacking small, innocent populations?

Allow "We the People" to decide how our tax money is spent, not the crooks who are stuffing *our* money into *their* pockets. Realistic, practical, and sane management of the treasury will never happen as long as the people raking in the largesse are making the laws, voting on them, and cutting us out of the decision-making process.

But we digress. It gets worse. The Vietnam War ended in 1975, after which there was a short pause in American open warfare. In the meantime, behind the scenes, black ops from the United States engaged in clandestine efforts to assassinate foreign leaders and overthrow democratically elected governments around the world, using the "offense spending" account.

All of it was being done at taxpayers' expense. How many billions of tax dollars do these secretive quasigovernment entities eat up? We don't know. It's a secret. What happens to the trillions of tax dollars the U.S. military budget has swallowed up? We don't know that either. The military has never passed an audit, and trillions of tax dollars allotted to the military remain unaccounted for. Did the American taxpayer vote for this? No, of course not. You don't have a vote in a fake democracy. You can only stand there and watch your tax money gobbled up, much of it unaccounted for, while unelected, behind-the-scenes, shadow government actors bloat their off-shore bank accounts.

On September 11, 2001, a group of men hijacked airliners, flew two of them into the World Trade Center and one into the Pentagon, presumably as an act of retribution against the CIA and U.S. military occupying, overthrowing, and terrorizing Arab and Muslim nations in the Middle East. As reported by the U.S. government, the 19 men included 15 from

How Google Stopped the Red Wave

Google and other tech companies want you obsessing about conspiracy theories so you won't look at how they tampered with the 2022 midterm elections

Robert Epstein

Based on my team's research, Google, and to a lesser extent, Facebook and other tech monopolies, not only took steps to shift millions of votes to Democrats in the midterms, but they are using their influence to spread rumors and conspiracy theories to make sure people look everywhere for explanations–except at them.

Google Is Influencing Elections by Flipping Votes on 'Massive Scale'

Search engine results that favor one political candidate were found to influence undecided voters so much that up to 80 percent of such people in some demographic groups shifted their voting preferences after only a single search.

"Carefully crafted search suggestions that flash at you while you are typing a search term can turn a 50/50 split among undecided voters into a 90/10 split with no one knowing they have been manipulated,' Robert Epstein writes.

"A single question-and-answer interaction on a digital personal assistant can shift the voting preferences of undecided voters by more than 40 percent."

Ahead of the 2022 election, "a high level of liberal bias" is being seen in Google search results in swing states like Arizona, Florida, and Wisconsin, Epstein wrote. Search results from Bing did not indicate such bias.

A Sampling of Recent Election Fraud Cases from Across the United States

1,500	1,276	56
Proven instances of voter fraud.	Criminal Convictions	Civil Penalties
	Heritage Foundation's Election Fraud Database	

Majority of American Voters Rightly Concerned About Vote Fraud

Saudi Arabia, two from the United Arab Emirates, one from Egypt, and one from Lebanon.

On the other hand, credible witnesses suggested that this was an "inside job." The same shadow government that assassinated JFK and pushed us into the Korean and Vietnam wars was responsible for the nearly 3,000 people killed on 9-11, they insisted. The government vehemently denied any part in this act of terrorism and instead came up with its own well-thought-out and perfectly sane explanation: Iraqis did it. That's right, the people of Iraq, and those from another Middle Eastern country, Afghanistan, were held responsible for an attack largely committed by Saudi Arabians.

If that sounds completely insane, that's because it is. Uncle Sam, in his current incarnation, is insane. The response to 9-11 was absolute proof of that. Three thousand innocent civilians were murdered in New York City in a coordinated plot conducted by foreigners, or so we're told. This was such a horrible crime that the only reasonable response was to commit a horrible crime of far greater magnitude: the murder of a million innocent civilians in foreign nations that had nothing to do with the 9-11 attack.

This does not come from the minds of sane people. But wait! Think about how much money can be made from another massive war operation against other small countries. Never mind the lies, deception, propaganda, censorship, and evil required to carry out more massive needless wars. Never mind the millions of people who would be killed and wounded. Never mind the unbelievable destruction we would inflict on nations of innocent people, many of whom probably never heard of the World Trade Center. There was lots of money to be made and lots of weak-minded TV watchers to milk for their tax dollars.

After 9-11, the mainstream propaganda platforms and the brainwashing machines revved into high gear, working overtime to marinate the brains of the boiled frogs with lies and misinformation. A 20-year war was launched against Afghanistan, while Iraq was bombed "back to the stone age," invaded, occupied, and massively assaulted by Uncle Sam, while TV watchers stared blankly at their brainwashing machines as their tax dollars vanished into thin air to pay for it all. When money disappears

Wall Street Apes

Countless Videos Surfaced Showing Voter Fraud From Our Recent Elections But What Did We Expect? Videos Like This Came Out Previously & NOTHING Is Ever Done To Secure Voting

California San Joaquin Sheriff Patrick Withrow Discoveries Regarding Voter Rolls:

-93 people registered w/ birthdate of 1850

-4,144 voters registered over the age of 90 (there's only 10.3k residents over 80 in that county...this number would drop off significantly at 90)

-232 registered at local prisons

-125 registered to a non-profit, NGO or business

~300 voters with no first name

-110 potential double voters - same name, DOB, and address but different Voter ID numbers

-Registered voter named Jesus Christ

Democrats & Mainstream media call you conspiracy theorists, is this sheriff a conspiracy theorist too?

Now multiply this by every county in every state nationwide. United States elections are rigged. Our intelligence agencies/ Deep State are stealing our elections and we're all paying the price.

The whole Uniparty & Deep State belong behind bars.

Voter Fraud Cases Stemming From Jailhouse Voter Registration Drive in Florida

Biden 'Won' 2020 Election with Mail-in Ballot Fraud, Study Confirms

A bombshell new study has confirmed that President Joe Biden only got the votes required to "win" the 2020 election through widespread ballot fraud. A new study examining the likely impact that fraudulent mail-in ballots had in the 2020 election concludes that the outcome would "almost certainly" have been different without the massive expansion of voting by mail.

DeSantis Announces Election Crime Crackdown: 20 Arrested for Voter Fraud

from the U.S. treasury, it doesn't just vanish — it is funneled into the pockets of the people orchestrating the heist.

Costs of the 20-year "war on terror" are estimated at $8 trillion, leaving at least 900,000 deaths in its wake, a number that is widely viewed as very low compared to the actual number of dead and wounded. Imagine being able to rob someone of $8 trillion. That's $8,000 billion. All you need is a fake threat and a population of ignorant, compliant, obedient conformists. Bingo! The perfect crime.

These wars were pushed by the Republican Party, primarily by President George W. Bush and his associates Dick Cheney, Condoleezza Rice, Colin Powell, and Donald Rumsfeld, with significant assistance from the Democrat Party, especially Joe Biden and Hillary Clinton.

None of these people were ever punished or brought to justice for crimes against humanity. Instead, as this book is written, George W. Bush enjoys a lifetime pension and lifetime secret service protection at the expense of American taxpayers. According to online sources in 2024, his net worth was reported to be $50 million. The others are as follows: Hillary Clinton, $120 million; Donald Rumsfeld (now deceased) $200 million; Dick Cheney: $150 million; Colin Powell: $60 million; and Condoleezza Rice: $12 million. Not a bad accumulation of wealth for people who are supposed to be employed as public servants.

To put this into perspective, U.S. federal employee salaries averaged $143,643 in total compensation in 2022, while the median annual wage in the United States in 2021 was $45,760. The median net worth of all American families in 2022 was $192,700. *Our national debt, per household, was $406,000 at that time.* Looks like there's some gross incompetence taking place with our nation's finances.

In 2022, there were also 22.7 million people with a net worth of over a million U.S. dollars in the United States, 6.7% of the population, more than any other country in the world. China was second, with 6.2 million individuals worth more than $1 million. The obvious question here is how can China be a communist country when it has so many millionaires (and billionaires) in a system where private property is supposed to be prohibited? Could the greed gene be infecting the People's Republic of China?

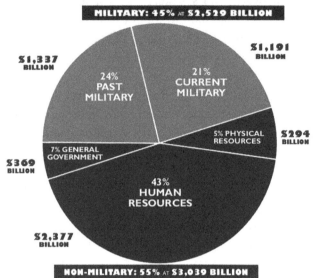

WHERE YOUR INCOME TAX MONEY REALLY GOES

U.S. FEDERAL BUDGET **2025** FISCAL YEAR

MILITARY: 45% AT $2,529 BILLION

$1,337 BILLION

24% PAST MILITARY

$1,191 BILLION

21% CURRENT MILITARY

5% PHYSICAL RESOURCES

$294 BILLION

7% GENERAL GOVERNMENT

$369 BILLION

43% HUMAN RESOURCES

$2,377 BILLION

NON-MILITARY: 55% AT $3,039 BILLION

The Financial Legacy of Iraq and Afghanistan

Abstract: The Iraq and Afghanistan conflicts, taken together, will be the most expensive wars in US history – totaling somewhere between $4 to $6 trillion. This includes long-term medical care and disability compensation for service members, veterans and families, military replenishment and social and economic costs. The largest portion of that bill is yet to be paid.

Alternative Brown University, Watson Institute Estimate

The United States federal government has spent or obligated $4.8 trillion dollars on the wars in Afghanistan, Pakistan, and Iraq. This figure includes: direct Congressional war appropriations; war-related increases to the Pentagon base budget; veterans care and disability; increases in the homeland security budget; interest payments on direct war borrowing; foreign assistance spending; and estimated future obligations for veterans' care. This total omits many other expenses, such as the macroeconomic costs to the US economy; the opportunity costs of not investing war dollars in alternative sectors; future interest on war borrowing; and local government and private war costs. The current wars have been paid for almost entirely by borrowing. Unless the US immediately repays the money borrowed for war, there will also be future interest payments. We estimate that interest payments could total over $7.9 trillion by 2053.

These statistics are listed here not to suggest that being wealthy is bad or wrong. Some people inherit their wealth unintentionally. Others are showered with wealth on behalf of their artistic talents. Many work hard, engage in useful, valuable, honest enterprises, and have earned their wealth. Others, obviously, make their money from phony wars and other crooked enterprises.

The question that should be obvious is this: if 6.7% of the U.S. population is made up of millionaires, a truly representative body in Congress should also be approximately 6.7% millionaires, not the 50% or more that is currently residing in Congress. A realistic, truly representative ratio can be achieved when representatives are chosen through a process of random intelligent selection. Random selection of representatives, coupled with direct citizen voting on legislation, is a means by which democracy can be fortified without warfare and bloodshed.

What happened after 9-11? Well, Afghanistan was invaded and occupied by the United States, at taxpayer's expense, of course. The Taliban, the country's ruling party, was pushed out of power. It was, at the time, considered a brutally repressive regime made up of religious fundamentalists who excluded women from employment and education, destroyed non-Islamic artistic relics, and implemented harsh criminal punishments. No one liked the Taliban.

Twenty years later, the United States withdrew from Afghanistan; the Taliban immediately rushed back in, took control, and became the recipient of billions of dollars of high-quality military equipment that the U.S. left behind. In the meantime, the ravages of war had been visited upon the nation: the murder and wounding of tens of thousands of men, women, and children; rape; massive destruction of property and infrastructure; the creation of widows, widowers, and orphans, while homes, businesses, and livelihoods were destroyed and lost, and so on.

Afghans and Iraqis who resisted the invasion were classified "enemy combatants" by the U.S. government. People who had the audacity to try to defend themselves and their families and communities from a violent foreign invasion were given their own criminal classification by the invaders, rounded up, imprisoned, and tortured by the tens of thousands, if not killed outright.

The Pentagon fails its fifth audit in a row

If the Defense Department can't get its books straight, how can it be trusted with a budget of more than $800 billion per year?

"I would not say that we flunked," said DoD Comptroller Mike McCord, although his office did note that the Pentagon only managed to account for 39 percent of its $3.5 trillion in assets.

Costs of the 20-year war on terror: $8 trillion and 900,000 deaths

A report from the Costs of War project at Brown University revealed that 20 years of post-9/11 wars have cost the U.S. an estimated $8 trillion and have killed more than 900,000 people. "The Pentagon and the U.S. military have now absorbed the great majority of the federal discretionary budget. The death toll, standing at an estimated 897,000 to 929,000, includes U.S. military members, allied fighters, opposition fighters, civilians, journalists and humanitarian aid workers who were killed as a direct result of war, whether by bombs, bullets or fire. It does not, the researchers noted, include the many indirect deaths the war on terror has caused by way of disease, displacement and loss of access to food or clean drinking water. "The deaths we tallied are likely a vast undercount of the true toll these wars have taken on human life." [2021]

Defense Contractors Benefited From Nearly Half of $14 Trillion Spent for Afghan War: Study

A study that illuminates how defense contractors benefitted from the war in Afghanistan showed that they pocketed up to half of the $14 trillion spent by the Department of Defense since 9/11.

What We Left Behind in Afghanistan

An impressive amount of U.S. military hardware: 22,174 armored Humvees, 42 pickup trucks and SUVS, 64,363 machine guns, 162,043 radios. 16,035 night-vision goggles, 358,530 assault rifles (the real ones, not the "assault rifles" that Joe Biden warns about in the United States), 126,295 pistols, and 176 artillery pieces.

And that's just for starters. The United States also generously left behind more than 100 helicopters, including 33 Blackhawks, four C-130 transport planes, and about 60 other fixed-wing aircraft.

If you ever feel useless, remember, it took four presidents, 20 years, and trillions of dollars, to replace the Taliban with the Taliban.

War profiteers made mountains of money, enough to buy plenty of influence in Congress and elsewhere. $14 trillion was spent on the war, according to *Newsweek*, half of which went to military contractors like Halliburton, of which Vice-President Dick Cheney was the former CEO. Halliburton received more than $30 billion.

"Any member of Congress who doesn't vote for the funds we need to defend [the United States] will be looking for a new job after next November," threatened the vice president of Boeing.

How is this possible? All members of Congress require lots of money to run for election. Where does that money come from? Obviously, from very wealthy people who have the money and who are likely to benefit financially by selecting the Congresspersons of their choice, then keeping them in power by financing their reelections. If representatives were chosen through a process of random selection, this would be impossible. No money would be needed for an election because it would be a different type of election, a selective election, not a financed election.

The money that one military contractor, Lockheed Martin, got from Pentagon contracts was one and a half times the entire budgets of the State Department and the U.S. Agency for International Development (USAID). Billions of unmonitored loose American dollars poured into the Afghanistan War, funding unspeakable corruption.

Iraq? Same thing only worse. At the time of this writing, the war in Iraq is ongoing, 20 years after it started. Wars are easy to start but hard to stop. As long as a war continues, war profiteers rake in the money.

The propagandists in the United States had insisted that our military forces needed to invade Iraq to eliminate their leader, Saddam Hussein, falsely claiming the Iraqis were manufacturing weapons of mass destruction. In fact, Saddam Hussein refused to trade Iraqi oil for U.S. dollars, thereby threatening U.S. financial dominance in the oil industry.

The Unired States subsequently sent 170,000 soldiers over, causing massive death, destruction, political instability, widespread violence, and the rise of militant groups, creating an enormously destructive human, social, economic, and environmental toll. A low estimate is that 315,000 people died from direct war violence in Iraq, a hundred times more than Americans who died on 9-11, although other estimates put the death toll

War Is Always Inflationary

While the United States is ostensibly not at war with anyone, our government is spending taxpayers' money as if it were. This year, the budget for the U.S. Department of Defense is $844 billion. The United States spends nearly three times more on defense than does China and 10 times more than does Russia. [2024]

Interest Costs Just Surpassed Defense and Medicare

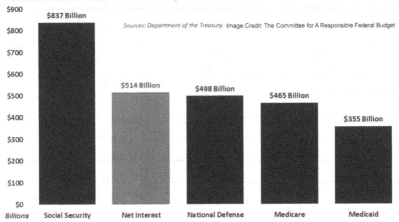

Sources: Department of the Treasury. Image Credit: The Committee for A Responsible Federal Budget

| | $837 Billion | $514 Billion | $498 Billion | $465 Billion | $355 Billion |
| Billions | Social Security | Net Interest | National Defense | Medicare | Medicaid |

US Spends Billions on Overseas Wars, But Who Really Benefits?

Numerous analysts believe that the administration's supplemental spending request, in addition to its record-breaking defense funding, would effectively serve as a massive transfer of wealth to the defense sector from U.S. taxpayers. Stephen Semler, co-founder of the Security Policy Reform Institute think tank, said defense contractors stand to reap billions from the administration's requested supplemental spending request, which would go "mostly to just a few companies." [2024]

Jamie Dimon Warns of 'Rebellion' as Government Debt Balloons, Economy Heads Towards 'Cliff'

The CEO of JPMorgan Chase warns of a potential market 'rebellion' due to Washington's unchecked spending escalating U.S. government debt.

US Household Debt Surges to Record $17.8 Trillion

of upward around 2 million due to indirect causes such as displacement, poor access to safe drinking water, lack of medical care and supplies, and preventable diseases. Estimated costs for the Iraq war are around $3 trillion; however other estimates are much higher.

More than 7 million people from Iraq and Syria were refugees in the early 2020s; nearly 8 million people were internally displaced in the two countries. The devastation to local infrastructure and the environment, including harm to local and regional ecosystems, endures long after major fighting has ended. U.S. forces continue to strike Iraq from the air and the ground. It's also estimated that 6 million people, or about 15% of all Iraqis, are now disabled. Of those, about 200,000 required an orthotic or prosthetic limb. This was done to them in response to the 9-11 attacks, although they had nothing at all to do with those attacks.

It should be noted that the Afghan and Iraq/Syria wars have been five times more expensive than World War I, more than five times more expensive than the Korean War, and nearly 2.5 times more expensive than the Vietnam War. There is lots of blood money to be made, just keep the boiled frogs securely mesmerized in front of their brainwashing machines so they don't interfere, and use dark money to maintain control of the houses of representatives, judges, police, governors, media, and lawyers.

A handful of Saudis committed a crime of terror at the World Trade Center, and Americans responded by slaughtering and terrorizing Afghans, Iraqis, and neighboring countries such as Syria. How can this be possible? Quite frankly, our congress is bought and paid for. Before we spend $14 trillion to commit another crime against humanity, let's vote on it. Oh wait, we can't. We have a fake democracy and a corrupt House of Representatives controlled by special interests lacking in conscience and infected by a lust for money.

Our shadow government, comprised of unidentified, unelected, powerful actors who control your "representatives," as well as many government agencies, don't care what party anyone belongs to. They comprise a sort of "UniParty," which preys on easily corrupted, pliable government "representatives" and three-letter agency directors who will do their bidding given sufficient financial incentives.

Most expensive ever: 2020 election cost $14.4 billion

Political spending in the 2020 election totaled $14.4 billion, more than doubling the total cost of the record-breaking 2016 presidential election cycle. That's according to OpenSecrets' analysis of Federal Election Commission filings. OpenSecrets previously estimated that the 2020 election would cost around $14 billion. The extraordinary spending figure makes the 2020 election the most expensive of all time by a large margin. Donors also fueled record spending in congressional races, capping off the 2020 election with the all-time most expensive Georgia Senate runoffs.

Not Making Headlines... George Soros Dumps $750,000 into Wisconsin Midterms as Democrats Gear Up for the Steal

The Wisconsin Election Commission admits they have 7.1 million in the database but only 3.68 million are eligible to vote. Even dead voters are not separated out. Other investigations show data missing in required fields, thousands of identical 1918 birth dates, illegible text entries, missing last names or addresses, up to 25 Voter ID's for one registration, and other inexcusable issues. Charging $13,500 to investigators who asked for voter data helped hide these atrocities.

Fairfax County Virgina Received Over $1.2 Million in Zuckerbucks in 2020 Election – Does This Explain the Three 300,000 Biden Ballot Drops on Election Night?

Three 300,000 Biden Vote Dumps Late on Election Night

in Virginia Cannot Be Adequately Explained or Tied to Final Results

Cryptocurrency magnate, new GOP megadonor, sunk millions into primaries

50 Richest Members of Congress

The median net worth of a senator is a staggering $3.2 million. For representatives, it's $900,000. [2016]

CHINESE MILLIONAIRES

According to Credit Suisse, the number of millionaires residing in China totaled 6.2 million individuals, ranking second after the United States. [2023]

FTX Poured Millions Into Political Campaigns Before Bankruptcy

It Keeps Going

Although we're touching upon some of the more notable examples of brainwashing, censorship, and mass insanity demonstrated by human beings and especially by the American people since WWII, this simple review is far from complete. As an example, the United States invaded the island nation of Grenada in 1983. This small Caribbean nation north of Venezuela had gained independence from Great Britain just a decade earlier. The leader, Maurice Bishop, a socialist, was considered a "Communist" by American politicians, many of whom used the terms "Socialist" and "Communist" interchangeably, and many still do today.

Bishop was a popular international speaker, like Cuban leader Fidel Castro was, and his speeches were reported in international newspapers but not in the United States. In fact, the U.S. population only received information that the U.S. government allowed people to see — anything else would be "communist propaganda." One of Bishop's speeches before an international body revealed that he expected the United States to invade the island and to assassinate him. Shortly thereafter, he was killed. "Better dead than red" was a popular American saying at the time.

Ronald Reagan, the U.S. president in 1983 and a rabid anticommunist, got on TV and showed the alarmed American population a spy satellite photograph of an airport being built in Grenada, declaring that it was designed to be used for sinister purposes by communists. The United States then bombed the airport and invaded the island to protect America from the purported communist invasion. In the meantime, the airport construction was being financed by the British for large international flights of tourists. This fact had been conveniently omitted by Reagan, who believed socialists had to be stopped at any cost, even if it meant lying to the American public on television.

The morning after the invasion, the headline in a major London newspaper had only one word, printed in very large letters across the top of the front page: OUTRAGE! The British were incensed that their island protectorate had been invaded under false pretenses by the Americans and that their prized tourist airport had been destroyed. The American general population knew none of this. The brainwashing ma-

Pennsylvania 2021 & 2022 Elections

SALARIES FOR ELECTED AND APPOINTED OFFICIALS RECEIVING SALARIES CONTAINED IN ACT 1995-51

PREPARED NOVEMBER 15, 2023

POSITION	ANNUAL SALARY EFFECTIVE 1/1/2023	COLA ADJUSTMENT	ANNUAL SALARY EFFECTIVE 1/1/2024	DAILY RATE EFFECTIVE 1/1/2024	BIWEEKLY EFFECTIVE 1/1/2024
Governor	$229,642	3.5%	$237,679	$649.40	$9,091.55

PA Governor: $122 million raised to run for a $229 thousand salary?

"The Most Secure Election in American History"

In **Georgia**, the Secretary of State, Brad Raffensperger, signed a settlement agreement in March of 2020 in a suit that was filed by the Democratic Committee that essentially obliterated the signature verification process in Georgia. It made it virtually impossible to disqualify any ballots no matter how unlike the signature on the ballot was to the signature in the registration file.

Were They Told to Stand Down? The DOJ's Arizona Election Fraud Investigators Go AWOL Following 2020 and 2022 Elections – Where Are They Today?

More Than 8,000 Double-Registered Voters Found on New Jersey Rolls

Bodycam Footage Shows Texas Man Admitting to Brazen Cash-for-Ballots Scheme

Election Fraud Issues Are Not Limited to Swing States

Election integrity issues in South Dakota

Ex-Democrat Congressman Pleads Guilty to Voter Fraud in Multiple Pennsylvania Elections

A Democrat former U.S. congressman has pleaded guilty to voter fraud charges spanning multiple elections in Pennsylvania. 79-year-old ex-Rep. Michael "Ozzie" Myers (D-PA) bribed election judges for two South Philadelphia wards from 2014 to 2018 to add fake votes for his candidates. Democratic Party operative Myers pleaded guilty to conspiracy to deprive voters of civil rights, bribery, obstruction of justice, falsification of voting records, and conspiring to illegally vote in a federal election, the

In a 54-year period, up until the year 2000. . . we [United States government] interfered in the elections of 81 countries. And then also, during that period of time, significant assassinations of 50 that were directed by our CIA that they documented. Some they brag about. Ron Paul, Liberty Report

chines were working full-time and were quite effective.

To provide another example, in 1953 the CIA overthrew the democratically elected government of Iran. Prime Minister Mohammed Mosaddegh had made the mistake of trying to wrest control of Iran's vast oil reserves from the British and to return the nation's natural resources to the Iranian people. The CIA put a stop to that, pushing Mosaddegh out of office and installing Mohammad Reza Shah Pahlavi, the "Shah of Iran," who subsequently tortured and executed thousands of political prisoners while violently suppressing dissent.

In 1979, the Iranians finally overthrew the Shah, and Islamic nationalist Ayatollah Khomeini took power. Subsequently, Islamic students stormed the U.S. Embassy in Tehran and took 52 American employees as hostages. They were held for 444 days, then released on January 20, 1981, minutes after Ronald Reagan was sworn in as the republican president of the United States.

Remember Jimmy Carter, the democrat president, sworn in in 1977, who had promised to grant amnesty to all "draft dodgers" after the Vietnam War, a promise he kept? He was a popular president who was reviled and hated by anticommunist Republicans. After the American hostages were taken, an oil embargo drove the price of oil up, followed by steeply climbing interest rates, leaving Carter's presidency in turmoil, facing crisis after crisis. Republicans attacked him from all sides. If only he could secure the release of the hostages to bolster his chances for reelection.

But the Iranians held the hostages until the very minute Ronald Reagan was sworn into office, then they were all suddenly and "unexpectedly" released without comment. Seem a little fishy? Was there a backdoor deal here between the Republicans and the Iranians aimed at undermining American support for Jimmy Carter?

How many billions of our taxpayer dollars are used to bribe foreign actors? How can the United States government be run like a criminal enterprise with impunity? Why don't citizens have any say about how their tax dollars are spent? How much of our money is sucked up by Black Ops and used to undermine democracy around the world, including domestically in the United States?

If you want an in-depth glimpse of behind-the-scenes American government malfeasance, read the book *Killing Hope: US Military and CIA Interventions Since World War II*, by William Blum, 472 pages of fine print detailing covert CIA operations, interventions, murders, overthrown governments, and other clearly undemocratic, cruel, criminal, deplorable activities paid for by U.S. citizens with their hard-earned tax dollars during the 50-year period from World War II (1945) until the book's publication in 1995.

The book you're reading now was written 30 years after that. A lot has happened since then. Mr. Blum would be spinning in his grave. It should be no surprise that the words "truth, justice, and the American way," are nowhere to be found in his book.

Most young American adults today know little to nothing about the mafia-like nature of the United States government, especially the unelected shadow government that sucks up our tax dollars like giant leeches draining the blood out of our nation's back.

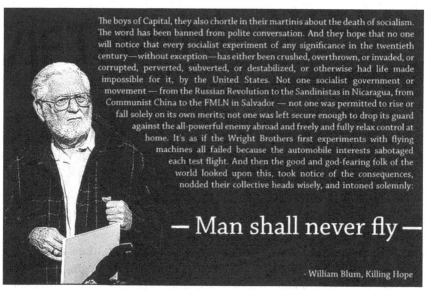

The boys of Capital, they also chortle in their martinis about the death of socialism. The word has been banned from polite conversation. And they hope that no one will notice that every socialist experiment of any significance in the twentieth century—without exception—has either been crushed, overthrown, or invaded, or corrupted, perverted, subverted, or destabilized, or otherwise had life made impossible for it, by the United States. Not one socialist government or movement — from the Russian Revolution to the Sandinistas in Nicaragua, from Communist China to the FMLN in Salvador — not one was permitted to rise or fall solely on its own merits; not one was left secure enough to drop its guard against the all-powerful enemy abroad and freely and fully relax control at home. It's as if the Wright Brothers first experiments with flying machines all failed because the automobile interests sabotaged each test flight. And then the good and god-fearing folk of the world looked upon this, took notice of the consequences, nodded their collective heads wisely, and intoned solemnly:

— Man shall never fly —

- William Blum, Killing Hope

"Consciously or unconsciously, [the American people] have certain basic beliefs about the United States and its foreign policy...The most basic of these basic beliefs, I think, is a deeply-held conviction that no matter what the U.S. does abroad, no matter how bad it may look, no matter what horror may result, the government of the United States means well." William Blum (1933-2018)

7

Scamdemic

"If human equality is to be forever averted — if the High as we have called them, are to keep their places permanently — then the prevailing mental condition must be controlled insanity." George Orwell, 1984

Take a look at the *"What's Wrong with This Picture"* illustration on the next page. What that illustration shows is that the "COVID-19 Global Pandemic" was, at best, an American disaster of gross incompetence; at worst, it was a scam perpetrated on the American people, a fraud, a hoax, a crime. Or all of the above.

The author of this book is an international consultant in two unrelated fields. Neither of these are medical fields. At no time is the author, age 72 at the time this book was published, trying to misrepresent himself as a medical authority or professional scientist. The author is a person who has lived through some of the eras discussed in this book, starting with the Korean War, then Vietnam, Central American proxy wars, Iraq, Afghanistan, anti-communism, pervasive media propaganda, and now this awful power grab being called a "pandemic."

He is also a person who has not watched commercial television since the age of 18 (1970) and is acutely aware of the growth of media propaganda over time, propaganda that has metastasized like a spreading disease into numerous other media forms. The effects these propaganda outlets are having on the collective human mind of the TV-watching world are very disturbing and destructive.

It doesn't take an expert to know that the "19" in COVID-19 stands for the year 2019. That's the year the "pandemic virus" was released. This was a respiratory virus, which typically occur every year in a cyclical manner. The "cold and flu season" starts in October and lasts through May — every year. Year after year, during the coldest months, people come down with colds and flu. The official season produces an annual bell curve of fatalities, usually in the very young, the elderly, or the already unhealthy. Then the virus mutates, season to season, producing different symptoms with each mutation.

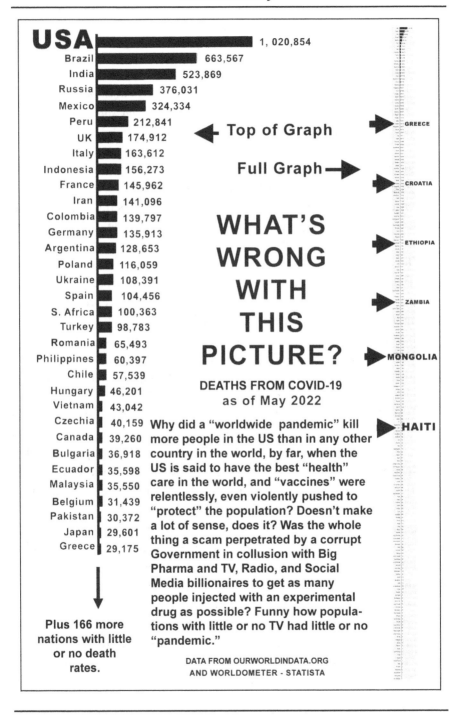

USA — 1, 020,854
Brazil — 663,567
India — 523,869
Russia — 376,031
Mexico — 324,334
Peru — 212,841
UK — 174,912
Italy — 163,612
Indonesia — 156,273
France — 145,962
Iran — 141,096
Colombia — 139,797
Germany — 135,913
Argentina — 128,653
Poland — 116,059
Ukraine — 108,391
Spain — 104,456
S. Africa — 100,363
Turkey — 98,783
Romania — 65,493
Philippines — 60,397
Chile — 57,539
Hungary — 46,201
Vietnam — 43,042
Czechia — 40,159
Canada — 39,260
Bulgaria — 36,918
Ecuador — 35,598
Malaysia — 35,550
Belgium — 31,439
Pakistan — 30,372
Japan — 29,601
Greece — 29,175

Plus 166 more nations with little or no death rates.

← Top of Graph

Full Graph →

GREECE
CROATIA
ETHIOPIA
ZAMBIA
MONGOLIA
HAITI

WHAT'S WRONG WITH THIS PICTURE?

DEATHS FROM COVID-19 as of May 2022

Why did a "worldwide pandemic" kill more people in the US than in any other country in the world, by far, when the US is said to have the best "health" care in the world, and "vaccines" were relentlessly, even violently pushed to "protect" the population? Doesn't make a lot of sense, does it? Was the whole thing a scam perpetrated by a corrupt Government in collusion with Big Pharma and TV, Radio, and Social Media billionaires to get as many people injected with an experimental drug as possible? Funny how populations with little or no TV had little or no "pandemic."

DATA FROM OURWORLDINDATA.ORG
AND WORLDOMETER - STATISTA

Most medical professionals are not *health* professionals. Let that sink in for a moment. Their expertise is in medicine and related technologies, such as surgery, trauma care, pharmaceuticals, and so on, and we are all very grateful for that. We all respect and are indebted to anyone who can help people overcome sickness and suffering. However, when the entities that control medical doctors, the pharmaceutical industry, the hospital industry, and the insurance industry, also control the *government*, then we have a very big problem.

Humans have natural immune systems that remain strongest when they eat natural foods and lead healthy lifestyles, which has nothing to do with pharmaceutical medicine. Your health comes primarily from your food and secondarily from your environment. Our natural immune systems have allowed *Homo sapiens* to become predominant on the planet for hundreds of thousands of years. Yet, natural immunity was remarkably scoffed at and derided by the medical establishment during the "COVID pandemic." Doctors and others who spoke out in defense of natural immunity at that time were ridiculed, fired, or demoted.

The United States, with the world's most expensive and advanced medical services, also has a very high percentage of unhealthy people. It seems that no illness can be cured without a medical solution, according to the medical experts. Take a pill or get a shot. This includes colds and respiratory viruses. The solution to these pesky, perennial illnesses? Vaccines. "Get your flu vaccine" is oft repeated year-round in U.S. media, pushed at drug stores, and urged on TV and radio commercials, even on pregnant women. What's not promoted, however, is natural health.

The author of this book had traveled to approximately 64 countries by the time the "pandemic" was announced in early 2020. The COVID respiratory illness had largely come and gone by the end of May 2020, according to the fatality bell curve, although the media hysteria remained unabated, and the push for "COVID vaccines" remained relentless.

The author got a phone call at the end of the pandemic year, in December 2020, asking if he would go back to Mongolia, a country where he had already visited three times for work. Mongolia seems like the perfect place for a respiratory virus to spread. The people are poor. The average income when the author worked there was about $2 per day. Members

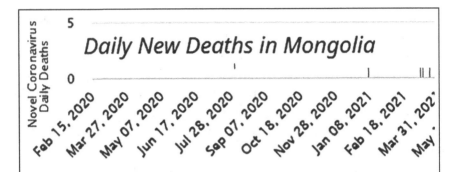

The five countries with the most Covid vaccinations were also the five countries with the most deaths.

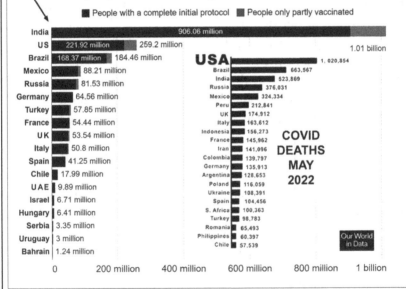

Number of people vaccinated against COVID-19, Jun 20, 2022

Experts Puzzled By Why Haiti Has One of the Lowest COVID-19 Death Rates In the World Despite Administering Zero Vaccine Doses: 'We Don't Know'

Haiti has lower coronavirus death counts with few restrictions. Why?
Nobody is sure, but scientists are trying to find answers.

of parliament were paid about $300 a month. The people, traditionally nomadic, were moving in large numbers to the few population centers that existed, such as the capital city, Ulaanbaatar (UB), where the air pollution was quite bad. UB was also considered "the coldest capital city in the world." Many people lived in "gers," (rhymes with "bears"), which we would call yurts, made of canvas draped over a portable wood frame. Add that all up, and you have a very unfortunate combination that surely would render the Mongolian people extremely vulnerable to the purported worldwide respiratory virus that had Americans scared to death.

After hanging up the phone, the author wondered how bad COVID had hit Mongolia. The United States had sunk deeply into a frenzy of death and fear. What about that remote nation sandwiched between China and Siberia? This was December 2020, after COVID had purportedly swept across the globe and killed so many people.

After searching online, the author came upon "Our World in Data," a product of the Oxford Martin school, "a world-leading center of research at the University of Oxford," in Oxford, England, *"dedicated to the study of large global problems, including poverty, disease, hunger, climate change, existential risks, inequality, and war."* This seemed like a good place to start investigating. *Worldometers* and *Statista* were additional tools added to the search. To make a long story short, there were six reported COVID deaths in the entire nation of Mongolia by December of 2020! Six! Six months later, a year and a half into the "pandemic," on June 8th, 2021, the total COVID death count in Mongolia amounted to 324.

Well, this started to raise some suspicions. The author had also traveled to Haiti four times, working there amongst the poorest of the poor (as in Mongolia). Haiti was the poorest nation in the western hemisphere, where sanitation was abysmal and medical services were often beyond the reach of the average person. A medical doctor who had accompanied the author on one of his trips to this island nation southeast of Cuba, remarked woefully at the outset of the "pandemic" that the Haitians were "going to be hit so hard." She was almost in tears at the thought of these poor people defenseless against the hideous airborne assassin we were so relentlessly being warned about in the American media. So, the author looked Haiti up on the data sites. There were 234 deaths attributed to

! COVID-19 VACCINE BOOSTER UPDATE

Who should get a booster? • Everyone ages 5 and older

Who should get a **second** booster?

• Everyone ages 50 and older

cdc.gov/coronavirus

• Everyone ages 12 and older who has a weakened immune system

---

DO YOU RECOGNIZE DISCRIMINATION WHEN YOU SEE IT?

"The Nazis established many new anti-Jewish laws. These were introduced slowly at first, so that the civilian population would not realize the extent of [them]" British Library

IN 2020 WE WERE TOLD, "2 weeks to flatten the curve", "the vaccine will get us back to normal". Mandate by mandate we have now reached a point where, *everyone*, whether vaccinated or not, must surrender sovereignty over their bodies and show "papers", or lose employment, income and access to fundamental life services. Those vaxxed become unvaxxed if they decline any of the endless boosters. *This is not about public health.*

"Those who cannot remember the past are condemned to repeat it." George Santayana

---

THE NUREMBERG CODE 1947

The 10 principles of the Nuremberg Code *oblige* any doctor or official conducting a medical experiment on human subjects *to ensure that consent of the human subjects is voluntary, fully informed, obtained without coercion in any form and respects their body sovereignty.* These principles are part of medical codes worldwide, in ethics and in law.

Government has embarked on an aggressive campaign to inoculate an unsuspecting and ill-informed populace with the product of a technology never before used in humans. This untested "medical device" of genetic modification has been deliberately mislabelled a "vaccine" even though it is still in the phase three experimental testing stage. The inoculation campaigns *constitute egregious and multiple violations of every single paragraph of the Nuremberg Code.* Government "vaccine" campaigns, with complicit media, have used *fraudulent declarations of public emergency, censorship of critical information, unlawful mandates, overreaching controls, fraudulent data and protocols, and coercive social and economic force to induce the entire populace to submit to taking part in the experiment.*

A Host of Notable COVID-19 Vaccine Adverse Events, Backed by Evidence

Some are widely acknowledged, like blood clots and myocarditis. Others are less publicly discussed.

28 Types of Kidney Complications Following COVID-19 Vaccination

---

The number of Americans who say they won't get a COVID shot hasn't budged in a year

About 66% of Americans are fully vaccinated. But as the United States approaches a million deaths from COVID-19, the virus mortality rate is being driven mainly by people who are not vaccinated, according to the Centers for Disease Control and Prevention. Nationally, about one in six Americans say they "definitely will not get the vaccine," according to the Kaiser Family Foundation. For the record, COVID-19 vaccines are FDA-approved, and recommended by the CDC because they're safe and effective at preventing serious or fatal cases of the virus."The ones that have been most likely to say they're definitely not going to get the vaccine have been Republicans and people living in rural areas, as well as white evangelical Christians." 20 percent of those who say they'll never get the vaccine identify as Democrats or politically independent, and 28% live in cities or suburbs. NPR

COVID in this nation of 11 million people by December of 2020, fewer than what were recorded in the author's rural county in Pennsylvania, which had about 300 deaths. Only about 1.6% of Haitians had received at least one dose of the COVID injections by May 2022. What?

More people had died of COVID in the author's rural, agrarian, highly "vaccinated" Pennsylvania county, than in the entire nation of Haiti, where people did not mask, did not "socially distance," and did not get the injections. American doctors who visited Haiti were "baffled." Their advice to the Haitians: mask up, start social distancing, and get injected — the same advice they were forcing on the American population.

These statistics ate away at the author's mind until finally, a year and five months later, in May 2022, he went back to the database and graphed total COVID deaths for every country in the world, which is what you see in *"What's Wrong with This Picture."* The results should shock any intelligent person. *COVID deaths were mainly in the United States, a country with only 4% of the world's population!*

Most of the world apparently did not have a "pandemic" that amounted to anything at all. Brazil was second in death rate, far behind the United States, and India was third. The population of India in 2022 was over 1.4 billion people, nearly half of whom didn't have access to proper sanitation. Some of the most polluted, unsanitary, and impoverished population centers in the world were in India (where the author had also worked). Surely, they would have experienced worse outcomes from a "global pandemic" than in the highly developed United States, a nation with the most advanced "health care" system in the world.

Impoverished, polluted India with nearly five times as many inhabitants as the United States, had about half as many COVID deaths. What was going on here? That's not what we saw on TV! The United States was leading the world in the response to COVID-19, or so we were told.

The pandemic "heroes" in the United States included Dr. Anthony Fauci, Dr. Deborah Birx, Dr. Ashish K. Jha, and Dr. Rochelle Walensky, to name a few. Biden's former "COVID Czar," Dr. Jha, stated in 2024: *"These [COVID] vaccines ended the pandemic, they saved millions of lives. Thousands of Americans were dying every day at the height of the pandemic; the vaccines totally turned it around. So, there's no question in my mind that*

Report Criticizes 'Catastrophic Errors' of COVID Lockdowns, Warns of Repeat

'Granting public health agencies extraordinary powers was a major error,' says Johns Hopkins economist Steve Hanke.

"A much wiser strategy than issuing lockdown orders would have been to tell the American people the truth, stick to the facts, educate citizens about the balance of risks, and let individuals make their own decisions about whether to keep their businesses open, whether to socially isolate, attend church, send their children to school, and so on," the report states.

How the authorities systematically lied to the public about the threat of COVID-19 in 2020

The WHO was reporting figures strongly at odds with then-existing expertise within epidemiology and infectious disease. Why would the World Health Organization intentionally provide figures that it knew were false?

[case fatality rate]

To make matters worse, the media relentlessly amplified WHO's 3.4% figure, and public health officials not only did not correct the record and put the brakes on the hysteria, but made policy consistent with it. The media then relentlessly ridiculed Trump for reporting the figures that were more consistent with prevailing scientific opinion within the field; the media denounced these figures as "misinformation."

Trump was later vindicated: his 0.5% figure was later confirmed by scientists as almost exactly the median death rate globally: 0.47%. (It turned out to be around 0.07%, or 1-in-1500, in those under the age of 70.)

The public health establishment, through the mouthpiece of the World Health Organization, was responsible for promoting a dramatically inflated figure. Meanwhile, the media was responsible for amplifying this figure and selectively neglecting and suppressing figures that were much more consistent with the scientific evidence *at the time.*

Every House Democrat Voted AGAINST Stopping the Government 'Monitoring And Prosecuting' Unvaccinated Americans.

All House Democrats on the Judiciary Committee voted against a proposed amendment to a domestic terrorism bill that would have prevented American intelligence and security agencies from receiving taxpayer funds to "monitor, analyze, investigate or prosecute" Americans unvaccinated against COVID-19.

COVID-19 'Vaccines' Are Gene Therapy

Not a vaccine in the medical definition, the COVID-19 'vaccine' is really an experimental gene therapy that does not render immunity or prevent infection or transmission of the disease.

Further evidence supports controversial claim that SARS-CoV-2 genes can integrate with human DNA

A team of prominent scientists has doubled down on its controversial hypothesis that genetic bits of the pandemic coronavirus can integrate into our chromosomes and stick around long after the infection is over.

these vaccines were extremely effective, they were largely very safe."

Dr. Deborah Birx stated in May of 2024 that *"[The COVID vaccines] were very effective for what they were supposed to be used for, which was prevent severe disease and hospitalization and death. And that's what the vaccines were studied to do in this country, and that's what they did."*

The remainder of the medical establishment fell in line and repeated the same false propaganda. Those who didn't were swiftly punished.

This book is about politics and saving what remains of American democracy. But it was this graph, *"What's Wrong with This Picture?"* that expedited the book project. It was our government, "captured" by Big Pharma, who imposed the "global pandemic" farce on the American taxpayer, once again robbing the U.S. treasury of trillions of dollars in the process. It was our government, not a virus, not a pandemic, that deprived Americans of their fundamental rights, stripped them of their dignity, forced experimental drugs into their bodies, lied to them, and continues to lie to them today.

It was *the U.S. government* that forced the Korean War upon Americans; that forced the war against Vietnam upon them; that funded the proxy wars in Central America; that invaded Iraq and Afghanistan and made American sons and daughters die there while taxpayers paid for it. *The government is the problem.* It is rotten to the core. If "we the people" don't fix it, it won't get fixed. That's what this book is about.

Incidentally, once the "vaccines" were introduced into Mongolia, the deaths skyrocketed, as they did in many other small nations around the world when the jabs were forced on the people. No doubt these deaths were classified as "deaths from COVID-19."

The Virus Hysteria

Fake "pandemics" now marked the advent of a new and sinister threat to humanity: medical terrorism. What if the U.S. Constitution could be scrapped and the Bill of Rights cast aside? What if humans could be corralled like cattle, convinced to willingly be injected with experimental, untested, DNA-altering drugs, including pregnant women and babies as young as six months of age? What if most of the population

California Nurse: "I Want People to Know What I Lost to this Vaccine. I am Living a Nightmare, It's Not Worth it."

"Do not cave because you do not want to be like me," she says. "I don't want anyone to lose their health. I was a thriving 50-year-old.

CDC Changes Definition of Vaccine So It Can't Be 'Interpreted to Mean That Vaccines Are 100% Effective'

Emmy Award-winning investigative reporter and Epoch Times contributor Sharyl Attkisson said the new definition was made to "meet the declining ability of some of today's 'vaccines,' including the COVID-19 vaccine," adding that "after the COVID-19 vaccines were introduced, and it was discovered they do not necessarily 'prevent disease' or 'provide immunity,' CDC altered the definition of vaccines again to say that they merely 'produce protection.'"

Rep. Thomas Massie (R-Ky.) took to Twitter about the CDC's definition change and compared it to George Orwell's "1984," writing, "They've been busy at the Ministry of Truth."

Vaccination (pre-2015): Injection of a killed or weakened infectious organism in order to **prevent** the disease.

Vaccination (2015-2021): The act of introducing a vaccine into the body to produce **immunity** to a specific disease.

Vaccination (Sept 2021): The act of introducing a vaccine into the body to produce **protection** from a specific disease.

The White House is Controlled by the Medical-Industrial Complex

Last February, the serving White House (WH) Chief of Staff (COS) quietly resigned, and a new one was ushered in. But a comparison of the outgoing and incoming WH Chief of Staff demonstrates striking similarities. A careful reading of the bios of Biden's two chief of staff picks reveals a disturbing trend. Both choices appear consistent with - first and foremost - the capture of both the "health"-related administrative state and the levers of the Biden administration itself by the pharmaceutical-medical industrial complex.

Why is this important? Because the WH Chief of Staff is the most critical political appointee of the President, and functionally serves as the head of the Executive Office of the President of the United States in addition to being a cabinet position. The position is widely considered the most important and powerful job in the Executive branch of the US Government, next to the sitting POTUS.

COVID Vaccine Gene Could Integrate Into Human Cancer Cells

could be denied basic human rights under the guise of an approaching, impending, unavoidable, worldwide, and horrible public health threat that would lay waste to the human race unless everyone complied with lockdowns and other draconian mandates such as forced drug injections imposed by medical authorities?

We have seen how groups of humans can be influenced into committing horrendous crimes against their own species through propaganda, coercion, and authoritarian tyranny. As bad as the witch burnings, carpet bombings, invasions, occupations, assassinations, mass murder, rapes, and other unspeakable crimes that have occurred over the course of the past few centuries were, what happened in the 2020s was shocking.

The communist doctrine of the mid-1800s was a response to ultra-wealthy rulers who owned nearly everything and controlled almost every aspect of the lives of the working class. Their control was often cruel, punctuated by a domineering, egotistical arrogance that repulsed the sensitivities of common, hard-working folks. People who simply wanted to live in peace and raise happy, healthy families on a sacred piece of Earth, had to deal with an oligarch thrusting his or her militant control over their homes, families, villages, farms, herds, orchards, and community. The communist solution was to strip humanity of private property altogether, thereby erasing wealthy people from existence, and to disable the basic building block of humanity, the family, putting it under the control of the communist state.

Fast forward a couple centuries and we see that the communist experiment, in hindsight, revealed two things. First, it is not human nature to be denied private property, and people will fight to the death to preserve their basic rights not only to own private property but also to raise and educate their children as they see fit, to exercise freedom of speech, of religion, of assembly, and so forth.

Second, however, the communist experiment also revealed the horrid reactions and depths of cruelty that the wealthy minority is capable of in response to the threat of losing their substantial properties. Mass murder of all ages and all walks of life became commonplace throughout the world during the anticommunist persecutions. When American capitalists finished their slaughter in Korea and then in Vietnam, they moved

SHOULD VACCINATED PEOPLE WORRY THEY ARE SPREADING THE VIRUS THAT CAUSES COVID-19?

• If you get vaccinated, your risk of infection is lower, and your risk of getting ill, being hospitalized, or dying from COVID-19 is much lower.

• Emerging science suggests some vaccinated people can be infected with the Delta variant and spread it to others.

• In areas with substantial or high spread, CDC recommends that everyone wear a mask in public indoor settings to prevent further spread.

Austria to fine unvaxed citizens over $15,000 a year

Corruption of the WHO is the Biggest Threat to the World's Public Health of Our Time

Due to the influence of private money at the World Health Organisation ("WHO"), the corruption of the WHO is the "biggest threat to the world's public health of our time."

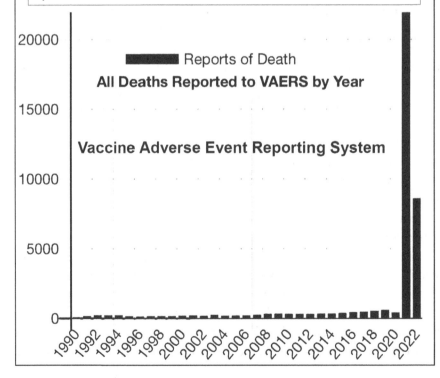

All Deaths Reported to VAERS by Year

Reports of Death

Vaccine Adverse Event Reporting System

on to Central America where they armed and financed "death squads" to wipe out anyone who supported "socialism" or "communism." Men, women, children, babies, nuns, priests, entire villages, community organizers, and so on, were murdered. Much of this carnage was charged to the American people, paid for by their tax dollars taken straight out of the U.S. treasury. None of this is hyperbole. It is all a historical fact.

It's worth reminding the reader that, just because someone has more material wealth than just about everybody else, it doesn't mean they are more intelligent, more wise, more mature, healthy, stable, benevolent, or in possession of any virtuous attributes at all. Extreme wealth in the hands of unstable, deranged individuals presents a grave threat to all humanity. The communists understood this. And despite their misguided efforts to find a solution to this problem, the problem persists even today. But it has shifted in a way that few could have foreseen.

One of the most valuable attributes a human being can possess is humility. Humility is the understanding that we are capable of errors. Grave errors. We can alleviate the chances of committing grave errors by soliciting the opinions of others. *Two heads are better than one*, as the saying goes. This is why democracy presents such an appeal to thinking people. Let's discuss the issues that we are faced with and try to arrive at some sort of consensus without authoritarian rule, without dictators forcing their way upon everyone else, without strong-arm fascism being shoved down our throats. One way we can do this is by the citizenry creating, openly debating, then voting directly on legislation. This would cut out the middlemen, the paid political prostitutes who take our votes away from us.

Instead, we find ourselves trying to be controlled by "the smartest people in the room." At least that's how they would describe themselves. Their intelligence, arrogance, and lack of wisdom dwarf their humility. In the twenty-first century, the "smartest people in the room" are also the wealthiest people in the world, plus their entourage. They have convinced themselves that they can save the world by controlling humanity. The most holy on high will take over, push the commoners and populists out of the way, and create a world in their desired image. But how?

Well, one brilliant group of scientists, college professors, business

'The Power of Natural Immunity': COVID Challenge Trials Struggle to Infect Participants, Even at High Doses

U.K. scientists attempting to deliberately reinfect healthy people with COVID-19 for vaccine and treatment testing found that even doses 10,000 times higher than the original could not induce sustained infection in participants with natural immunity from prior infection, as reported in The Lancet Microbe.

THE BIG LIE: The 'Powers That Be' Overcount COVID Deaths and Undercount Vaccine Deaths All for Money and Power

Spreading Vaccine 'Misinformation' Puts Medical License at Risk, U.S. Boards Tell Physicians

Three U.S. medical certifying boards have warned doctors they risk losing their certification and license if they spread COVID vaccine misinformation, but the boards offered no clear definition of "misinformation."

Emails Reveal CDC Changed Definition of "Vaccine" and "Vaccination" Because Their Experimental COVID Shots Didn't Work as Advertised

The 'false' pandemic: Drug firms cashed in on scare over swine flu, claims Euro health chief [2009]

The swine flu outbreak was a 'false pandemic' driven by drug companies that stood to make billions of pounds from a worldwide scare, a leading health expert has claimed.

Double Digits: Biden Admin Tells Americans It's Almost Time for Their 10th COVID Shot

Dose number NINE: CDC panel green lights yet another Covid mRNA shot

For the vax compliant, that's nine doses in only three years. FEB 29, 2024

Time for your EIGHTH dose: Pfizer says latest booster won't be tested on humans but it works great on mice!

Government green-lights SEVENTH covid shot

mRNA madness: FDA authorizes both 4th and 5th COVID shots

EFFECTS OF LOCKDOWNS ON COVID-19 MORTALITY

While this meta-analysis concludes that lockdowns have had little to no public health effects, they have imposed enormous economic and social costs where they have been adopted. In consequence, lockdown policies are ill-founded and should be rejected as a pandemic policy instrument.

COVID-19 injections neither safe nor effective

The conclusion of the interim report by the independent commissioners for the National Citizen's Inquiry is that the COVID-19 products known as vaccines are neither safe nor effective.

owners, politicians, doctors, and other influencers concluded that the human being can be "hacked" using drug injections designed to alter the DNA of the individual. By injecting billions of people with experimental drugs, commoners can theoretically be controlled, en masse, from the inside, through artificial, laboratory-created biochemical influences.

But how can a group of wealthy elitists achieve the goal of injecting 8 billion people with experimental drugs, thereby creating a complacent, subservient, underclass of humans who will allow themselves to become the subjects of sinister experiments willingly and even eagerly?

The answer presented itself in 2020: orchestrate a fake "Pandemic," or a "Scamdemic," or a "Plandemic" as many victims of this ruse called it. Scare the weak-minded TV watchers into having their government, under the control of "big pharma," inject experimental drugs into their bodies and their children's bodies, into the bodies of pregnant women, into the bloodstreams of perfectly healthy individuals, repeatedly, while constantly reassuring them that it was "safe and effective."

When the effective drug turned out to be not effective at all, and people who had been injected with it became *more* susceptible to viral infection and were getting sick, well that's because they needed a *second* injection. Duh. That first injection didn't work because you weren't "fully vaccinated." You needed a second shot, then a third. Then a fourth, fifth, sixth, seventh, eighth, ninth, and so on!

Anyone who dared to question or disagree with this ludicrous scheme was loudly denounced on mainstream propaganda platforms as a selfish, boorish, ignorant, antiscience, buffoonish "antivaxxer" wearing a tinfoil hat, unworthy of human rights or respect. Constitutional rights, charter rights, and basic rights such as freedom of speech, of assembly, of religion, and so forth, were denied to independent thinkers on the grounds that they were threats to society. How dare they be so selfish as to doubt the smartest people in the room? How dare they ask questions? They must be punished, and punished they were.

Dr. Leana Wen, a practicing physician, healthcare executive, op-ed columnist for The Washington Post, CNN medical analyst, guest contributor for NPR, PBS, BBC, and MSNBC, a World Economic Forum's Young Global Leader, and TIME magazine's 100 Most Influential People,

CNN's Leana Wen: The Unvaccinated Should Not Be Allowed To Leave Their Homes

"You have the option to not get vaccinated if you want," said the doctor. "But then you can't go out in public."

1,884 Athlete Cardiac Arrests in 2.5 Years, 1,310 Dead

Proposed Brazil Laws To Imprison Anti-vaxxers

DEFINITION OF "INSANITY": GET VAXXED. GET BOOSTED. GET COVID. REPEAT.

Alcohol-related deaths surged during the first year of the pandemic

IHME's Global Burden of Disease study: 8.7 million die from tobacco use every year

Prenatal Exposure to COVID-19 mRNA Vaccine BNT162b2 Induces Autism-Like Behaviors in Male Neonatal Rats: Insights into WNT and BDNF Signaling Perturbations

More extensive studies are needed to confirm these observations in humans and to explore the exact mechanisms. A comprehensive understanding of the risks and rewards of COVID-19 vaccination, especially during pregnancy, remains essential.

New York Legislation Provides for Indefinite Detention of Unvaccinated at Governor's Whim.

Conflict of Interest: Reuters 'Fact Checks' COVID-Related Social Media Posts, But Fails to Disclose Ties to Pfizer, World Economic Forum

WHEN THE TRUTH comes out you can't UNVAX YOUR KIDS

stated live, on TV: *"That when vaccinated and unvaccinated people are mixing, unless there is proof of vaccination, everybody should still be wearing masks. So, I actually support what the CDC is now doing, which is going back to this indoor mask requirement, because frankly we know that we can't trust the unvaccinated. That they have been walking around without masks, and in fact that's what led to the surge that we're seeing."*

She also equated normal people, those who choose not to be injected with experimental drugs, with drunk drivers. *"You can remain unvaccinated if you so choose, but if you want to be in public and could be potentially infecting others with a dangerous and sometimes fatal disease that's highly transmissible, then there's an obligation to society . . . At the end of the day, I don't really understand why people have the choice to be infecting our vulnerable children or immunocompromised people, or even others who have taken the responsible choice to be vaccinated."*

Of course, no mention is made of natural immunity, of the millions of people who already had the illness and had no need for any injections, or of the millions of people who can take care of their own health without the need for experimental medical interventions. She seemed to be totally unaware of the fact that masks were scientifically proven to have little or no effect on the prevention of respiratory illnesses. She used the often-repeated propaganda that normal, uninjected people are *"infecting"* and potentially killing *"our vulnerable children"* and *"immunocompromised people,"* like grandma. This "fear porn" was relentlessly repeated on mainstream media and was especially effective on young mothers, many of whom insisted that their healthy husbands get the shot "to protect the children." After all, that's what they were told on TV.

Nor does the good doctor explain why people already "vaccinated" are threatened by normal, uninjected people. If the "vaccines" are effective, then there is no risk from others. If the vaccines are not effective, then people pushing them are akin to carnival barkers, making ludicrous claims that are unsubstantiated and dangerous.

The Good Doctor

An unspoken presumption has been foisted upon society that if some-

GOVERNMENT "HEALTH EXPERTS" IN THE 2020s

Belgium's Health Minister

Quebec's Health Minister

US Assistant Secretary for Health

Britain's Health Secretary

Africa is only 6% vaccinated, and covid has practically disappeared... scientists "baffled"

THEY SOMEHOW MANAGED TO DEMONIZE COUGHS, SNIFFLES AND HAVING NO SYMPTOMS AT ALL... BUT NORMALIZED STROKES, BLOOD CLOTS, NEUROLOGICAL DISORDERS AND 'DIED SUDDENLY'

one has a medical degree, an MD, or a Doctor of Medicine status, whatever they say is true and can only be doubted by fools. Yet, despite the incredible successes and advances of drugs and medicine over the centuries, colossal errors have punctuated the history of the medical and pharmaceutical industries.

In the case of the 2020 scamdemic, all that was needed was a declaration of a "pandemic" by international "health" organizations, particularly the World Health Organization, to push everyone out of the way and insert medical doctors into the driver's seat of society. Millions of people were going to die, and everybody had to listen very carefully to the "health" professionals and do what they were told without hesitation, question, or doubt. The result: *More people died "from COVID" in the United States than in any other country in the world, by far,* following the dictates of the medical "experts." How was that possible?

In Pennsylvania, the top health professional, "Rachel Levine MD," Pennsylvania physician general and secretary of the Pennsylvania Department of Health, was born a male named Richard. In his adulthood, after being married and fathering two children, he concluded that he was actually a woman. Unbelievably, Levine was then named *USA Today's Woman of the Year* in 2022. When a social media channel named *The Babylon Bee* posted a parody meme of Levine declaring him to be "Man of the Year," they were suddenly and permanently banned by the dominant social media platform *Twitter* for "hate speech." This is not a joke; this is an example of life in the early 2020s.

Levine was the person in charge of the state of Pennsylvania's "health" system, a state with a population of 13 million people. He was installed, promoted, and congratulated by then Governor Tom Wolfe, a democrat, who was apparently incapable of locating anyone else out of Pennsylvania's 13 million people better suited to oversee the health of Pennsylvania's residents. Never mind Levine's gender confusion; every citizen in Pennsylvania became subject to his/her authority.

As an example of Levine's health acumen, she/he ordered the following state-wide mask mandate in November of 2020, well after the 2019-2020 COVID "pandemic" had passed: *Masks are required to be worn indoors and outdoors when away from home. When outdoors, a mask must be*

Pennsylvania officials tell residents to wear masks in their homes when guests are over

The Pennsylvania Department of Health is telling residents in the state to wear face coverings inside their homes when guests are over, part of expanded tactics by officials to bolster the state's COVID-19 orders. The agency stated that "masks now required anytime you're with people outside of your household, even if you're socially distant. Applies to all indoor facilities + if you have people in your home not part of your household." Pennsylvania Health Secretary Rachel Levine included the new provisions in an updated mask order on Tuesday.

The Babylon Bee

Man *of the* Year

Rachel Levine Was a Disaster in Pennsylvania But Is Now Headed to Washington

This is potentially good news for Pennsylvanians, who will finally be rid of her after having had to endure her disastrous Covid lockdowns and restrictions for nearly a year, but is likely bad news for the rest of the country.

Woman who refuses to wear mask arrested in West Boca

Celebrities Call For 'Total Hollywood Strike' Until Every Last Person Gets Jabbed

We support Hollywood striking until EVERYONE is vaccinated.

Woman Arrested At School Board Meeting After 'Improperly' Wearing Mask
A NY woman was arrested and detained by sheriff's deputies after refusing to fully cover her nose when she was wearing her mask.

Police With No Gloves, No Mask Arrest Father For Playing With Daughter At The Park

Israeli study proves 4th COVID jab ineffective

worn if you are not able to stay at least 6 feet away from someone not in your household the entire time you are outdoors. When indoors, masks will now be required even if you are physically distant from members not in your household. This means you will need to wear a mask inside if with people other than members of your household. The order applies to every indoor facility, including homes, retail establishments, schools, gyms, doctors' offices, public transportation and anywhere food is prepared, packaged or served."

Levine mandated that you have to wear a mask inside your own house when someone who is not part of your household is also inside your house. You were also ordered to otherwise wear a mask all the time no matter where you were. Levine also imposed a long list of other restrictive orders, explaining that it was *"our responsibility for the common good of everyone in Pennsylvania."*

The fact that mask wearing has been scientifically proven to have no positive impact on public health measures, but does have negative effects on personal health, not to mention the obvious assault on personal liberty and autonomy, seemed to have escaped everyone, as the TV-watching public dutifully wore masks or were forced to by business owners. Businesses had to impose the mask mandates on their customers or face having their business licenses revoked and their businesses shut down by politicians. The clear message was that Levine and the politicians controlling the government were somehow smarter than everyone else and should be obeyed no matter how ludicrous their dictates were.

When the democrats took over the U.S. presidency in 2020, under very loud accusations of credible, if not blatant, election fraud, Levine was immediately promoted to a national position, United States Assistant Secretary for Health, then was sworn in as a four-star admiral — the highest-ranking official of the U.S. Public Health Service Commissioned Corps. But let's not get too far into the weeds on this issue — we will circle back to mask mandates and gender confusion later.

Let's make one thing very clear. An MD is a Doctor of *Medicine*. Not a Doctor of *Health*. A person with an MD degree is neither a Doctor of Business Administration, nor a Doctor of Civil Affairs, nor a Doctor of Law, Education, Commerce, Constitution, Social Security, Finance, Community Organization, Civil Rights, Engineering, History, Politics, Con-

Canadian Doctor Faces Prison for Warning of Covid Shot Side Effects

Suspended Doctor Reveals How Regulators Punished Her For Prescribing Ivermectin

Doctor sues Queen's University for allegedly pushing him out of job over his COVID opinions

Florida Doctor Reinstated After Losing Board Certification for Criticizing COVID-19 Vaccines

Doctor: Pharmacists Continuing to Refuse Ivermectin Prescriptions, Raising Ethical Concerns

Doctor Fired for Warning Senate about Covid Shots

Fired Over Ivermectin, ER Doctor Fights for Medical Freedom

Military Doctor Facing Discharge for Giving Exemptions to COVID-19 Vaccine

Top Doctor Put in Psych Ward by Police for Covid 'Misinformation'

Authorities determined that Binder, who has held a private practice for 24 years, should be examined for mental illness in response to his public criticism of Covid restrictions, mandates, and testing. On the day before Easter of 2020, he was confronted outside his home by about 60 armed police officers, including 20 with the canton of Aargau's anti-terrorism unit, ARGUS.

Doctor in Mississippi Fired for Administering Ivermectin

Pennsylvania Doctor Fired for Prescribing Ivermectin

Doctor Suspended From Houston Methodist for Backing Ivermectin and Opposing Vaccine Mandates Sues Hospital

Top ICU Doctor Suspended After Suing Hospital for Banning Life-Saving COVID Treatments

servation, the Environment, or any of the myriad categories that play very important roles in all of our lives.

Yet, based on the declaration of a "pandemic" by a group of unelected medical professionals deeply embedded with the pharmaceutical industry, medical doctors were suddenly handed total control over all aspects of people's lives around the world. They were afforded the authority to regulate almost every element of our day-to-day existence, to strip us of basic human rights, to deprive us of our jobs, our freedom of speech, association, religion, education, and to be backed up with ruthless violence carried out by dutiful police and military when ordered by their government overlords.

Trust the Experts

At one point during the scamdemic, 40 million people were suddenly put out of work in the United States alone; thousands of businesses were forced to close, many to go bankrupt and never reopen; people were forced to cover their faces when in public to "protect the vulnerable"; even healthy people had to cover their faces, even people who already had the respiratory illness, had recovered, and had natural immunity.

Many people had no symptoms at all, despite "testing positive," yet they were still forced to get a series of experimental drug injections or be fired from their jobs, including doctors, professors, or anyone who insisted on controlling their own health without medical intervention.

The so-called experts behind the hideous repression and tyranny were the same people who brought upon our nation *the highest total death count from COVID in the entire world*, while at the same time declaring, even in congressional hearings, that men can be women, get pregnant, and have abortions, or that women can have penises. Most of this lunacy came from the Democrat Party and from the unelected, behind-the-scenes actors who controlled President Biden and Congress. And all of the insanity was spoon-fed into the minds of the boiled frogs on a daily basis. Many eagerly lapped it up.

Claims of natural immunity were ridiculed and became a nuisance to be ignored by medical professionals, despite hundreds of thousands of

'Institutional Corruption': Big Pharma Money Permeating Global Drug Regulators

Though drug regulators were originally set up to regulate the drug industry, a new investigation by the British Medical Journal (BMJ) shows that conflict of interest (COI) is pervasive within agencies globally. Pharmaceutical companies are the biggest funders of major regulatory agencies. The study found some national drug agencies are almost exclusively reliant on pharmaceutical money, serving as a "prime example of institutional corruption," said Donald Light.

The Simple But Forgotten Open Air Factor in Infection Control

Documented in medical journals for almost two centuries but seemingly forgotten nowadays, breathing fresh outdoor air could be key to defending against airborne bacteria and viruses, including COVID-19, disease expert from the Australian National University (ANU) suggests.

Michigan Bans Many Stores From Selling Seeds, Home Gardening Supplies, Calls Them "Not Necessary"

The shutdown follows an executive order from last month that's been widely interpreted by many in the industry as banning greenhouses, independent garden centers, and plant nurseries from selling to the public, as part of a larger crackdown on activities deemed "not necessary to sustain or protect life." (Curiously, the state's list of "not necessary" items doesn't include lottery tickets and liquor.)

OSHA Vaccine Mandate: 84 Million Workers Face Jan. 4 Deadline

The Biden administration has released the new rule from the Occupational Safety and Health Administration (OSHA) that requires 84 million private-sector workers to get vaccinated against COVID-19.

More than two-thirds of Congress cashed a pharma campaign check in 2020, new STAT analysis shows

WASHINGTON — Seventy-two senators and 302 members of the House of Representatives cashed a check from the pharmaceutical industry ahead of the 2020 election — representing more than two-thirds of Congress, according to a new STAT analysis of records for the full election cycle.

Nurse Sounds Alarm On Heinous Medical Malpractice: Immediate Intubation, Remdesivir Killed Covid Patients

"They were dying because doctors were immediately intubating patients and providing them with Remdesivir, an expensive drug that does nothing to treat Covid or respiratory illness, but shuts down the organs," the nurse, who worked at **Cleveland Clinic Indian River Hospital** exclusively during Covid, recollected.

years of adaptation by the human immune system. The Medical Industrial Complex had spoken. There was a horrible pandemic sweeping across the globe, and the medical professionals were now in charge of everyone, of every aspect of their lives. The only way out of this horrible situation, the ONLY way, was through a series of experimental drug injections, or so they were told, over, and over again. The boiled frogs got the message, and the boiled frogs complied.

It has long been a goal of the medical-industrial establishment to convince humans that the primary way to achieve optimum health is through medical drugs. Injectable pharmaceuticals provide the answer to disease, or so they say. Bill Gates, founder of Microsoft, with a net worth in 2024 estimated to be $141 billion, making him one of the richest people in the world at the time, was also perhaps the world's greatest proponent of "vaccines" worldwide. It seems that his goal was to convince people around the globe that injected pharmaceuticals are the single most important solution to global health problems. Never mind that he was a major financial investor in the vaccine industry with a reported 20:1 rate of return on his investments, which would appear to be a massive conflict of interest under any other circumstance.

Gates was a businessman, not a doctor, scientist, or health professional. He owned a collection of private jets worth nearly $200 million. His mansion in Washington state was valued at upward of $170 million. It's hard to imagine how someone of this socioeconomic status could conceive of realistic lifestyle solutions for the 3 billion people in the world who don't even have toilets. Injecting them with drugs, starting at birth, to "protect their health" may be a well-meaning *suggestion*, especially when it's a financial investment that yields very attractive returns. But is it a realistic *solution*?

Here's an authentic well-meaning suggestion: Mr. Gates should live for one full year without electricity, running water, or a flush toilet, on an expense account of less than $10 per day, as billions of people do around the world. It's that simple. The insight he would gain regarding the plight of the less fortunate would be eye-opening, even miraculous. Injecting the impoverished masses with drugs may no longer look nearly as important as improving their sanitation, enhancing their soil fertility,

6-Foot Social Distancing Rule During COVID Not Based On Scientific Evidence, Ex-NIH Director Testifies

latimes.com Column: Mocking anti-vaxxers' deaths is ghoulish, yes — but necessary

Health officials gain guardianship of baby whose parents refused 'vaccinated blood' transfusion

CDC: Fully Vaccinated People Should Wear Masks

The research indicates that vaccinated people who contract the Delta variant have the same viral load, or amount of virus, as unvaccinated people, and that vaccinated people can transmit the variant.

providing better nutrition, protecting their housing security and access to arable land, providing and supporting honorable and safe livelihoods, cleaning up their environments, and so on.

All of these things can arguably be achieved with smaller financial investments than injectable drugs. The results would produce substantial, long-term dividends for *all* the people, not just for the wealthy investors. It may come as a surprise that, given clean drinking water, safe and comfortable housing, food security, ecological sanitation, right livelihoods, an unpolluted environment, and the other necessities required for a healthy human condition, public health issues will resolve themselves without the need for mass drug injections.

The vaccine industry seems to be making an all-out effort to convince the public that injectable pharmaceuticals deserve an almost religious reverence. So-called vaccines cannot be questioned in any manner and certainly cannot be criticized. All vaccines are "safe and effective," as we are repeatedly told. This mantra is reiterated on mainstream propaganda platforms over and over, akin to the propaganda scenarios described in George Orwell's *1984*. There are plenty of books, research papers, and medical professionals that would dispute this mantra.

It must be added that the two declared attributes of the vaccine mantra, namely, "safe" and "effective," are conveniently (and certainly intentionally) *omitting* two other equally important and necessary attributes. Vaccines and any injected drug or medicine should also be "needed," and must also be "wanted." This recognizes that the person receiving the drugs has the right to decide what is injected into his or her body and has the right to choose an alternative healthcare option based on their own personal research, experience, preference, and autonomy.

For example, there are no vaccines for cholera, a disease that killed many thousands of people over many generations. We don't need a vaccine for cholera because we now know what causes this disease, namely, the drinking of water polluted with sewage. When the cause of the disease was understood and the polluted water removed, the cholera epidemics declined or ceased to exist altogether. Most people would admit that they don't *need* a cholera vaccine. However, there are those in the pharmaceutical industry who could make money from such a vaccine, and there are

CBS: Soaring Heart Attacks Due to Lack of Masking

CBS News's medical expert has claimed that the unprecedented spike in the number of young people suffering sudden heart attacks is due to a lack of masking and a failure to keep up to date with vaccinations.

CCP government 'intentionally released' COVID-19 'all over the world', Chinese virologist says

Dr. Li Meng Yan says the CCP underestimated the virus' transmissibility

PEOPLE WHO GOT THE VACCINE WERE NOT COUNTED AS VACCINATED UNTIL 14 DAYS PASSED, SO ALL SIDE EFFECTS AND DEATHS THAT HAPPENED UNTIL THEN WERE COUNTED AS UNVACCINATED!

Piers Morgan Imagine being scared of having a safe, well-regulated, 4-second vaccine shot, when previous generations braved gun shots for years on end to save us all from tyranny? **Anti-vaxxers** really are a bunch of spineless pussies.

Public Health Knew Vaccinated Could Carry Same Viral Loads as Unvaccinated Before Mandates Imposed

Study Finds Majority of Patients With Long COVID Were Vaccinated

WEBMD HEALTH NEWS

Unvaccinated People Create Higher Risk for Vaccinated, Study Says

Vaccinated People Show Long COVID-Like Symptoms

The findings indicate that the persistence of spike proteins was likely the driver for symptoms of long COVID and post-vaccine syndrome.

REMEMBER WHEN ONE OF THE SYMPTOMS WAS HAVING NO SYMPTOMS

those individuals who would *want* to take such a vaccine and would pay for one anyway, whether they needed it or not. That is their prerogative.

We decide what we want injected into *our* bodies in the name of preventative or prophylactic health. Our bodies are our temples, and nobody can force us to have drug injections we don't *want*. Or *need*. Forced drug injections, especially with experimental drugs, represents a sinister tyranny of the worst kind, a form of medical terrorism.

In the 2020s, doctors who questioned the safety of COVID drug injections were fired from their positions, or their medical licenses were revoked, or their hospital privileges were suspended. Citizens who suffered from COVID vaccine injuries and spoke out were censored, attacked, ridiculed, and kicked off social media platforms without warning. Medical doctors must conform to the edicts set forth by their masters, or have their careers destroyed. The state medical boards make sure this happens. This is an inconvenient truth.

"Health care" is free to everyone; "medical care" can be prohibitively expensive or impossible for many. Health care means a good night's sleep, fresh air, a nutritious diet, freedom from stress, a comfortable living habitat, and a pollution-free environment, among other things. None of these needs require the medical industrial complex. Emphasis on *health* rather than *drugs* could vastly improve the human condition. Drugs are important, even essential and lifesaving at times, and they do make a lot of money for the pharmaceutical industry, but they should not be considered a basis or foundation for optimum human health. They should be used only when needed.

If people can be convinced that their physical and mental health depends on the pharmaceutical industry more than anything else, then they can be influenced to take drugs and receive drug injections on a routine basis, whether they need them or not.

The influence of the medical establishment is aided by government medical agencies (CDC, NIH, FDA, etc.) that have become "captured" by the pharmaceutical industry and other arms of the medical industrial complex, with industry members sitting on government boards and committees, thus affording for themselves decision-making authority.

Add to this the fact that mainstream media is also controlled by the

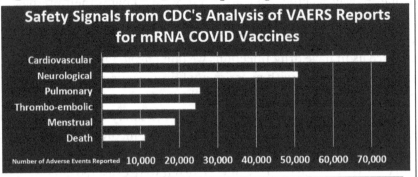

CDC's VAERS Safety Signal Analysis

Safety Signals from CDC's Analysis of VAERS Reports for mRNA COVID Vaccines

Cardiovascular
Neurological
Pulmonary
Thrombo-embolic
Menstrual
Death

Number of Adverse Events Reported   10,000   20,000   30,000   40,000   50,000   60,000   70,000

Court-Ordered Pfizer Documents They Tried To Have Sealed For 55 years Show 1223 Deaths, 158,000 Adverse Events in 90 Days Post EUA Release

The CDC waited 15 months **before** doing its first safety signal analysis. The CDC didn't want to release it either - this data is ONLY available because of a Freedom of Information Act (FOIA) request by Zachary Stieber at the Epoch Times.

Drugmakers' Secret Royalty Payments to Fauci's NIAID Exploded After Pandemic: Report

Covid Shots Are SOLE Cause of Soaring Child Heart Failure, Top Study Confirms

NIH scientists made $710M in royalties from drug makers — a fact they tried to hide

Adam Andrzejewski June 2, 2024

Nearly 30 fully vaccinated Louisiana residents have died with COVID-19

Pope Francis urges people to get vaccinated against Covid-19

Pfizer's COVID Vaccine Could Become Most Lucrative Drug in the World

Pfizer's vaccine is already the second-highest revenue-generating drug in the world.   03/18/21 · BIG PHARMA › NEWS

BREAKING: In a major blow to vaccine efforts, senior FDA leaders stepping down

Two of the FDA's most senior vaccine leaders are exiting from their positions, raising fresh questions about the Biden administration and the way that it's sidelined the FDA.

pharmaceutical industry due to the torrent of drug advertising dollars that the media has come to rely upon and enjoy, plus the millions of campaign dollars donated to senators and congresspersons by industries associated with the medical industrial complex, and you have a perfect storm. Throw in a heavy dose of censorship, sweeten it with a constant barrage of propaganda, add a small army of corrupt politicians and media talking heads and — voilà! A plandemic of epic proportions can be thrust upon the people, including a massive campaign to force experimental drug injections into as many human bodies as possible.

Bill Gates and Klaus Schwab (founder of the World Economic Forum) famously stated that everyone on Earth must be injected with pharmaceutical drugs, aka "vaccines," especially the COVID experimental drug, and until that is achieved, "nobody will be safe." The implication being that anyone who refuses to be injected is a threat to humanity.

People who exercise their right to decide whether they want a drug injected into their body or not, and refuse such an option, become a problem for the authoritarians who are pushing the jabs. When a laboratory-manufactured pathogen is intentionally or accidentally released, and people become ill and some die, the reason, according to the government and the media, is because some people refuse to get a mandated drug injection. People who got the COVID drug injections literally stated that their "vaccines" weren't working because some "anti-vaxxers" didn't get injections. Not only did they believe this absolute nonsense, but this deception was relentlessly pushed by mainstream propaganda on TV.

Normal (un-injected) people were blamed for the manufactured COVID health threat and for the associated health problems, including deaths, *of other people*, while the weak-minded TV watchers nodded their heads in agreement. Normal, uninjected people were labeled "dirty," and became targeted by deranged medical extremists and by ignorant members of the public. When a man forcibly injects semen into another person against his or her will, he is committing rape. When drugs are forcibly injected into people against their will, they are being medically raped. When a government agency, acting under the control of the pharmaceutical industry, mandates widespread medical rape, then we have a government that is totally out of control.

Doctors Warn COVID-19 mRNA Jabs Can Cause Primary Cutaneous CD4 Small/Medium T-Cell Lymphoproliferative Disorders And Cutaneous Lymphomas! *Thailand Medical News*

Vaccinated People Are Immune Imprinted, Unusual Response to COVID-19 mRNA Boosters

Immune imprinting occurs when previous exposures leave such a strong immune memory that the body continues to produce antibodies targeting the past experience.

Vitamin D proves superior to the Covid "vaccines"

Systematic Review

Preventive Vitamin D Supplementation and Risk for COVID-19 Infection: A Systematic Review and Meta-Analysis

Pfizer's pivotal mRNA trial in adults did not show any statistically significant reduction in all-cause mortality, and in absolute terms there were actually more deaths in the treatment arm versus in the placebo. Statement COVID-19 Vaccines Safety and Efficacy by Dr Aseem Malhotra MD for Mika Vauhkala

Japanese Researchers Warn About Risks Associated With Blood Transfusions From COVID-19 mRNA Vaccinated Individuals

Thailand Medical News

The Covid death rate is higher after mass vaccinations

There is a discernible reduction in the rate of Covid deaths in only 38 out of the 202 countries studied (19%). Therefore, in the vast majority of countries, both the rate and the number of Covid deaths after vaccination programs are higher than before. In fact, the Covid death rate (deaths per million per day world average) rises from 1.4 to 2.0 after mass vaccinations begin, an increase of 42%.

Japan's Experts Baffled by High 'Covid' Deaths From Heart Problems Despite High Vaccination Rate

Doctors 'baffled' by sudden uptick in "Sudden Adult Death Syndrome" despite Government data proving COVID Vaccine is to blame

Doctors 'Baffled' over Global Surge in Deadly Turbo Cancers

America vs America

The American deep state, the shadow government, the CIA, the FBI, the unelected players who control the nation behind the scenes, the entities who orchestrated the wars, invasions, assassinations, and death squads, who fomented the anti-communist psychopathy, which morphed into anti-terrorist psychopathy, which metastasized into a deep and destructive collective human cancer fueled by a lust for power and wealth, turned its destructive sights in the twenty-first century 180 degrees. Not content to attack populations and governments outside the borders of the United States, the target became America itself, its government, and its citizens.

What stands in the way of a malevolent takeover of the planet by an unelected world government is, among other things, the pesky *Bill of Rights*. The *Bill of Rights* affords people basic human rights, including the right to bear arms, and it must be destroyed if the globalists are to have their way. The 2020 scamdemic provided a test opportunity to attack the *Bill of Rights* in the United States and attack it they did.

It didn't happen overnight. An earlier attempt occurred when the 2009 H1N1 flu virus prompted the WHO to declare a pandemic. Experts warned that this flu could "wipe out 120 million people." Once a formal pandemic declaration occurs, nations that enter into agreements to buy millions of doses of flu vaccines become contractually obligated to pay for them and to receive delivery of them. Clearly there is a perverse incentive to declare a seasonal flu to be a pandemic. The problem was that not enough people died during that flu season to scare people into getting a "flu vaccine" or even to justify calling it a pandemic.

The definition of "pandemic" hinged upon death rates being abnormally high. When this didn't happen in 2009, the definition of pandemic was quietly modified so that the conditions required to declare a pandemic could be more easily obtained in the future. Once a pandemic has been declared, experimental drugs can be provided with "Emergency Use Authorization" (EUA). This simply means that the drugs need not undergo the rigorous testing protocols required of virtually all pharmaceutical drugs, nor are the recipients of the drugs provided with "informed

Virologist Predicts Imminent 'Tsunami of Death' Among COVID Vaccinated

World-renowned Belgian virologist Geert Vanden Bossche issued a grave warning of an imminent "massive tsunami" of COVID illnesses and deaths among the vaccinated that will collapse hospitals and cause financial, economic and social "chaos."

Let this sink in: For the first time in human history, we can transmit a disease we don't have to those who are immunized against it!

Aaron Siri

FDA asks federal judge to grant it until the year 2076 to fully release Pfizer's Covid-19 vaccine data. So, the gov't mandates Pfizer's product, grants it immunity for injuries, and wants to hide its safety data for 55 years. Who does the gov't work for?

Although 13-Year-Old Boy Died 10 Days After Receiving 2nd Dose of Pfizer Vax, Coroner Can't be Certain of Myocarditis Source

Saudi Arabian Study: 27.11% of Study Population Report Cardiac Complications Post COVID-19 mRNA Vaccination

HOT TOPICS   TOUGH NEW WA LAWS

Unvaxxed parents to be banned from visiting kids in WA hospitals.

We don't hire the unvaccinated, go home.
Unite against COVID-19

Find out more at Covid19.govt.nz

Chapter 7: Scamdemic

consent," since the emergency drugs need not reveal their ingredients or side effects to the public.

Furthermore, the emergency drugs can be forced upon the public in the name of public health and disaster prevention with no liability for the manufacturers or for the people selling, advertising, distributing, or administering the drugs. If any already existing drugs have been shown to be effective in treating whatever illness gave rise to the emergency situation, no emergency drug can be authorized. However, once an emergency drug has been authorized, it, by definition, has no other competing medicine and therefore can reap huge profits for the drug manufacturer.

If this looks like potential corruption and abuse, then you're paying attention. Corrupt politicians and captured government agencies staffed by industry insiders issue emergency authorization for experimental drugs, then they buy billions of dollars' worth of them from the pharmaceutical industry at high prices, paid for by taxpayers with borrowed money since the United States is already deeply in debt. Then, with the help of compromised political leaders such as the president of the United States, in this case democrat Joe Biden, as well as governors of individual states, both democrat and republican, under the guise of a public health emergency, they force "we the people" to be injected with the drugs.

Don't want a drug injection? Then you're fired from your job! Think you can take care of your own health without being injected with an experimental medical drug that has no long-term studies? Then you're forced to cover your face in public; you're banned from common public places such as restaurants, movie theaters, churches, sports, and other entertainment venues, you're blocked from continuing your college education, and you're not allowed to enter hospitals, even to see your own children, or a dying loved one!

Mainstream propaganda networks were employed to bombard the weak-minded TV watchers with false, confusing, disturbing, and misleading information, relentlessly, day in and day out, with a backdrop intoning mounting death tolls displayed on the TV screens. The boiled frogs responded by frantically lining up to get injected as if they were lemmings lining up to jump off a cliff. The propaganda was relentless and effective.

Standing

Sitting

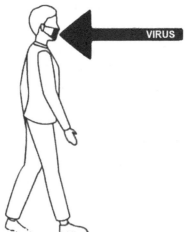

How the virus works in restaurants

What Are They Hiding?—Dr. Robert Malone on the Pfizer Documents and Evidence of Cardiotoxicity, Birth Defects, and the Rise in All-Cause Mortality

This is fundamental. We believe in the Constitution. This isn't radical. If we are right-wing Nazis because we believe in the Bill of Rights and the Constitution, then something is seriously wrong with how the press is positioning all this information. We declare that Pfizer, Moderna, BioNTech, Janssen, AstraZeneca, and their enablers withheld safety and effectiveness information from patients and physicians, and they should be indicted for this. Again, this is an incontrovertible fact. We have the GAO report from the government side. We have the forced disclosure of the Pfizer information package, which is still being released. It reveals that a lot of the propaganda and information that's been pushed on us about vaccine efficacy and safety is fraudulent.

Dr. Malone: The shocking thing, and I don't know how else to say it, one had assumed and what we were being told and basically marketed by our governments was that these vaccines would protect us from infection, replication, and virus spread, at a minimum. As those pillars fell, the data became clear that the vaccines were not effective in any way. A traditional vaccine would be considered to be effective if it is preventing infection and spread. The fallback position of the government has always been that they protect you from severe disease and death. Now those pillars are falling.

The data from the U.S., from Europe, from Israel, and from the UK and Scotland until they stop sharing the data, demonstrates that the more genetic vaccines, particularly the RNA vaccines, that an individual patient receives the higher your risk for infection, disease, and death, compared to those that remain "unvaccinated."

Abbott Quietly Renews COVID Disaster Declaration

The latest extension makes it 1,046 days that Texas has been in a state of emergency over the virus.

Gyms and beaches were closed during the declared COVID "health" emergency, but strip clubs, liquor stores, fast food restaurants, junk food corner stores, and marijuana shops were allowed to be open. You weren't allowed to bring your own grocery bags to grocery stores in some locations, but you were allowed to wear your own clothes into the same stores. In some cases, you had to enter a restaurant wearing a mask while standing or walking, but when you sat down you could take your mask off, then you had to put it back on to stand up or to go use the toilet. You were only allowed to *walk in one direction staying six feet apart* down grocery store aisles "to save lives." Arrows were painted on the floors to make sure everybody obeyed these orders.

Schools were closed, some for years. People needing organ transplant operations were heartlessly denied them if they weren't "vaccinated." Playgrounds were closed, swing sets and park benches roped off; open beaches were deemed "unsafe" and closed, but crowded Walmarts and other billionaire-owned box stores were wide open. It seemed like the asylum was being run by lunatics, with police only too eager to enforce the absurd restrictions, violently, if necessary.

Dr. Anthony Fauci, one of the main architects of the COVID response in the United States, initially declared that no facemasks were necessary, then he changed his opinion to require one mask, then two masks, one on top of the other. Subsequently, he publicly wore one mask over another as if to confirm the necessity of this peculiar behavior. If you complied with the drug injections, you were told you could take the masks off, but that changed, too. You were still required to wear masks even *after* you had the injections. People wore masks while swimming in swimming pools. They wore masks, and little else, while sunbathing at the beach. They wore masks while riding motorcycles "to be safe," although they didn't wear helmets. They wore masks while riding alone in their cars.

The most comprehensive analysis of scientific studies conducted on the efficacy of masks for reducing the spread of respiratory illnesses, including COVID-19, was published in the *Cochrane Database of Systematic Reviews* in 2023. Tom Jefferson, the Oxford epidemiologist who was its lead author, summarized the results of the study in an interview with the

Arrest warrant issued after woman rejects mask at Texas bank

Snowboarder Arrested For Not Wearing Mask at Canadian Ski Resort

Idaho man arrested for not wearing mask at outdoor worship service: 'Unbelievable'

He told Laura Ingraham the Moscow, Idaho coronavirus order is 'tyrannical'

Canada Post suspends mail delivery to 2 Toronto highrises after some residents seen without masks

Service will resume once all residents wear masks in common areas, Crown corporation says ⊕CBC

Woman seen in viral Galveston mask refusal video sentenced to 12 days in jail

GALVESTON COUNTY, Texas - A woman, who made national headlines for refusing to wear a mask inside a Galveston business, during the height of the COVID-19 pandemic, was sentenced to 12 days behind bars.

2 Georgia Republicans Rack Up Fines for Defying House's Mask Mandate

Not wearing a mask during COVID-19 health emergency isn't a free speech right, appeals court says U.S. NEWS

Murray-Nolan, who had testified before lawmakers on her skepticism toward the efficacy of masking, attended an early 2022 Cranford school board meeting without a mask despite a requirement for them. Less than a month later at the board's next meeting, she was arrested on a defiant trespass charge after attending without a mask. A lower court found officers had probable cause to arrest her because she failed to wear a mask as required under the law at the time. She appealed.

Wyoming teenager arrested after refusing to wear mask on school grounds, family says

A 16-year-old girl in Wyoming was arrested Thursday at her school after she refused to wear a mask on school grounds, she and her father said. Grace Smith, a junior at Laramie High School, told state Sen. Anthony Bouchard, R-Cheyenne, in an interview posted online, that police placed her in handcuffs for trespassing after she was suspended for not following the school's mask mandate and refused to leave school grounds. Smith's arrest also led to a "brief lockdown."

Woman tasered after refusing to wear face mask at Ohio school football game

An Ohio woman was tasered and forcibly removed from a middle school football game on Wednesday evening after refusing to wear a face mask. Smith reportedly asked the woman to wear a face mask, but she refused claiming she has asthma.

New York Times: *"There is just no evidence that masks make any difference. Full stop."* According to the Cochrane research, *"We included 12 trials comparing medical/surgical masks versus no masks to prevent the spread of viral respiratory illness. Wearing masks in the community probably makes little or no difference to the outcome of laboratory-confirmed influenza/SARS-CoV-2 compared to not wearing masks."*

In the meantime, the U.S. Centers for Disease Control's "Face Mask Recommendations" from their website stated, *"Masking is a critical public health tool for preventing spread of COVID-19, and it is important to remember that any mask is better than no mask."* This is exactly the opposite of what the science tells us. It seems that the CDC, at that time directed by Rochelle Walensky, was just taking a wild guess, not based on science at all, or on any data whatsoever. In fact, most of the CDC's advice and mandates related to the COVID-19 debacle appeared to have been wild guesses.

If you have any doubt about this, or want to jump to the defense of the CDC, take another look at the graph at the beginning of this chapter titled *"What's Wrong with This Picture?"* More people died from COVID-19 in the United States than anywhere else in the world *by far*. Four percent of the world's population had 20% of the world's COVID deaths! This is indefensible, even criminal, and it represents the epitome of public health incompetence. It's also information that is almost entirely unknown among the American public. It is information that is *completely censored* from the weak-minded TV watchers by all the mainstream propaganda platforms, especially the ones that pushed the masks and shots so relentlessly. Instead, the public has been repeatedly told by both the government and the media that millions of lives were *saved* by the courageous and brilliantly intrusive "public health" measures that, on the contrary, severely damaged America.

Thanks to the CDC and "health experts" such as Fauci and Walensky, forced masking was the rule rather than the exception throughout the United States and much of the TV-watching world in the early 2020s. People not wearing masks in public were rudely evicted from public spaces, even open-air parks and beaches. They were attacked by police, violently assaulted, arrested, fined, and treated like despicable criminals.

Dad Facing Jail for Refusing to Wear Mask Outdoors Wins Case in Court

Fauci Pushes Indoor Mask Requirements

NPR Has Corporate-Snitching Platform To Rat Out Anti-Mask Coworkers

BY ORDER OF LA PUBLIC HEALTH DEPARTMENT

MASKS ARE REQUIRED FOR EVERYONE

Man Denied Treatment, Forcibly Removed from Hospital for Refusing to Wear Mask

A Canadian man has been denied treatment at a Toronto hospital and forcibly removed from the facility by security staff because he wasn't wearing a face mask.

Pennsylvania Woman Arrested at Doctor's Office, Declined Care Over Refusal to Wear a Face Mask

House Republicans Fined for Violating Pelosi's Mask Mandate Appeal to Supreme Court

Los Angeles students must wear non-fabric COVID masks at all times, including sports

Washington Orders Restaurant That Defied Mask, Vaccine Mandates to Close

Washington health authorities on Tuesday ordered a restaurant that openly defied the city's mask and COVID-19 vaccine mandates to close.

Florida 2nd Grader Suspended for Refusing to Wear a Mask

Surgeon Fired After Speaking Against School Mask Mandate

Home Depot Says All Employees Must Mask Up

New Jersey School Nurse Suspended After Saying Masks Are Harmful to Students

Dangerous pathogens found on children's face masks

Although the ineffective masks weren't needed for public health purposes, they were needed for "virtue signaling." People had been convinced that they needed to wear masks "to protect others." Anyone not wearing a mask was therefore "an asshole." Furthermore, people not wearing masks were considered to be "right-wing extremists" and "Trump lovers," as the propaganda platforms repeated ad nauseum. This was particularly effective on the people burdened with the Trump Derangement Syndrome, a mental illness that primarily infected democrats.

Masks reminded everyone to be frightened of the air they were breathing. The public was assured they would be saved from the deadly but invisible threat floating in the air once they received the life-saving experimental drug injections. In the meantime, they were ordered to keep their faces covered. Ironically, even *after* they got the injections, they *still* had to cover their faces to remind *everyone else* to remain fearful until they got *their* injections.

Propaganda, Censorship and Brainwashing

It was clear to many at the onset of the "pandemic" that the COVID "vaccine" was not being created to curb a global health threat, but that the "pandemic" was being created to push experimental drugs on as many people as possible.

Theories were abundant. For example, it seemed plausible that administering a series of drug injections could create a subservient underclass of humans that could be easily controlled by the billionaire cabal who had concocted the conspiracy. Once a significant proportion of a population was coerced into agreeing to have unknown, experimental drugs injected into their bodies, their children's bodies, their babies' bodies, and the bodies of pregnant women, while at the same time their constitutional rights were suspended, then game over. People who agreed to such a scheme became the most pliable of obedient conformists. They lacked independent research skills or the ability to think for themselves. Their lack of courage justified them shrinking from confrontation, refusing to stand up for their rights, and avoiding expressing an opinion that was contrary to the forced narrative.

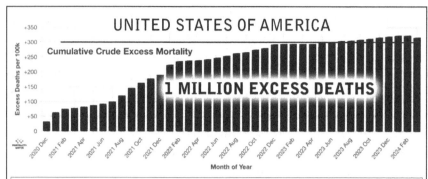

Japanese Leader Apologizes to the Unvaccinated: You Were Right, Vaccines Are Killing Millions of Our Loved Ones

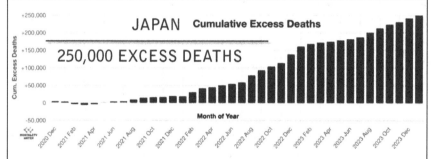

Shocking Words by Vaccine-injured Japanese MP & Minister
@kharaguchi Calls mRNA shots a Biological Weapon that cost many lives, Apologizes to the vaxxed, Shares his own & other MPs post-vaccine turbo cancers & lashes out at WHO & censorship by NHK TV

Philippines' House of Representatives Investigates 290K+ Excess Deaths Correlated with Experimental Vaccines

A Critical Analysis of All-Cause Deaths during COVID-19 Vaccination in an Italian Province
COVID-19 vaccination did not "save lives" as so many in Washington have proclaimed without evidence. The trend was for multiple vaccine doses to increase COVID-19 mortality and there was an important signal for increased all-cause death with one or two doses.

Ireland sees 42% more deaths in past two months compared to pre-COVID levels
'When we see death rates 3,000 higher in a small six-week period than they were in a six-week period pre-COVID, we can't have the Government standing idly by,' said Deputy Peadar Tóibín.

Respected Researchers' Investigation Demonstrates COVID-19 Vaccination Correlates with Excess German Deaths Across Federal States

Perhaps the drug injections would cull out a portion of the population by including a time-released death mechanism (spike proteins?), which would manifest as an improbable rise of sudden deaths, including in young, healthy people such as athletes. The "fact checkers," on the payroll of Big Pharma or the government, would very loudly proclaim that the deaths had nothing to do with the COVID injections that the healthy young people had received.

A disturbing, statistically significant spike in "all-cause mortality" would appear among populations around the world where COVID injections had been widely distributed. Although baffled medical experts had no idea what was causing the high rate of unexpected deaths, they could agree on one thing — it had nothing to do with the COVID drug rollout.

"Turbo cancers" exploded. People who had overcome cancer and were in remission suddenly had a new bout after receiving a jab, then died a short time later. Young people were developing colon cancer, heart attacks, and myocarditis. The medical industrial complex was raking in the profits by medically treating the increasing number of sick people.

Injecting pregnant women with an experimental drug with unknown ingredients seems not only ludicrous, but insane. However, if the intent was to prevent future pregnancies from happening by inducing miscarriages and stillbirths, plus rendering young women sterile, then the method behind the madness becomes apparent.

The reports of death and injury from the COVID jabs were censored from public view. And of course, the dead can't talk. Their survivors, their loved ones, the parents, husbands, wives, sons, and daughters of people who were injured or killed by the COVID jabs certainly could still talk, and many did, but they were also censored by mainstream propaganda outlets, the ones the boiled frogs were glued to daily. The TV-watchers remained unaware of this disturbing information.

Take, for example, the "Trusted News Initiative" (TNI), a group of media giants that "work together to ensure that legitimate concerns about future vaccinations are heard while harmful disinformation myths are stopped in their tracks." They took on this initiative ostensibly to "save lives during the pandemic," by "leading the way in countering dangerous disinformation which puts public health at risk."

TRUSTED NEWS INITIATIVE TO COMBAT SPREAD OF HARMFUL VACCINE DISINFORMATION

The partners within the TNI are: AP, AFP; BBC, CBC/Radio-Canada, European Broadcasting Union (EBU), Facebook, Financial Times, First Draft, Google/YouTube, The Hindu, Microsoft, Reuters, Reuters Institute for the Study of Journalism, Twitter, and The Washington Post.

'Trusted News Initiative' Antitrust Litigation

CHD has filed a first-in-the-country **antitrust lawsuit** against members of the "Trusted News Initiative" ("TNI") for collusively censoring online news.

Davos and its danger to Democracy

We are increasingly entering a world where gatherings such as Davos are not laughable billionaire playgrounds, but rather the future of global governance.

MSM PLOT EXPOSED: 'Trusted News Initiative' Leads Coup Against President Trump

11,000 politicians and elites received an exemption for the Covid vaccination: "This is shocking."

Japan's Most Senior Oncologist, Prof. Fukushima Condemns mRNA Vaccines as 'Evil Practices of Science'

It's as if *we've opened Pandora's box and are now encountering all sorts of diseases.* We're facing them. **Autoimmune diseases, neurodegenerative diseases, cancer, and infections**. All of these, including rare and difficult diseases, even those rare conditions are happening. **Even diseases unheard of are being encountered by ordinary doctors.**

Anti-Science is reading a notice on a mask box that it doesn't protect against viruses, and wearing one to protect against a virus.

Warning: This product is an ear loop mask. This product is not a respirator and will not provide any protection against Covid-19 (Coronavirus) or other viruses or contaminants.

In 2020 the TNI included the Associated Press, AFP (Agence France-Presse), BBC (British Broadcasting Corporation), CBC/Radio-Canada, European Broadcasting Union (EBU), Facebook (owned by Meta), Financial Times, First Draft, Google, YouTube (owned by Google), The Hindu, Microsoft, Reuters, Twitter, and The Washington Post. Later, ABC and others joined the group.

In the early 2020s, Mark Zuckerberg owned Meta (Facebook, Instagram, WhatsApp, etc.) holding 13.68% equity and 61.2% of the voting rights. He also donated hundreds of millions of dollars for "get out the vote" campaigns in the 2020 presidential election, including financing ballot drop box schemes in primarily democrat strongholds.

Robert F. Kennedy Jr., one of the most knowledgeable and respected Americans regarding pharmaceutical drugs in general, and particularly vaccines, was censored by Instagram, Facebook, and YouTube, based on claims of "vaccine misinformation." Rather than providing "misinformation," Kennedy was providing inconvenient truths. He explained:

"When they use the term "vaccine misinformation," they are using it as a euphemism for any statement that departs from official government policy and pharmaceutical industry profit taking. It has nothing to do with whether it's true or false, it only has to do with what the political implications are.

And who is doing this censorship? It's government officials in league with Bill Gates [vaccine entrepreneur worth $141 billion in 2024], with Larry Ellison [worth $128 billion in 2024], with Mark Zuckerberg [worth $177 billion in 2024], with Sergey Brin from Google [worth $110 billion in 2024], and with all of these internet titans.

They have engineered not only the destruction of our democracy and our civil rights, but they have engineered the biggest shift of wealth in human history. $3.8 trillion from working people to these handful of billionaires, many of them from Silicon Valley.

This pandemic has impoverished the world and created 500 new billionaires. And those are the people who are strip mining our economy and making themselves rich. And is it a coincidence that these are the same people that are censoring criticism of the government policies that are

COVID Vaccination is 'Safe' but Remains Clinically Untested for Pregnant Women: Health Canada

"I was amazed that we were even going to contemplate giving this to a pregnant woman, because we never give a pregnant woman, for very obvious reasons, anything new out of the gate. Prior to 2020, if I had ever given a pregnant woman a new product or medication, that's malpractice. The miscarriage rate was 80 percent in the Pfizer trials. They knew that. Sadly, [after the Covid injection rollout] I noticed that my miscarriage rate from year to year had gone up by 100 percent." Dr. Kimberly Biss, board-certified OBGYN

Vaccines Recommended during Pregnancy CDC

The Centers for Disease Control and Prevention (CDC) recommends the following vaccines during pregnancy:

COVID-19
Everyone age 6 months and older, including pregnant women, should stay up to date on **COVID-19** vaccines

Flu (Influenza)
Everyone age 6 months and older, including pregnant and breastfeeding women, should get vaccinated against **flu** every year.

Respiratory Syncytial Virus (RSV)
There are 2 ways to protect babies from getting very sick with **RSV**. Pregnant women can get vaccinated against RSV, or babies can receive a preventive monoclonal antibody after birth.

Whooping Cough (Pertussis)
Pregnant women should get vaccinated against **whooping cough** during each pregnancy.

CDC issues urgent health advisory, strongly recommends #COVID19 vaccination for those pregnant, recently pregnant or trying to become pregnant or who might become pregnant in the future to prevent serious illness, deaths, & adverse pregnancy outcomes.

PREGNANT PEOPLE with symptomatic COVID-19 have a
70% INCREASED RISK OF DEATH CDC

Alberta Health Services ✅

"A benefit of getting the vaccine in pregnancy is that the antibodies that your body makes from the vaccine are transferred to the baby," says Dr. Erin Bader. "And then the baby is born w/ protection against COVID-19." Vaccines are safe & effective.

Teachers Should Tolerate Bullying Towards Unvaccinated Children
The New York Times

bringing them trillions of dollars? The people who are benefitting are the people who are squeezing away our constitutional rights and engineering the destruction of democracy worldwide."

Robert F. Kennedy Jr. being interviewed on Dr. Phil, 2024:
"About 50% of the FDA's budget comes from regulated industries, mainly the pharmaceutical industry. You have 'agency capture' on steroids. The principal objective of FDA today is to serve the mercantile interests of pharmaceutical companies. For example, the Moderna vaccine: NIH [National Institutes of Health] *owns half of that vaccine, 50%. So, the billions of dollars that that vaccine makes, half of that goes to NIH, the agency. But there's also individuals, at least four and maybe six individuals who work for NIH who are high-level deputies under Anthony Fauci who get to collect $150,000 a year forever, not just for their lives but for their children's. As long as that mRNA technology is on the market, they're gonna be making money from it. That is a conflict. If you talk about this kind of thing, you get censored by YouTube. You will not be allowed on the mainstream media to talk about these issues. It used to be that you could, but nowadays you cannot."*

Of course, Kennedy's posts, speeches, and publications were labeled "misinformation" by the "Trusted News" watchdogs and "fact checkers," and censored. Furthermore, *anyone* who exposed the truth behind the scamdemic was labeled a "far right extremist." How do you know this? Just do a search on Google, once a trusted search engine, now a censorship and propaganda platform. That's what the boiled frogs do, unknowingly being directed where Google wants them to go, while finding trusted sources such as Kennedy, and many others, labeled conspiracy theorists, spreaders of disinformation, and far right extremists.

Let's look at a small number of examples of propaganda and brainwashing in the early 2020s, out of thousands. Start with the assurances that if you get the COVID injection, you won't get sick:

"You're OK. You're not going to get COVID if you have these vaccinations." President Joe Biden

CDC ✪ @CDCgov Getting a COVID-19 vaccine when pregnant helps protect you & your baby from serious illness that could lead to hospitalization.

Government Gave Millions to American College of Obstetricians and Gynecologists to Promote COVID Vaccines to Pregnant Women

COVID-19 vaccinated pregnant women continue to die unexpectedly from perinatal complications: stillbirths, blood clots, bleeding, infections and more DR. WILLIAM MAKIS MD

Spike in Miscarriages and Stillbirths Directly Linked to Covid Shots, Study Finds

OB-GYN Testifies on Alarming Miscarriage Spike among Vaxxed Women

COVID vaccines and pregnancy: > 172,000 spontaneous abortions due to the vaccine

Former Pfizer VP warns childbearing-age women: 'Do not accept these vaccines'
Dr. Michael Yeadon discussed recent findings indicating that experimental COVID-19 vaccines concentrate ovaries and induce an 'autoimmune attack' on the placenta.

We have never seen so many young women presenting with stage 4 cancers. They all were forced to take the COVID-19 vaccines. Same thing with colon cancer. We have never seen so many stage 4 presentations of colon cancer in young people. Again, the only thing they have in common is that they've taken COVID-19 vaccines. They grow extremely rapidly. They metastasize very quickly. And they're resistant in many cases, they are completely resistant to conventional chemotherapy or radiation therapy.

Radiologist, oncologist, and cancer researcher Dr. William Makis

NEJM Editor-in-Chief Eric Rubin PhD and *NEJM* Managing Editor Stephen Morrissey PhD host HHS CDC Director Rochelle Walensky on April 16, 2021 promoting the safety and efficacy of COVID-19 vaccines in pregnancy published 5 days later on April 21, 2021 in *NEJM*.[21]

During this interview, Rubin and Walensky promoted the safety of the COVID-19 vaccines in pregnancy. They used scare tactics to push the vaccines in pregnancy alleging excess morbidity and mortality in pregnant women, preborns, and newborns with COVID-19 when the literature showed the opposite. Pregnant women with COVID-19 infection had a 75% reduction in risk of mortality compared to non-pregnant women,[27] consistent with other studies.[28,29]

Shimabukuro CDC Vaccine Safety Official and 20 other authors (all federal employees) publish a flawed article on April 21, 2021 in the NEJM promoting the safety and efficacy of novel, untested COVID-19 vaccines in pregnancy.[24] The authors[24] reported a 12.6% miscarriage when their study documented an 82% miscarriage rate, a pregnancy loss rate on par with the abortion pill, RU486 (mifepristone).[25,26]

"COVID-19 vaccines are safe, and data from the past two years have shown that these vaccines are effective in preventing severe disease, hospitalization, and death." Rochelle Walensky, CDC Director

"Our data from the CDC today suggest that vaccinated people do not carry the virus, don't get sick, and it's not just in the clinical trials but it's also in real world data." Rochelle Walensky, CDC Director

"The science is clear; these vaccines will protect you and those you love from this dangerous and deadly disease." former president George W. Bush. *"They could save your life,"* former president Bill Clinton.

"This vaccine means hope. It will protect you and those you love from this dangerous and deadly disease." former president Barack Obama.

"Now we know that the vaccines work well enough that the virus stops." Rachel Maddow (MSNBC)

"When people are vaccinated, they can feel safe that they're not going to get infected." Dr. Anthony Fauci

"If you're vaccinated, you're not going to be hospitalized. You're not going to be in the ICU unit, and you're not going to die." President Joe Biden

Now let's look at some of the many comments that later adamantly claimed that the people who got the jabs were not safe after all. Instead, they were now vulnerable to a different threat — the *"unvaccinated,"* who were simply people capable of thinking for themselves and who had the personal integrity to ignore the incessant bleating of the propagandists. Or the "unvaccinated" were simply people who already had the virus and now had natural immunity and didn't need or want any drug injections. Or they were perfectly capable of tending to their own health without medical interference.

Note that none of the ludicrous and dangerous statements listed below were banned, censored, or blocked by the "Trusted News Initia-

ALTERNATIVE NEWS SOURCES
A SMALL SAMPLE OF

VIDEO PLATFORMS
Rumble
Odysee
Brighteon
Bitchute
onevsp.com
UGETube
NEWS:
153 News
Childrens Health Defense
Citizen Free Press
Compact Magazine
Epoch Times
Evol News
Highwire
InfoWars
Joe Rogan
Kim Iversen
N/A (News Addicts)
People's Voice
Prickly Pear
Rebel News (Canada)
Slay News
Sovren Media (Ben Swann)
Stew Peters
Substack
Telegram
Trial Site News
Tucker Carlson
Tulsi Gabbard
Twitter
Vigilant News
X

OTHER RESOURCES:
Academy of Ideas
America's Frontline Doctors
Ben Tapper
COVID-19 Critical Care Alliance
Christiane Northrup
Global Covid Summit
How Bad is My Batch?
Joseph Mercola
O'Keefe Media Group
OpenVAERS Project
QuestioningCovid.com
RAIR Foundation
Renz Law
Russell Brand
Sharyl Attkisson
Sherri Tenpenny
Sunfellow
Vaccine Safety Research Foundation

ON X
CITIZEN JOURNALISTS
and News Sources on X (there are many more)

Aseem Malhotra @DrAseemMalhotra
Ben Tapper @DrBenTapper1
Blake @_BlakeHabyan
Bret Weinstein @BretWeinstein
Brownstone Institute @brownstoneinst
Catturd @catturd2
Chief Nerd @TheChiefNerd
Christine Anderson @AndersonAfDMdEP
Citizen Free Press @CitizenFreePres
Clown World @ClownWorld_
Dan Bongino @dbongino
Elijah Schaffer @ElijahSchaffer
Elon Musk @elonmusk
Epoch Times @epochtimes
Five Times August @FiveTimesAugust
Flyover @TheFlyoverNews
Gain of Fauci @DschlopesIsBack
Jeffrey A Tucker @jeffreyatucker
Jessica Rojas @catsscareme2021
John Davidson @BrokenTruthTV
Judy A. Mikovits @DrJudyAMikovits
Kanekoa The Great @KanekoaTheGreat
Kevin Bass @kevinnbass
Maria Zeee @zeee_media
Mary Talley Bowden @MDBreathe
Matt Walsh @MattWalshBlog
MAZE @MazeMoore
Megyn Kelly Show @MegynKellyShow
Midwestern Doctor @MidwesternDoc
Mike Benz @MikeBenzCyber
Neil Oliver @thecoastguy
Overton @OvertonLive
Peter A. McCullough, MD @P_McCulloughMD
Robert Epstein @DrREpstein
Robert W Malone, MD @RWMaloneMD
Seth Holehouse @ManInAmericaUS
Sonia Elijah @Sonia_Elijah
Stew Peters @realstewpeters
Tom Renz @RenzTom
Tucker Carlson @TuckerCarlson
Tulsi Gabbard @TulsiGabbard
UngaTheGreat @UngaTheGreat
Vigilant Fox @VigilantFox
Vigilant News Network @VigilantNews
Viva Frei @thevivafrei
Wendy Bell @WendyBellPgh
Western Lensman @WesternLensman
Whitney Webb @_whitneywebb
Wide Awake Media @wideawake_media

tive" or by the "fact checkers." Apparently, the following comments were to be trusted and certainly didn't constitute disinformation:

"You are the unvaccinated. You are the problem. It is the unvaccinated who are the problem period, end of story." Mika Brzezinski, MSNBC

"The only people you can blame, this isn't shaming, this is the truth (maybe they should be shamed), are the unvaccinated." Don Lemon, commentator on CNN's *Don Lemon Tonight.*

"It's time to start blaming the unvaccinated folks, not the regular folks." Alabama Republican Governor Ivey on CNN.

"Don't get me started on the lunatics who won't take any of the COVID vaccines... Anyone you came into contact with will blame you. As will the rest of us who have done the right thing by getting vaccinated." MSNBC TV, The Sunday Show, with Jonathan Capehart

"Because frankly we know that we can't trust the unvaccinated." Dr. Leana Wen on *Democracy Now!*

"I think it's time to get our moral house in order, Anderson [Cooper]. It's the unvaccinated who are the threat." Commentator on CNN, with a TV screen subtitle that stated, *"Biden makes urgent plea for vaccination and orders new requirement for federal workers: 'It's about life or death.'"*

"People are not behaving honorably. The unvaccinated are basically saying, 'Well, it's open season for me. I can do whatever I want as well'." Dr. Leana Wen on CNN, with a TV screen subtitle that stated, *"New Covid Cases Rising in Every State."*

"The unvaccinated are basically beating their breasts, running around the country saying, 'Ha ha, we don't care, we're living free, and

U.S. Covid-19 Deaths in 2021 Surpass 2020's
Pandemic continues to exact huge toll despite vaccines as Delta variant spreads

No "vax" for HIV after 40 yrs of research. No vax for cancer after more than 100 yrs of research. No vax for the Common Cold. And yet a virus mysteriously appears & within 12 months a "vax" is found by FOUR Pharma companies all within 1 week & we are all mandated to take it. **Joseph Boaz**

But there is something "mysterious" going on in Africa that is puzzling scientists, said Wafaa El-Sadr, chair of global health at Columbia University. "Africa doesn't have the vaccines and the resources to fight COVID-19 that they have in Europe and the U.S., but somehow they seem to be doing better," she said. Fewer than 6% of people in Africa are vaccinated. For months, the WHO has described Africa as "one of the least affected regions in the world" in its weekly pandemic reports.

Concerns regarding Transfusions of Blood Products Derived from Genetic Vaccine Recipients and Proposals for Specific Measures

Abstract: The coronavirus pandemic was declared by the World Health Organization (WHO) in 2020, and a global genetic vaccination program has been rapidly implemented as a fundamental solution. However, many countries around the world have reported that so-called genetic vaccines, such as those using modified mRNA encoding the spike protein and lipid nanoparticles as the drug delivery system, have resulted in post-vaccination thrombosis and subsequent cardiovascular damage, as well as a wide variety of diseases involving all organs and systems, including the nervous system. In this article, based on these circumstances and the volume of evidence that has recently come to light, we call the attention of medical professionals to the various risks associated with blood transfusions using blood products derived from people who have suffered from long COVID and from genetic vaccine recipients, including those who have received mRNA vaccines.

Egyptian Physician Asks Why Were COVID-19 Death Rates So Much Higher in the West vs. Africa?

Numerous peer-reviewed entries have addressed the African COVID-19 paradox. A review of Worldometers recorded COVID-19 deaths finds America far at the top in related deaths.

The Egyptian provider-research shares in the journal: "In Africa we've been able to live without anxiety or mandates throughout the pandemic because we trust science and adopted early treatment using safe, and effective repurposed drugs that have saved the majority of COVID-19 patients.

so forth...'" commentator on MSNBC with a TV screen subtitle that stated, *"CDC Sparks Debate With Masks for Vaccinated as Unvaccinated Pose Main Risk."*

"We've been patient, but our patience is wearing thin . . . This is not about freedom or personal choice . . . Those who are not vaccinated will end up paying the price . . ." U.S. President Joe Biden on a televised public service announcement.

"The unvaccinated, a group that includes children, and people acting like children. And the rest of us are starting to get pissed off." Steven Colbert on his TV show.

"The vaccinated feel the unvaccinated are 'making me upset or angry'." TV analyst on Face the Nation, referring to a CBS News poll in California. The TV screen showed that 59% of the *"fully vaccinated"* believe that the *"unvaccinated"* are *"putting people like me at risk,"* and nearly half of the *"fully vaccinated"* stated that the *"unvaccinated"* are *"making me upset or angry."*

"When are we going to stop putting up with the idiots in this country and just say, you know, it's mandatory to get vaccinated? Fuck their freedom, fuck their freedom." Howard Stern on the Howard Stern Show.

"The antivaxxers, they seem to have a thing, for death and home remedies." Joy Reid on her MSNBC TV show *The Reidout*. A TV screen subtitle stated, *"Breaking News: FDA Urges Anti-Vaxxers Not to Take Livestock Medicine."*

"The anti-maskers turned anti-vaxxers are not just putting their own lives at risk. If that was a key issue, we could just say that we can watch them compete to win, place, or show in the Darwin Awards." Commentator on CNN's *"Reality Check"* TV program. A TV screen subtitle stated, *"Yes, Vaccine Mandates are Constitutional."*

I lost my medical license in Ontario, Canada in part for reporting adverse reactions to the Covid vaccines. I was charged with professional misconduct and incompetence for every report I submitted. **Patrick Phillips, MD**

Part of Stay safe. Get vaccinated. Save lives.

Vaccine required

As of August 20, you must show proof of vaccination to go into bars, restaurants, clubs, gyms, large outdoor events, or any business or event serving food or drinks indoors.

In these places, anyone 12 or older will need to show proof of vaccination. You will still need to wear a mask in most of these places. SF.gov (San Francisco, California)

Hundreds of Thousands of Americans Sought Medical Care After COVID-19 Vaccination: CDC Data

Wait what? FDA wants 55 years to process FOIA request over vaccine data?

Maker of COVID Tests Says Pandemic is Biggest Hoax Ever Perpetrated

Joy Reid Blames GOP 'Death Cult of Disinformation' for COVID Spikes

"Well, it's no surprise since the right-wing talking heads are trying to get their viewers killed by smearing the vaccine,"

As America tops 4 million COVID cases, the cult of Donald Trump has become a death cult

People who refuse to wear a mask are bolstering their sore egos.

"Since...the vaccine rollout, we have 1.1 million excessive Americans dying, 4.0 million disabled—we estimate another 28.6 million injured... So, it's about 33 million Americans have been injured, disabled, or died from this vaccine." Former BlackRock fund manager, Edward Dowd   [May, 2024]

"We have to start doing things for the greater good of society. And not for idiots who think they can do their own research . . ." Don Lemon on the CNN TV show *"Don Lemon Tonight."* A TV screen subtitle stated, *"Patience Runs Out. TV Host Rips Unvaccinated: 'Stop Your Bullshit and Hurting World'."*

"We need to start looking at the choice to remain unvaccinated the same as we look at driving while intoxicated." Dr. Leana Wen, medical analyst on CNN's Cuomo Prime Time.

"Dr. Fauci said that if hospitals get any more overcrowded, they're going to have to make some very tough choices about who gets an ICU bed. That choice doesn't seem so tough to me. Vaccinated person having a heart attack, yes, come right on in — we'll take care of you. Unvaccinated guy who gobbled horse goo, rest in peace, wheezy." Jimmy Kimmel on the ABC late-night show *"Jimmy Kimmel Live!"*

"Pointing back to the unvaccinated who are really creating a problem in this country. Every death that we are seeing from COVID could have been prevented." Mika Brzezinski, co-host on Morning Joe, MSNBC TV.

"Literally, the only people dying are the unvaccinated. And for those of you spreading misinformation, shame on you. Shame on you." Chuck Todd on MTP Daily, MSNBC and NBC TV.

"That choice not to get vaccinated does put millions of other Americans at risk. Those who can't get the vaccine because they are immunocompromised or because they're children and the vaccine hasn't been approved for kids under the age of 12 yet. So, while this is a pandemic of the unvaccinated there are millions of children who can get sick because of adults who won't do something to protect them." Anderson Cooper on CNN TV.

"This is not fiction. This is not some kind of disinformation cam-

Arrested for paddleboarding in the ocean after "health" professionals had ordered everyone to stay indoors "to protect their health."

Paddle boarder chased by boat, arrested in Malibu after flouting coronavirus closures CALIFORNIA

Woman arrested for not wearing mask in NY subway to sue police for $10 million

Christians arrested for maskless outdoor church service to get payout from liberal college town

FBI Agents Arrest Woman Who Yelled At Man For Not Wearing Mask On Plane

Victoria-area man arrested, fined twice for refusing to wear a face mask

American Airlines passenger arrested after refusing to wear mask

Not Wearing a Mask Is Now a Crime in These Places
Face masks are now mandatory in 16 states and the District of Columbia.

Boise police arrested a man for not wearing mask in Costco. Now, he wants $4.5 million

Oakland man arrested for not wearing mask died of jail's 'outright refusal' to provide medical care: lawsuit

IMAGINE A VACCINE SO SAFE YOU HAVE TO BE THREATENED TO TAKE IT FOR A DISEASE SO DEADLY YOU HAVE TO BE TESTED TO KNOW YOU HAVE IT

MotherJones
Anti-Vaxxers Have a Dangerous Theory Called "Natural Immunity." Now It's Going Mainstream

FAIRNESS & ACCURACY IN REPORTING

The Dangerous Misuse of 'Natural Immunity' Against Covid Vaccination

paign. This is just a fact. If you are dying today in America from COVID *it's because you're unvaccinated. Why would you want to die?"* Xavier Becerra, HHS Secretary (wearing a mask) on CNN Live TV.

Dr. Anthony Fauci stated in a 2024 congressional hearing that *"Peter Hotez has done an analysis of this that shows that in people who refuse to get vaccinated for any of a variety of reasons, [they are] probably responsible for an additional 200,000 to 300,000 deaths..."*

The comments above are classic propaganda intended to brainwash TV watchers. Such comments could be considered a ludicrous clown show if they weren't so disgusting, sinister, and evil. The purpose of the propaganda platforms like the ones above had a single intent — convince as many people as possible to get injected with the COVID drug. Why?

The Injections

The COVID drug injections, officially referred to as "vaccines," were declared "safe and effective," but the drug manufacturers insisted on having no liability whatsoever for any deaths or injuries caused by the "safe" drugs. The government exempted drug manufacturers from all responsibility for any deaths or injuries caused by the injections. Pfizer had even petitioned the federal government to hide their vaccine safety data for 55 years. The damning safety data were only released after a lawsuit forced Pfizer to release it.

If someone died or was injured within 14 days of a COVID drug injection, that death or injury was, incredibly, listed as being in the *unvaccinated*! Yet, the Vaccine Adverse Event Reporting System (VAERS) indicated that the vast majority of deaths and permanent injuries from the COVID jabs occurred within 72 hours of the injection. Medical professionals conveniently, and perhaps criminally, recorded those vaccine deaths as *COVID* deaths in the *unvaccinated*!

A deadly aerosolized viral pathogen could somehow only be tested for by plunging a swab deep up a person's nasal passageway nearly all the way to their brain. If the pathogen is floating in the air and passes through

Robert W Malone, MD

I am going to speak bluntly. Physicians who speak out are being actively hunted via medical boards and the press. They are trying to deligitimize and pick us off one by one. This is not a conspiracy theory - this is a fact. Please wake up. This is happening globally.

COVID VACCINE INJURIES .COM

Garnet Harper was denied a kidney transplant because he wasn't vaccinated. No doctor or hospital in Ontario would perform the surgery, despite his two brothers volunteering to donate. Garnet tragically passed away on May 22, leaving behind his wife of 12 years and their 5 children. He was only 35.

Kentucky's largest school district requires masks regardless of vaccination status.

Sydney teen's lung transplant denied over Covid vaccination status

Parents of leukaemia-stricken teenager are grappling with a hospital's refusal to conduct a lifesaving transplant due to her lack of Covid-19 vaccination.

DOES IVERMECTIN WORK? GOOGLE: NO CAN MEN GET PREGNANT? GOOGLE: YES

REMEMBER WHEN THEY OUTLAWED FRESH AIR & SUNSHINE BECAUSE THEY CARED ABOUT YOUR HEALTH?

Study: Ivermectin can lead to "large reductions" in Covid-19 deaths

41% of Voters Believe Civil War Will Break Out By 2029

one's breath, and can be stopped with just a face mask, why not just swab the mouth or even have someone just breathe on the swab?

Five and a half billion humans were injected with the COVID "vaccine" by 2024; 13.57 billion doses had been administered globally in the early 2020s. The word vaccine is in quotes because the experimental drug being injected did not fit the traditional scientific definition of a vaccine. This problem was rectified by government agencies quickly changing the definition to fit the drug, as they had done with the word "pandemic."

If a new dose of the COVID drug had been manufactured every second, it would have taken 430 years to produce 13.57 billion doses. If 430 doses were manufactured every second, 25,800 every minute, 1,548,888 every hour, or over 37 million doses every day, nonstop, 24/7, for an entire year, you would have 13.57 billion doses. Explain how that degree of manufacturing occurred, not to mention that level of clinical administration, in response to a sudden, unexpected, "novel" pathogen over such a short period of time. 13.57 billion doses injected into human beings is equivalent to injecting *every single person in the United States* 40 times. Had the "vaccines" already been manufactured ahead of time? Was this whole thing planned in advance?

The drug package inserts associated with these EUA drugs were blank. There was no information on them, despite almost every other commercial pharmaceutical drug having package inserts that unfold like a newspaper and contain a plethora of fine print that lists side effects, contraindications, and drug incompatibilities. Not so with the COVID EUA drugs. The public had to search for relevant information using the Freedom of Information Act. Pfizer would not release its information until they were sued and lost. When Pfizer's lawyers told the court they needed 55 years to release the data, the court ruled that they had to release it much more quickly than that. When they did, much of it was redacted.

People formed long lines down sidewalks to have these drugs injected into them despite having no idea what was in the drugs or what long-term, or immediate, detrimental health effects might occur. They were bribed with promises of free hamburgers, free ice cream cones, free lottery tickets, savings bonds, gift cards, cash, marijuana, donuts, beer, jewelry, kitchen utensils, and free popcorn at movie theaters while congratulated

Amanda Marcotte

Vaccine refusers should lose their jobs. If they can't take this most basic step to protect colleagues and customers, they can't be trusted in any other way.

salon.com
It's time to start firing unvaccinated people: Trump fans are overdue for a lesson in consequences

Vaccination / Manufacturer	Lot / Dose	Site / Route
COVID19: COVID19 (COVID19 (PFIZER-BIONTECH)) / PFIZER/BIONTECH	- / UNK	- / OT

Administered by: Other   **Purchased by:** ?
Symptoms: <u>Death</u>, <u>Exposure via breast milk</u>
SMQs:, Neonatal exposures via breast milk (narrow)
Life Threatening? No
Birth Defect? No
Died? Yes   **VAERS ID:** <u>2428044</u>

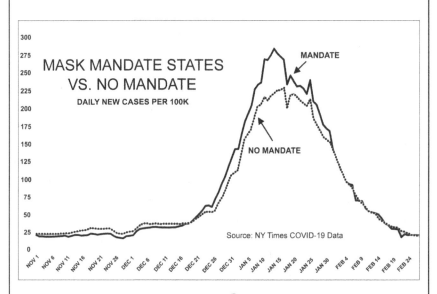

MASK MANDATE STATES VS. NO MANDATE

DAILY NEW CASES PER 100K

MANDATE

NO MANDATE

Source: NY Times COVID-19 Data

Certificate of Achievement
awarded to
THE UNVACCINATED
FOR SURVIVING THE GREATEST
PSYCHOLOGICAL FEAR CAMPAIGN IN HUMAN HISTORY

for being willing to experience "the miracle of vaccines."

The people who chose to remain normal and not be injected with any unwanted and unneeded drug were soundly condemned by mainstream propaganda platforms such as CNN which labeled them *"malevolent actors"* who were *"undermining Americans' public confidence in vaccines,"* and *"mainstreaming formerly fringe antivaccination sentiments"* in *"response to a terrifying pandemic."*

We had discussed earlier in this book how malicious propaganda can cause massive death and suffering, such as in Vietnam, a country that Americans attacked based on lies from the U.S. government and media. In the end, Vietnam won the war and the lies became exposed but were rarely, if ever, discussed in public. Our "way of life" in America wasn't destroyed as we had been warned. The "Reds" didn't invade and take over our country, even though we lost the war. In the case of COVID, the "terrifying pandemic" petered out in most of the world, manifesting itself as little more than a normal flu season. The very worst outcomes happened in America. Forcing people to get the injections didn't help anything — it made everything worse.

The government forced the COVID injections on people who already had the virus, had recovered, and had natural immunity, as well as people who had virtually no chance of dying from the illness. People who tested positive but had no symptoms were forced to get the injections. Pregnant women were told by the CDC that they would have healthier babies if they got an untested experimental drug injection. At the same time, doctors were cautioning pregnant women to avoid fish, lunch meat, soft cheeses, fresh-squeezed organic fruit juices, salt, alcohol, caffeine, tobacco, raw sprouts, and even herbal tea. But a mysterious, untested, experimental drug was not only okay for pregnant women and their fetuses but beneficial. What? And pregnant women believed this? And medical doctors promoted this? Yes, they did.

Seven hundred and seventy "safety signals" had presented themselves during the COVID drug trials. 1,223 *deaths* and 158,893 adverse events were listed in the Pfizer data over the three-month trial period; 1.6 million adverse events associated with the COVID injections were recorded in VAERS, assumed to be only 1/10 to 1/100 of the actual total.

2,602,082

REPORTS OF VACCINE ADVERSE EVENTS IN VAERS

37,544 COVID Vaccine Reported Deaths / **47,847 Total Reported Deaths**

216,213 Total COVID Vaccine Reported Hospitalizations/305,847 Total Reported Hospitalizations

1,637,441 COVID Vaccine Adverse Event Reports Through April 26, 2024

openvaers.com

Sudden death epidemic: Excess mortality among young, middle-aged Americans skyrockets

"We had to really move at the speed of science ..we had to do everything at risk" -Pfizer Exec

In fact you didn't risk anything, you made sure of that. You told the world it was safe and effective. You made deals with governments to escape liability, no one was allowed to sue you. You paid media across the world to promote the vaccine. You hid the risk, you hid the data, in fact you wanted 75 years to release the data. Reminder, the vaccine inserts/risk warnings were left blank. We all saw it. And you made tens of billions of dollars.

Breakthrough COVID infections show 'the unvaccinated are now putting the vaccinated at risk' pbs.org

health experts say that rare "breakthrough infections" among vaccinated people are not a sign that vaccines are failing. Instead, they are a warning of how vaccine holdouts can endanger their inoculated neighbors.

MSM Silent As Court Holds PCR Covid Tests 97% Inaccurate - Unfit for Purpose

Ask your doctor if a drug with 1291 side effects listed on 32 pages, including blood clots, strokes, and heart attacks, is right for you.

A 2024 research paper stated: *International analyses of excess mortality indicate that COVID-19 vaccinations may have had serious largescale consequences. In a careful study of mass vaccinations throughout Europe in 2021-2022, Aarstad and Kvitastein analyzed the potential interplay between COVID-19 vaccination coverage in 2021 across Europe and subsequent monthly excess mortality through 2022. Utilizing a well curated dataset encompassing 31 nations, the authors applied population-weighted analyses and found the following: (a) increases in All Cause Mortality during the initial nine-month period of 2022 were positively correlated with increases in 2021 vaccination distribution; and (b) each percentage point increase in 2021 vaccination coverage was associated with a 0.105% increase in monthly mortality during 2022. An extensive, multi-country ecological analysis by Rancourt and colleagues estimated that COVID-19 vaccination resulted in 17 million excess deaths, with a global vaccine-dose fatality rate of approximately 0.1%. Rancourt's 180-page report showed that the COVID-19 vaccine rollouts were synchronously followed by peaks in All Cause Mortality in many countries.*

The part that the government and Big Pharma don't want you to see bears repeating: *"COVID-19 <u>vaccination</u> resulted in 17 million excess deaths."* Not only was the published, peer-reviewed research paper forced to be abruptly retracted, but the same propaganda platforms that hysterically pushed the COVID injections, relentlessly condemned the research paper as false and blocked it from public view. Good luck finding it on Google.

The SARS CoV2 (COVID) virus was reportedly developed by the U.S. military in cooperation with U.S. "health" agencies, partnering with Chinese scientists, using U.S. tax dollars. It appears that they had genetically altered what would otherwise be called a flu-like virus (SARS-CoV-1), causing it to infect human beings more easily. The genetic mutation theoretically allowed the virus to block the uptake of the oxygen molecule by the hemoglobin molecule in human blood. The resultant effect was to cause infected people to inhale but not get the amount of oxygen they would normally absorb. This caused a "shortness of breath" symptom that was alarming and frightening, especially for people who were already unhealthy, such as nicotine smokers, sugar addicts, and the obese, poor health conditions that burdened a large percentage of American citizens.

Influenced by nonstop TV propaganda, many people panicked and

MEDICAL EXAMINER
So You're Triple-Vaxxed and Still Got COVID. Now What?

Day 6 of Covid. Now my wife and kids have it too. All of us vaxxed; wife and I both boosted not long ago. Everybody we know who has omicron was vaxxed; most also boosted. So I gotta ask: what's the point of vaccine passports now? Security theater? Prepping social credit system?

Scientific Publications Directory
Collection of peer reviewed case reports and studies citing adverse effects post COVID vaccination.

Here, we share an ever growing list of peer-reviewed studies specific to Covid vaccine adverse events by our dedicated staff of injured PhDs and medical professionals.

Showing total of 3,580 entries   https://react19.org/science

Pfizer reportedly withheld presence of cancer-linked DNA in COVID jabs from FDA, Health Canada

According to information released by the Epoch Times, Pfizer purposefully failed to advise drug regulators, including Health Canada, the U.S. FDA and the European Medicines Agency, that the cancer-linked SV40 DNA enhancer was present in their experimental COVID shot.

HEALTH AND SCIENCE

You can't sue Pfizer or Moderna if you have severe Covid vaccine side effects. The government likely won't compensate you for damages.

Hospital Whistleblower: Covid Shots Kill Patients 'So Horrifically, So Quickly'

A hospital whistleblower has gone public to raise the alarm after witnessing how hospital patients are killed "so horrifically, so quickly" by Covid mRNA shots. The medical industry insider, who goes only by "Zoe," described the horrific side effects patients experienced after taking the experimental COVID mRNA vaccines in 2021 and 2022 and how doctors were inadequately prepared to handle them. "It was insane, I've never seen anything like that."

flocked to hospitals at the urging of their doctors, certain that they would otherwise die of COVID.

The genetically engineered mutant virus appeared to have been released intentionally, some say accidentally, in several places throughout the globe simultaneously, including China, New York City, Italy, Iran, and Brazil. These outbreaks were frantically reported on the mainstream propaganda platforms, showing helicopter views of mass graves in New York City, reports of bodies being cremated on sidewalks because there was no more room left at the morgues, and box trucks loaded with corpses being taken out to the countryside because there was no room left in the city for more dead bodies. Of course, the reports did not show the contents of the trucks. Nor did they mention that NYC already had mass graves for homeless people who pass away with no next of kin, and so on. Facts didn't matter. Fear did.

A few months before the release of the virus, a practice scenario known as "Event 201," hosted by the World Economic Forum and the Bill and Melinda Gates Foundation, enacted a simulated dry run of what was expected to happen during a worldwide health catastrophe: panic, widespread death, overrun medical facilities, nuisance persons who would not follow orders, and the need for censorship and propaganda.

Upon release of the virus, a vast, internationally coordinated propaganda effort was mounted to stir panic among the masses. A *polymerase chain reaction* (PCR) testing procedure was used to determine whether anyone was infected, and frightened people lined up to take the test, which was later proven to be unreliable for diagnostic purposes. The inventor of the test mechanism, Dr. Kary Mullis, winner of the 1993 Nobel Prize in chemistry for his invention of the process on which the PCR test is based, had publicly stated that the PCR test could not be used for the diagnosis of disease. He was also an outspoken critic of Dr. Anthony Fauci. Dr. Kary Mullis' 2019 death at age 74 "of pneumonia," at the beginning of the "pandemic," seemed suspicious to many people.

Nevertheless, positive PCR test results grew exponentially, even among people with no symptoms. The increasing "positive" tests were ominously displayed on TV screens alongside the climbing COVID-19 death toll. President Joe Biden grimly warned, *"We are looking at a winter*

COVID-19 RNA Based Vaccines and the Risk of Prion Disease

The folding of TDP-43 and FUS into their pathologic prion confirmations is known to cause ALS, front temporal lobar degeneration, Alzheimer's disease and other neurological degenerative diseases. The enclosed finding as well as additional potential risks leads the author to believe that regulatory approval of the RNA based vaccines for SARS-CoV-2 was premature and that the vaccine may cause much more harm than benefit.

The Pharmaceutical Conspiracy to Silence Online Dissent is Bigger Than You Think

• There has been a coordinated campaign to attack and defame anyone who has spoken out against the COVID-19 response. This has primarily been restricted to social media (e.g., getting people deplatformed) but it has also been weaponized in real life (e.g., getting medical licenses revoked).

• This coordinated campaign was the result of a "non-profit" known as The Public Good Project (PGP), which was actually directly linked to the pharmaceutical industry. The PGP used the industry funding it received to defend industry interests.

Non validity of "PCR test" and consequences

Dr Astrid Stückelberger PD PhD

The PCR test was no reason to act on the healthy public and to enforce unnecessary and unreliable test with high amplification cycles. Moreso, it induces 97% of false positives in Finland.

Given the Coronavirus COVID-19 (SARS-CoV2) mutates and disappears within a few months, it is scientifically not possible to maintain the declaration of a COVID-19 "pandemic" beyond 2020 nor any public health measures, nor to impose its diagnostic with a misleading test over time.

Possible toxicity of chronic carbon dioxide exposure associated with face mask use, particularly in pregnant women, children and adolescents – A scoping review

Results: Fresh air has around 0.04% CO_2, while wearing masks more than 5 min bears a possible chronic exposure to carbon dioxide of 1.41% to 3.2% of the inhaled air. Although the buildup is usually within the short-term exposure limits, long-term exceedances and consequences must be considered due to experimental data. US Navy toxicity experts set the exposure limits for submarines carrying a female crew to 0.8% CO_2 based on animal studies which indicated an increased risk for stillbirths. Additionally, mammals who were chronically exposed to 0.3% CO_2 the experimental data demonstrate a teratogenicity with irreversible neuron damage in the offspring, reduced spatial learning caused by brainstem neuron apoptosis and reduced circulating levels of the insulin-like growth factor-1.

How Africa Defeated COVID so Decisively Without Vaccines

It so happens that two of the most effective treatments for COVID, ivermectin and hydroxychloroquine, are also routine prophylactic weekly medicines throughout equatorial Africa, because they happen to be known for a half-century as the most effective, applicable and safest anti-parasite medications.

of severe illness and death for the unvaccinated — for themselves, their families and the hospitals they'll soon overwhelm." But no one with natural immunity was going to have severe illness and death. No one who already had the "novel" virus and gotten over it needed to have anything to worry about. According to Biden and the democrats however, none of that mattered. The only thing that mattered was whether you got the COVID drug injected into your body. Why? Why were they so desperate to have this untested drug injected into everyone, even healthy people, even children and pregnant mothers?

Almost anyone who died during this time period (early 2020s) was declared a COVID-19 death. This included murder-suicides, automobile accident deaths, and people who died in the hospital after being put on ventilators and injected with drug combinations that were likely to cause organ failure and death. The more people who were proclaimed dead from COVID, the more hysteria and fear the media could drum up and the more they could point the finger at the "unvaccinated" as the cause of the deaths. The TV watchers lined up in great masses thinking they were saving themselves and their loved ones by getting the shots.

Some nurses reported that 95% of hospital patients who were diagnosed with COVID-19 and put on ventilators and drugs died. Ventilators are machines that mechanically replace the work of the lungs. They're typically used in cases such as coma victims, where artificial lung action is needed to keep a patient alive. The COVID-19 laboratory virus was genetically altered to block the uptake of oxygen. It did not stop the muscular architecture of the lungs from working.

Ventilators not only seemed useless in the treatment of this virus, but, according to witnesses, they were deadly. A nurse working in the Elmhurst Hospital in Brooklyn during the outbreak, Erin Olszewski, reported undercover that what was happening in her hospital could be described as murder. She wrote a book about her experiences (*Undercover Epicenter Nurse*) in which she stated:

> *"The COVID crises could be an opportunity for us to confront the true state of healthcare in America, before it's too late. Or it could be another invitation to further denial, that will only prolong the suffering that so*

U.S. FDA ✔ @US_FDA · Aug 21   🔗 fda.gov

You are not a horse. You are not a cow. Seriously, y'all. Stop it.

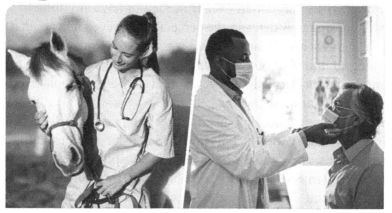

Why You Should Not Use Ivermectin to Treat or Prevent COVID-19.

Using the Drug ivermectin to treat COVID-19 can be dangerous and even lethal. The FDA has not approved the drug for that purpose.

FDA Settles Ivermectin Case, Agrees to Remove Controversial 'Stop It' Post

Doctors score win, forcing FDA to remove statements about ivermectin.

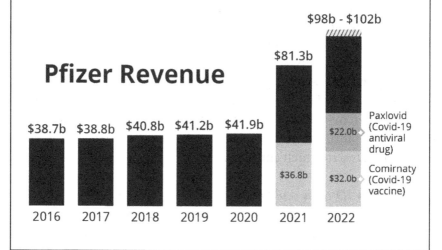

many people will face. In the meantime, they're murdering patients, and nurses who are supposed to be patient advocates are just not doing anything because they're scared."

She added, *"COVID-19 is real, and it can kill people. What I have been trying to illustrate, however, is that most of the people dying didn't have to. Most are not dying of* COVID. *Generally, they're dying of mismanagement, fraud, gross negligence, and greed."* Olszewski received death threats for speaking out.

Another nurse, Nicole Sirotek, who worked at another hospital in New York City, witnessed similarly disturbing scenarios:

"We're not treating the COVID guys. Like for real, we're not treating the COVID. You know, every day we try to get these guys off the vents . . . We still have a hundred percent fatality rate in the ICU unit. It's like going in the fucking Twilight Zone . . . Like guys, they are not dying of COVID, okay . . . And the worst part is when they die, it's just going to go down and it's like, oh, they died of COVID . . . I mean, how many people have to die before people get their shit together? They're not dying of coronavirus . . . I'm not fighting coronavirus here, people. I mean, I'm not. I'm fighting fucking stupidity. That's what I'm fighting right now."

Early in the "pandemic," NY doctor, Cameron Kyle-Sidell, sent out a warning to all doctors across the nation by video saying:

"I believe we are treating the wrong disease, and I fear that this misguided treatment will lead to a tremendous amount of harm to a great number of people in a very short time. I don't know the final answer to this disease, but I'm quite sure that a ventilator is not it." Later he added, *"I've run into a great deal of resistance within my institution . . . I could not morally, in a patient-doctor relationship I could not continue the current protocols . . . so I actually had to step down from my position in the ICU, and so now I'm back in the ER . . ."*

The climbing death toll was broadcast widely and loudly, throwing

WHISTLEBLOWER DROPS "DEEPLY DISTURBING" REPORT SHOWING THE CIA WAS PAID TO MISLEAD THE PUBLIC ON COVID

Myocarditis and Pericarditis Only Appear After COVID Vaccination: NHS Preprint
Adolescents had a higher incidence of post-vaccine myocarditis and pericarditis than children.

Doctors in Kentucky, California Received Millions in Bonus Payments for Vaccinating Medicaid Patients Against COVID

Saskatchewan Residents Deserve Apology From Province Over Vaccine Mandate, MLA Says

Doctors say they are seeing an alarming number of seemingly healthy younger patients having heart attacks. Now doctors at Mount Sinai are tracking patients to see if they can uncover the new risk factors behind the trend. @annenbcnews reports. @TODAYshow

The protected need to be protected from the unprotected by forcing the unprotected to use the protection that didn't protect the protected.

CDC Study confirms COVID Vaccination increases risk of suffering Autoimmune Disease affecting Heart by 13,200%

Israel Didn't Check Most Reports of COVID Vaccine Side Effects: Watchdog

Indian Study on AstraZeneca COVID-19 Vaccine: Troubling Atypical Adverse Event Rate-- 9.7% of Boosted Injured

Masks Found to Be Ineffective After First Omicron Wave: New Study
By the second Omicron wave, wearing masks was shown to offer no protection for adults and potentially increased the risk of infection in children.

Government Stockpiling Vaccines ahead of Pre-Election Pandemic

fuel on the panic gripping the TV-watching population.

A woman named Zowe, a medical coder who was forced to quit her job because she refused the COVID injections, during a live interview in 2024, explained:

"I knew they were killing people in the hospital. I would cry myself to sleep at night. There was so much death. It was almost unbearable. Hospitals became the place where people go to die instead of the place where people go to get better. They separated newborns from their moms. They let people die alone, without being able to say goodbye. They drugged them and they strapped them down and people died without being able to say goodbye to their family. Some of them just got a phone call. Some didn't get anything. Some of them just weirdly died in the middle of the night when there was a skeleton crew on and they had been doing fine up until that point and just all of a sudden overnight 'Oh they just crashed, I don't know what happened.' And that had never happened before the COVID protocol rolled out in 2020. So yeah, when they say they killed people I agree with them. I told people . . . don't go to the hospital. They're killing people in there, stay away. I don't know what's wrong. I didn't know what was doing it. I honestly didn't know it was the vents, I didn't know it was the remdesivir, until I looked into it later and I was able to kind of connect the dots. But I knew they were killing people."

At the same time, there were no reports of people *dying at home* from the virus. The homeless encampments in various cities should have had high death tolls, according to the hysteria being driven by the media. But they didn't. Refugee camps, poverty-stricken villages, poor people living in polluted environments around the world, should have been particularly vulnerable. But they weren't. In fact, the nation with the highest death toll attributed to COVID-19 was the United States, by a wide margin. Curiously, the United States, with what is often touted as the most advanced "health care" system on the planet, had more people die of the COVID-19 virus than any of the other 195 countries in the world.

It appeared that virtually all the United States deaths were taking place in hospitals. A single patient on a ventilator could reportedly rack

CDC Releases Hidden COVID-19 Vaccine Injury Reports

The agency was forced by a federal judge to disclose the reports.

The CDC, for years, declined to make the V-safe data public, instead publishing studies that described the reports as providing reassurance about the safety of the vaccines. However, according to data released in 2022, nearly 8 percent of the 10 million users required medical attention or hospital care after vaccination, and many others reported missing school, work, or other normal activities.

The first two tranches, made up of 780,000 reports from some 523,000 people, include dozens of reports of heart inflammation, hundreds of reports of facial paralysis, and thousands of reports of tinnitus.

Jessica Rose Breaks Down 1.6 Million Adverse Event Reports in VAERS, Definitive Evidence of Causality

Fact: Currently, 1,615,998 deaths have been successfully filed to VAERS in the context of the Covid-19 injectable products, with a staggering 1,013,442 reports filed in 2021 alone, when considering both the foreign and domestic data sets. The number of adverse events reported to the domestic VAERS data set for all vaccines combined has been on average 39,000 in total per year, and has been very slowly and steadily increasing in direct proportion to the increasing number of vaccine products on the market. Mar-07-2024

MN Senator and Doctor: Hospitals Get Paid More to List Patients as COVID-19 and Three Times as Much if the Patient Goes on Ventilator
"The CDC is Now Listing Vaccinated COVID-19 Deaths as Unvaccinated Deaths if They Die Within 14 Days of the Vaccine" – Dr. Simone Gold

Senator Dr. Scott Jensen: Right now Medicare is determining that if you have a COVID-19 admission to the hospital you get $13,000. If that COVID-19 patient goes on a ventilator you get $39,000, three times as much. Nobody can tell me after 35 years in the world of medicine that sometimes those kinds of things impact on what we do.

up an estimated $1 million in insurance payments for the hospital where the patient was bedded. Every patient *diagnosed* with COVID-19 yielded a bonus payment to the hospital from the Biden Administration. Every one of the patients who were then put on a ventilator racked up another bonus payment for the hospital, paid by taxpayers. Every patient who then died "of COVID" generated yet another bonus for the hospital, paid for by taxpayers under authority of big pharma's president of sales, Joe Biden.

Not only did Biden buy billions of dollars of COVID shots from big pharma using taxpayer money, he also spent billions of American tax dollars *advertising* the shots for Pfizer and the other drug manufacturers, then he mandated that most Americans get injected with the pharmaceutical products he was advertising, whether they wanted them or not. Biden was a politician who had demonstrated decades of political incompetence, now thrust into the American presidency through an election rigged by a cabal of unhinged billionaires, some of whom raked in the drug plunder hand over fist.

No treatments were allowed in the hospitals for patients diagnosed with COVID-19 except what was approved protocol according to the Centers for Disease Control (CDC), the same CDC that insisted, *"any mask is better than no mask."* The CDC mandated remdesivir, an experimental anti-viral drug originally used in Ebola trials in Africa, where its use was suspended when 53.1% of the patients on it died. It was then repurposed for COVID at a cost of about $3,000 per treatment. When this drug therapy was coupled with morphine and sedatives, it appeared that many patients under this treatment protocol simply died, especially when they had also been put on a ventilator. Their cause of death was listed as COVID-19, or "complications of COVID-19 infection."

SARS stands for "severe acute respiratory syndrome." It is a viral respiratory disease caused by the virus SARS-CoV-1, which, in 2002, was the first identified strain of the SARS-related coronavirus. SARS-CoV-2, the one we are discussing here, was referred to as a "novel" coronavirus in the media, implying that there were no cures since it was a new pathogen. Never mind that respiratory viruses readily mutate, which is why flu vaccines don't work very well, if at all. Virtually every flu virus

IM
In the 530 days since the CDC, with no evidence, recommended mask usage, Los Angeles has had only 37 days where masks were not mandated in all indoor areas. Their COVID death rate is in the top 10 worldwide

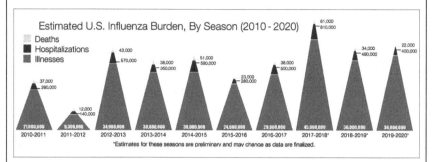

*Estimates for these seasons are preliminary and may change as data are finalized.

U.S. buys additional 200 million doses of Pfizer vaccine
The U.S. has now purchased 500 million of the 600 million possible doses negotiated between the Trump administration and Pfizer and BioNtech in July 2020.

$3 Billion of Taxpayer Money to Be Used on Ad Campaign to Increase Vaccine Uptake

9 New 'Vaccine Billionaires' Amass Combined Net Worth of $19.3 Billion During Pandemic

America's debt tops $34 trillion, but a commission to address it appears dead in Congress

Lars McMurtry
The CDC should roll out a new program: Get the shot or get shot. The unvaccinated need to be rounded up and lined up in front of open trenches. Their choice is simple, America has had enough of their virus. We need to get back to normal life. With or without them.

It was supposed to be a fight against the pandemic to protect the people

It became a fight against the people to protect the pandemic

mutates into something else by the end of the annual flu season. Otherwise, we'd continue to have the Spanish Flu every year, wouldn't we?

Despite the constant mutations of flu viruses, the new strains are not considered "novel" pathogens for which there is no curative treatment. The COVID virus, on the other hand, was deemed "novel" and therefore had no cure, which meant the public needed to run around like chickens with their heads cut off, scared to death they were going to die. There was no cure, but the government had one coming! Just wait for it. In the meantime, keep your face covered and remember to be terrified. But don't worry too much, because a "vaccine" is coming to save you.

Natural Health Care

Human beings have had to deal with respiratory viruses for millennia. As a result, our immune systems have provided us with natural defense mechanisms. This immune defense is bolstered by several things. For example, an unhealthy or weak body is more likely to suffer adverse consequences from a viral infection than a healthy one. People on unhealthy diets, especially overweight and obese people, are more likely to suffer.

The annual flu season is annual for a reason. Respiratory viruses appear to most successfully infect bodies that are cold, or when their body temperatures drop, such as when you "catch a chill." You may remember your grandmother telling you to bundle up when you go outside in cold weather or "you'll catch your death from the cold!" Ancient folk wisdom has provided solutions for recurring human illnesses.

Andrew Lwoff of the Pasteur Institute in Paris studied *"the paramount importance of factors such as temperature in determining the outcome of virus infections."* He pointed out that animals could overcome virus infections without relevant antibodies by using non-medical factors such as temperature augmentation (increase in body temperature). He noted that when mice were intentionally infected in a laboratory setting with a deadly Coxsackie B virus, a difference in their rectal temperature of only one degree meant the difference between 100% fatality and 100% recovery. Other laboratory experiments have shown that body temperature

YouTube Blocks Ivermectin Information

 This video has been removed for violating YouTube's Community Guidelines.
Learn more

New York Daily News

Hospitals in Oklahoma are being overwhelmed with patients overdosing on Ivermectin, an anti-parasitical treatment commonly used in farm animals.

Newsweek

Patients Overdosing on Ivermectin Are Clogging Oklahoma ERs: Doctor

Rolling Stone

Gunshot victims left waiting as horse dewormer overdoses overwhelm Oklahoma hospitals, doctor says

Rachel Maddow MSNBC

"Patients overdosing on ivermectin backing up rural Oklahoma hospitals, ambulances"
"'The scariest one I've heard of and seen is people coming in with vision loss,' he said."

KXMX - Local News   THE PROPAGANDA↑ THE FACTS↓

Ivermectin overdose NOT an issue at Sallisaw emergency room or hospital

Dr. Atsuo Yanagisawa, Former President of the International Society for Orthomolecular Medicine, SHOCKED at mRNA Adverse Reactions Data

Israeli Scientists Claim It's 'Pure Luck' They Were Already Working On A COVID-19 Vaccine Prior To The Outbreak

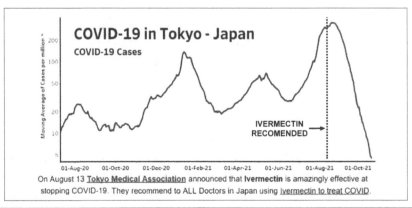

plays an important role in the multiplication of viruses — warmer bodies inhibit viral replication. Or as Lwoff put it, *"Slight differences in body temperature can govern the outcome of a virus infection."*

That was back in the 1960s. More recent research confirms these scientific observations. For example, a 2009 paper in the *Journal of Interferon Research* (Vol. 8, No. 2), reported that immersing human volunteers in warm water above 102°F (39°C) "rapidly alters the cell populations in the peripheral blood," producing as much as 10-fold more interferon-γ. Interferon-γ (γ = gamma) is a *cytokine* that is critical for immunity against viral, some bacterial, and protozoan infections. Its importance in the immune system stems in part from its ability to inhibit viral replication. Cytokines *"are the unsung heroes of the immune system, often acting as the first responders to a pathogen infection,"* according to LiveScience.com.

A 1987 paper in the *Journal of Interferon* published similar findings. Adult rhesus monkeys were placed in a climatic chamber maintained at 113°F (45°C) until their core body temperatures increased 2°C above control levels. The results showed a 4- to 16-fold increase in interferon-γ activity. This function is achieved naturally by the human body when it goes into a fever state. However, there is no need to wait until one is sick enough to become feverish. We can deliberately raise our own body temperature as soon as we feel a cold or flu coming on.

Clearly, soaking in a hot bath, as grandma told us, has therapeutic effects. Add a health regimen including plenty of sleep, healthy foods (or fasting), time off from stressful work, and simple remedies such as herbal teas, vitamins, sunshine, fresh air, and over-the-counter therapies, and one's natural immune system will take care of itself. Your body will most likely fight off whatever is ailing it.

Could this be why hot countries such as Haiti, where the people did not "social distance," nor did they wear masks or get drug injections and instead danced the nights away in hot, sweaty night clubs, yet had virtually no deaths from the respiratory flu that plagued America so much? It should be pointed out that Haiti eventually had about a 5% "vaccination" rate. It also had about a 5% rate of TV ownership. Coincidence?

Could this also be why the Scandinavian country of Sweden did so well with the "pandemic," despite not abiding by the lockdown dogma,

FDA on Ivermectin:

Ivermectin is not authorized or approved by FDA for prevention or treatment of COVID-19.

Ivermectin: enigmatic multifaceted 'wonder' drug continues to surprise and exceed expectations

Over the past decade, the global scientific community have begun to recognize the unmatched value of an extraordinary drug, ivermectin, that originates from a single microbe unearthed from soil in Japan. Work on ivermectin has seen its discoverer, Satoshi Ōmura, of Tokyo's prestigious Kitasato Institute, receive the 2014 Gairdner Global Health Award and the 2015 Nobel Prize in Physiology or Medicine, which he shared with a collaborating partner in the discovery and development of the drug, William Campbell of Merck & Co. Incorporated. Today, ivermectin is continuing to surprise and excite scientists, offering more and more promise to help improve global public health by treating a diverse range of diseases, with its unexpected potential as an antibacterial, antiviral and anti-cancer agent being particularly extraordinary.

The Journal of Antibiotics (2017) **70**, 495–505; doi:10.1038/ja.2017.11; published online 15 February 2017

New Hampshire governor blocks pharmacists from dispensing ivermectin to treat COVID-19

Ivermectin: Australian regulator bans drug as Covid treatment

Gov Parson signs law shielding doctors prescribing ivermectin, hydroxychloroquine | Fulton Sun

Patients Sue Pharmacies for Refusing Hydroxychloroquine, Ivermectin Prescriptions

Did official figures overestimate Britain's Covid death toll? The chaotic way mortalities were recorded during the pandemic could mean thousands were WRONGLY blamed on the virus

Judge Dismisses Ivermectin Lawsuit, Says Pharmacists Can Refuse to Fill Prescriptions

A federal judge has dismissed a lawsuit centered on pharmacists' refusals to fill prescriptions for ivermectin and hydroxychloroquine, ruling that the refusals were not illegal.

Feds Coming After Doctors & Pharmacies that Market Ivermectin as Effective & Safe for COVID-19

Written Date: **Last Filled:**

NOTES TO PRESCRIBER:

A NEW RX WAS SENT IN FOR IVERMECTIN 3MG #112 TABS, WITH THE DIRECTIONS OF 8 TABLETS 1 TIME A DAY

WE DO NOT FILL IVERMECTIN FOR COVID - IF THAT IS THE USE, SEND SOMEWHERE ELSE. IF NOT, PLEASE RESEND WITH THE DIAGNOSIS CODE
Invalid ePrescription - IVERMECTIN |

a country where hot saunas exist and are used in almost every household? Perhaps this is why people who are not on pharmaceutical drugs and who follow healthy dietary habits and have a healthy microbiome fared quite well against COVID regardless of any medical intervention? Was this studied by government or pharma scientists? Of course not.

Catching a cold or the flu? Tickle in your throat? Stay warm, stay home, soak in a hot bath or sauna, raise your body temperature daily, drink hot and nourishing liquids (such as chicken soup or hot tea), eat lightly and wisely, get lots of rest, and you'll be fine. None of these health care efforts require medical assistance; therefore there is no money to be made by the medical establishment, which may explain why there seems to be no professional medical interest in this approach.

There was almost no mention of these health care options by the media, by the government, or by medical officials during the COVID scare. On the contrary, people who valued natural immunity and non-medical approaches to health care were widely ridiculed and labeled "anti-vaxxers," tin-foil hat wearers, a danger to society, even murderers. There was *only one solution* to the widely advertised pandemic that gripped humanity by the throat, according to TV, and that was the COVID drug injection. Nothing else would work, therefore nothing else should be tried.

In the meantime, it was the *virus* that locked down our businesses. It was the *pandemic* that deprived us of our constitutional rights, made us cover our faces and "social distance." It was *COVID* that closed the parks and bankrupted our businesses, tore apart our families, blocked us from stores, shops, barbers, and hairdressers. It wasn't the *government* and the *media,* and the *medical "experts"* causing these problems. Who could be dumb enough to think such a thing?

Ivermectin and Other Remedies

One anti-viral drug shown in trials to have been effective against SARS viruses was Ivermectin. SARS-CoV-2 could very well have been treatable by Ivermectin, especially when combined with hot baths and rest, yet any doctor who prescribed it was reprimanded, if not outright

TORONTO STAR

WEATHER HIGH 33 C | CHANCE OF THUNDERSTORMS | MAP A22 THURSDAY, AUGUST 26, 2021

I have *no* empathy left for the wilfully unvaccinated. Let *them* die.

If they really want to save so many lives by now giving us all a vaccine, then why isn't insulin free? Why isn't cancer treatment free?
Somebody better open their eyes! **Salty Texan**

Billions of Copies of Residual DNA in a Single Dose of COVID-19 mRNA Vaccine: Preprint

A new preprint study up for peer review finds billions of residual DNA fragments in COVID-19 mRNA vaccine vials.

Excited to share that updated analysis from our Phase 3 study with BioNTech also showed that our COVID-19 vaccine was 100% effective in preventing #COVID19 cases in South Africa. 100%!

pfizer.com/news/press-rel... 01/04/2021 · Twitter Web App **Albert Bourla**

Covid-19 Vaccine Hesitancy In Populations That Actually Pay Attention

Journal of the Fucking Obvious, 2022

Regular Use of Ivermectin as Prophylaxis for COVID-19 Led Up to a 92% Reduction in COVID-19 Mortality Rate in a Dose-Response Manner: Results of a Prospective Observational Study of a Strictly Controlled Population of 88,012 Subjects Cureus

The FDA-approved drug ivermectin inhibits the replication of SARS-CoV-2 in vitro

April 03, 2020
Antiviral Research

Leon Caly, Julian D. Druce, Mike G. Catton, David A. Jans, Kylie M. Wagstaff

fired from their medical position, no matter how many decades of exemplary practice she or he had performed at his or her hospital.

Ivermectin was derived from a soil fungus in Japan and had been prescribed to humans over a billion times. It had one of the safest drug profiles of any drug in existence. Although the discoverers of Ivermectin won a Nobel Prize for it, the drug became so demonized by the medical establishment during the scamdemic that pharmacists were banned from filling prescriptions for it. In some states, pharmacists were required to contact the prescribing physician, ask what ailment the Ivermectin was prescribed for, and if it was for COVID-19, the prescription had to be denied. Pharmacists who did not comply with this mandate faced having their licenses revoked by state politicians.

People flying into Canada had their luggage checked and any Ivermectin was confiscated, as was reported on social media. Ivermectin sold for livestock use was locked up in farm and garden centers so people could not buy it. CNN described it as "horse paste." The FDA compared people who used Ivermectin as acting like "horses" and "cows." The government of Australia banned its use nationwide during the scamdemic.

Hospitals became like death prisons for many patients where alternative treatments such as Ivermectin and vitamin therapy were completely banned. Loved ones smuggled Ivermectin to their family members, many of whom later swore that it was the smuggled Ivermectin that spared their lives before the hospital could kill them.

Vitamin therapy was banned in medical hospitals, even though Vitamin D had been shown to be effective against respiratory infections. One study reported that *"As a safe, widely available, and affordable treatment, Vitamin D may help to reduce the severity of the COVID-19 pandemic."* Another study showed that Vitamin D administration resulted in a decreased risk of death and ICU admission and that the protective role of Vitamin D and ICU admission is conclusive. So, why would Vitamin D be banned?

Other scientists had similar results with Vitamin C, zinc, and hydroxychloroquine. A 2005 *Virology Journal* article concluded, *"Chloroquine, a relatively safe, effective and cheap drug . . . is effective in inhibiting the infection and spread of SARS-CoV in cell culture."* Another study concluded that *"HCQ can efficiently inhibit SARS-CoV-2 infection in vitro. In combi-*

nation with its anti-inflammatory function, we predict that the drug has a good potential to combat the disease." Yet these drugs were banned. Why?

If drugs like these, which cost pennies, could be effective against COVID-19, the emergency use authorization for the expensive experimental drugs would be suspended. But without competing remedies, the EUA drugs could be sold for top dollar. Biden bought billions of dollars of drugs from the pharmaceutical industry at high prices using taxpayer dollars, then mandated that American citizens have them repeatedly injected into their bodies or be fired from their jobs, while denying them alternative treatments. Pfizer generated $81 billion in 2021 and $100 billion in 2022. Their five-year average prior to that was $40 billion.

But that was a pittance compared to what was drained out of the U.S. treasury during the COVID plandemic. Four-*trillion* dollars vanished from the public coffers in a year, handed out as "COVID relief funds" primarily to mega corporations, especially those who implemented harsh lockdown mandates. That's $4,000 billion. Using fear porn, mass hysteria, relentless coordinated propaganda, threats, coercion, and violence directed toward a compliant population of boiled frogs, the robbery of taxpayer dollars had reached an unprecedented zenith.

What does any of this have to do with Direct Democracy? Probably nothing for those who continue to have themselves and their children injected with experimental drugs. But for the 20% of critical thinkers who are capable of free thought and independent research outside the constraints of mainstream propaganda and the brainwashing machines, it means everything. What we are witnessing today is a level of human greed that would be unthinkable at any other time in our history. We are witnessing the unfolding demise of the human species, being destroyed from within by a deeply rooted cancer that feeds on a deranged gluttony, unspeakable cruelty, and what appears to be a complete lack of conscience.

Someone once said that we should never doubt that a small minority of people can change the world. Twenty percent of the population is not small. And we can, and must, change the world.

8
The Evolution of Democracy

For generations, the American Democratic Party represented the working class. It was anti-war, pro-social justice, and pro-environment. The Republican Party represented the business class, the wealthy and the well-heeled. Republicans were largely pro-war and seemed to not really care about the environment.

In 2020, that flipped. Suddenly, the Democratic Party became the mouthpiece of "big pharma." It became pro-war, anti free speech, and pro-censorship. The republicans and conservatives became the voice of reason, freedom, anti-war, anti-big pharma, and pro free speech. What the hell happened?

It was embarrassing to watch. People who spent their lives speaking out against war, fighting for the environment, marching for freedom of speech, social justice, an end to racism and prejudice, and other endeavors that were hallmarks of the Democratic Party, did a complete about face. The propaganda machines had finally taken full effect. The frogs were boiled. Welcome to the "Uniparty," neither Democrat nor Republican, but a combination of the worst of both. The Uniparty was completely controlled by billionaires and other wealthy elites, plus Washington DC swamp creatures, and other unelected denizens of the shadowy underworld of government.

The World Economic Forum, founded by Klaus Schwab in 1971, also known as the WEF, appeared to play a major, if not controlling, role in the globalization of world government by a small minority of ultra wealthy individuals. Globalization, or World Government, is how the U.S. Bill of Rights can be destroyed and discarded. The Constitution is a product of the United States government. When superseded and replaced by a one-world government, the wealthy elite will make the rules and there will be no functional constitution.

It started with the *"Trump Derangement Syndrome,"* a mass mental disturbance in which the brains of many of the boiled frogs had become imbued with a hatred for one particular politician, Donald Trump. In a sense, it was similar to the deranged hatred for Jews that gripped German

The WHO's Pandemic Treaty: The End of National Sovereignty and Freedom

Contrary to popular opinion, the WHO is not an independent, unbiased, and ethical organization that aims to achieve the common good. In reality, its goals and agendas are set by its donors, including some of the world's richest countries and most influential philanthropists.

CDC-Funded Study of Nearly 100 Million COVID-19 Vaccine Recipients Reveals a Host of Adverse Events

Cases of a blood clot condition called CVST were found to be three times higher than expected among the vaccinated.

PROPAGANDA: IS THE USE OF FACTS, ARGUMENTS, RUMORS, HALF-TRUTHS, OR LIES TO INFLUENCE PUBLIC OPINION AND BEHAVIOR. PROPAGANDA HAS AN AGENDA AND A DELIBERATE PLAN WHICH RELIES ON MANIPULATION OF GROUPS OF PEOPLE, USUALLY FOR A POLITICAL PURPOSE.

Political parties exist to secure responsible government and to execute the will of the people. From these great tasks both of the old parties have turned aside. Instead of instruments to promote the general welfare they have become the tools of corrupt interests, which use them impartially to serve their selfish purposes. Behind the ostensible government sits enthroned an invisible government owing no allegiance and acknowledging no responsibility to the people. To destroy this invisible government, to dissolve the unholy alliance between corrupt business and corrupt politics, is the first task of the statesmanship of the day.

Theodore Roosevelt (1912)

A dog had his chain reduced one link at a time, every few days, until his chain was so short he could barely move. He never resisted because he was conditioned to the loss of his freedom slowly, over time.

citizens during the Nazi propaganda campaigns, or the abject contempt for "witches" in the 1600s, created by powerful but demented religious authorities and magnified by a compliant, malfeasant judiciary — hatred without reason, based on lies and punctuated by campaigns of fear.

Trump was an American businessman from New York City, a TV celebrity, author, and family man, but not a politician. Nevertheless, he ran for the office of President of the United States in 2016 and won in an upset victory against career politician Hillary Clinton, whom we have already mentioned. Trump campaigned on the promise to "drain the swamp," meaning expose and eliminate the shadow government, unelected bureaucrats, and behind-the-scenes actors who held a stranglehold grip on the U.S. government.

The United States Treasury, the bank depository for America's tax dollars, has been the largest accessible pot of money in the world. Robbing it was easy enough for the swamp creatures. Pilfering the people's bank account had developed into a fine science by the 2020s. Imagine being able to rob a bank in broad daylight in front of everybody and do it again and again without the need for even a gun — and get away with billions, if not trillions of dollars! When the government is controlled by criminals, that's what happens. Our tax money disappears by the trillions. And when it disappears, it doesn't just vanish, it goes into someone's pockets — out of the pockets of many hard-working American citizens and into the pockets of a few.

Direct democracy could wrest back control of the government's legislative body and put a lock and key on our treasury. Government control must be securely placed into the hands of the We the People. We can and we must put an end to the swamp creatures sucking our nation's blood out of the backs of the working class like gigantic parasitic ticks.

Trump's position as president had an incredible effect. He didn't succeed in draining the swamp, but he did succeed in lowering the water level enough to expose the many and various swamp creatures lurking underneath. Many of the boiled frogs weren't aware of any such thing because their minds had become infected with the Trump Derangement Syndrome and any information that was contrary to the narrative of the democrats, the WEF, and the "globalists," was simply censored and re-

Trump Indicted Over Efforts to Challenge 2020 Election Results

Democrat Donor Bought $1.3M of Hunter's 'Art' before Joe Biden Appointed Her to Prestigious Commission

The Pessimistic Case for the Future

The Security State Has Been Weaponized

Arguably the two most alarming spectacles of recent times are the Russia Hoax and the federal government's reaction to Jan. 6. Our intelligence agencies spied not just on American citizens, but on a presidential candidate and his senior-most aides, and then, after he won, on government officials. The FBI launched a phony investigation under false pretenses to prevent one candidate from winning the 2016 election and to lay the groundwork for his removal if he did. All of this was later uncovered. The guilty got away with it, and the agencies still have their budgets and all their powers. Indeed, the FBI was just given—with Republican votes—a $600 million raise!

As to the second, an unarmed, nonviolent protest (all four deaths were protesters, either directly or indirectly caused by the authorities) resulted in the largest (and still ongoing) manhunt in US history, widespread and ongoing pretrial detention, maximalist demands from prosecutors (up to and including "terrorism enhancements" in sentencing), forced confessions, and draconian sentences for minor crimes.

These same agencies—in particular, the FBI, and the Department of Justice—now routinely engage in predawn, no-knock raids and circus arrests before awaiting media (to whom time and place of said arrest have been pre-leaked) against the ruling class's perceived enemies, such as those the Jan. 6 Commission would like to feature in its show trial. These are the kinds of practices that, when Eastern Bloc Communist tyrannies did them, the US government condemned. Now our government does them itself.   *Michael Anton*   compactmag.com

O'Keefe Media Group Uncovers Disturbing Allegations of Money Laundering in Political Campaigns

Raffensperger Knowingly Ran Vulnerable Voting Machines during His 2022 Reelection, Covered It Up

Instagram Bans Robert F. Kennedy Jr's Account

Social media giant Instagram has suspended Robert F. Kennedy Jr.'s account and banned the 2024 Democrat presidential candidate from using the platform to communicate with voters.

YouTube Removes Another RFK Jr. Interview

placed with propaganda emanating from brainwashing machines.

Thereby, the globalists took over the Democratic Party and a portion of the Republican Party as well — the "RINOs" (republican in name only). Their agenda was to dismantle the U.S. Constitution, to force Americans to fund and ultimately fight new wars leading up to, and possibly including World War III, to rob as much money from the taxpayers in as short a time as possible, to undermine the United States as a sovereign nation, and to convince Americans and citizens of other nations around the world to accept regular, experimental, pharmaceutical drug injections as a requirement for living a "normal" life.

The one-world government wanted to control everyone's money through a digital currency system. *"You will own nothing, and you will be happy,"* according to the Schwabites. If they don't like the way you behave, they freeze your bank account and credit cards and/or seize your assets, as was demonstrated in Canada under Justin Trudeau's corrupt leadership when the truckers protested his insane lockdown mandates.

It's hard to believe that this is what the world was becoming in the 2020s, but it's a fact. Maybe not to the boiled frogs, however, who absorb their daily dose of brain pablum spoon-fed into their minds while they blankly sit in chairs staring at the brainwashing machines.

Trump was not a globalist. He, if anything, was an antiglobalist. A billionaire, he could not be easily bought, unlike so many politicians. He was considered a loose cannon by the swamp creatures, out of control, and a menace to their agenda. He had to be stopped.

The swamp creatures began their attack while Trump was on the campaign trail prior to his election victory in 2016. One of the first major examples of government malfeasance to be exposed was that the FBI was an organization that was corrupt at the highest levels — totally controlled by the swamp. The FBI was acting like a Mafia organization, or as a private security team for a police state, doing the bidding of politicians hiding in the shadows, attacking their political opponents, rounding them up, and throwing them into federal prisons.

Federal judges also exposed themselves during this era. Rather than pass judgment against defendants based on facts rooted in reality, many, not all, but many, especially in the DC circuit, rendered decisions that

Democratic Party Moved From Uncomfortable to Intolerable for Members: #WalkAway Founder

People were just noticing changes in the party, he said. They weren't always identifying what it meant, but they knew they didn't like how it felt, and quietly left. "But now, it's akin to cancer. Cancer doesn't stop growing and spreading just because people don't like it. And what's happening with the left is no different." "Particularly with them getting rid of Trump, installing Biden, and the Democrats taking full control of the government. This is a cancer that's rapidly growing and spreading now. And it's becoming not just uncomfortable, but I think intolerable, for a lot of people."

Democrats Commit Vastly More Dark Money Than Republicans for 2024

Democrats are outspending Republicans $800 million to $160 million.

Depleting America's Emergency Oil Supply to Elect Democrats

The drop in gas prices over the past couple of months is a brazen political maneuver to dampen certain Republican gains in Congress on Election Day. Biden has depleted the SPR by more than 160 million barrels to its lowest level in 37 years.

Robert Epstein: How Google Manipulates Us

A leading psychology researcher and Democrat denounces Google's partisan Democrat bias

Georgia Election Board Admits Rigging 2020 Election to Help Biden 'Stop Trump'

Fiscal watchdog group urges House not to pass $3.5T budget bill

"Taken together, passage of these efforts could set the stage for $4.3 trillion of new debt before extending any of its expiring policies, enough to lift debt to a massive 119 percent of the economy by the end of the decade."

were blatantly partisan in favor of the Democratic Party and their witch hunts against their opposition, especially Trump and his supporters.

By the time Trump's first term had ended, he had become widely popular, aside from the TV-watchers infected with the Trump Derangement Syndrome. Those people viscerally detested him. But Trump hadn't started any new wars, much to the consternation of the war machine. He was brash and spoke his mind, sometimes rudely, but he often said things that were more truthful than words spoken by most politicians.

For example, during a presidential debate, he stated that he could see no reason why the U.S. shouldn't have a better relationship with Russia. His democrat opponent, Hillary Clinton, sneered at him and accused him of being Putin's lap dog. He was right, she was wrong, and any person with functioning brain tissue could understand that.

Hillary had supported the bombing, invasion, and occupation of Iraq. The attack on Iraq was a misguided strategy cooked up by Republicans George W. Bush, Dick Cheney, Donald Rumsfeld, Condoleezza Rice, Colin Powell, and others. It was the worst crime against humanity to have occurred worldwide in the twenty-first century at that time. Unlike Hillary, Trump denounced the war against Iraq as a foolish strategy that needlessly drained our treasury and killed a lot of people who didn't need to die. The U.S. economy under Trump was booming. We were a nation of peace and prosperity. Trump was certain to win reelection by a landslide in 2020.

A billionaire cabal of unelected players behind the scenes were not going to allow that to happen. Trump's reelection would interrupt their scheme of world government, a world controlled by a powerful but tiny minority of ultrawealthy individuals. Trump had to go.

The COVID scamdemic was announced in early 2020. This was quickly used as an excuse to destroy the U.S. economy. First, the stock market crashed. Then the entire nation was shut down by government "health" professionals who had set up a virus task force in Washington, DC. Their edicts were foolish, their strategies were almost juvenile, and their mandates were extremely destructive. Their goals seemed to include destroying the economy, suspending the Constitution, subjugating the population, and, perhaps most importantly, getting as many people as

Delaware Supreme Court Strikes Down Voting by Mail, and Same-Day Registration

Jan. 6 Panel Votes to Refer Trump for Criminal Charges

As hundreds waited to vote in Houston, a dozen-plus polling sites ran out of ballot sheets

GOVERNMENTS LOVE PANDEMICS THE SAME WAY THEY LOVE WARS. It gives them power, it gives them control, it gives them the capacity to impose obedience on human beings.

Robert F. Kennedy jr.

Majority of American Voters Rightly Concerned About Vote Fraud

Watching the news, you'd be led to believe that vote fraud doesn't exist in the United States. Since the election on Nov. 8, news article after news article has simply dismissed any claims of vote fraud as "baseless" (New York Times and CNN) and "without evidence" (NPR, New York Times, and Washington Post). Republican gubernatorial candidate Kari Lake is lambasted for "stoking fears on mail-in ballots." And the news coverage was no different after the 2020 election.

But American voters aren't convinced. A Rasmussen Reports survey from late September found that 84 percent of likely voters were concerned about election integrity in this year's congressional elections. It was a belief shared by every category of voters, including liberals and Democrats, though they were less concerned than conservatives and Republicans.

FBI Agents Involved in Facebook's Suppression of Hunter Biden Laptop Story Were Democrat Donors

possible injected with an experimental COVID -19 "vaccine."

Restaurants were hit hard. Ordered by politicians to shut down, their fresh produce was forced to go to waste, rotting. All the large billionaire-owned big box stores were allowed to stay wide open. The little mom and pop businesses were forced to shut down, as were hairdressers, nail salons, barber shops, hardware stores, and even the churches, because "public health and safety had to be protected" as the "health experts" sternly reminded everyone.

Many restaurants were shut down for months; many went bankrupt and never reopened. Getting a hot meal or a nice salad was now considered a threat to public health if you ate in the presence of others. If a restaurant was allowed to open, the patrons had to wear masks over their faces, covering their nose and mouth. They were allowed to pull the masks down as they inserted food into their mouths, then cover their mouths and noses again when chewing, "to be safe." This would be laughable if it was just a joke. But it isn't.

People, even entire families inside restaurants who didn't cover their faces, were dragged out by the police, who roamed in bands from pizza shops to cafes looking for any sane people who wouldn't comply with the mass insanity. Those who wore masks but dropped them below their noses so they could breathe, were quickly pounced upon by store monitors and told they had to cover their noses or leave the building. Their exposed noses were a health threat to all the others on the premises, even though the others *had masks over their faces*. Those who didn't quickly comply were rudely ushered out the door. Some were arrested and thrown into police wagons after being forcibly masked. All of this mass insanity is verifiable by video footage.

Restaurants that didn't force their customers to follow the "public health" edicts were forced to close in New York City, and elsewhere, under the threat of armed, swarming police officers, while directly across the street the restaurants were allowed to stay open because they were in a different borough. People who had Thanksgiving dinner in the privacy of their homes willingly sat six feet apart, "for their safety." People who didn't cover their faces were branded "right-wing extremists," "Trump lovers," and followers of a "death cult." The lunacy was breathtaking.

"In the entire history of mankind there has never been a political elite sincerely concerned about the wellbeing of regular people. What makes any of us think that it is different now. - Christine Anderson European Parliament."

Pandemics as a Catalyst for a New World Order

The United Nations has morphed into a leviathan. Its various agreements and goals seek to centrally dictate the world's economy, migration, "*reproductive health*," monetary systems, digital IDs, environment, agriculture, wages, climate modifications, one world health, and other related globalist programs.

How Did American Capitalism Mutate Into American Corporatism in 2024?

Neither the left nor the right, nor Democrats or Republicans, nor capitalists or socialists, seem to be speaking clearly to the moment in which we live. The dominating force on both the national and global scene today is techno-corporatism that intrudes itself into our food, our medicine, our media, our information flows, our homes, and all the way down to the hundreds of surveillance tools that we carry around in our pockets. Excerpted from Jeffrey A. Tucker

U.S. government is now borrowing $100K every second, that means the debt is growing:
—$6,000,000 per minute
—$8,640,000,000 per day
—$60,480,000,000 per week
—$241,920,000,000 per month
—$2,903,040,000,000 per year

BBC Boasts it Got Vaccine Injured Support Group With 250,000 Members Removed From Facebook

The mass insanity was frightening.

In the meantime, anyone who sneezed in their hand, then grabbed a public doorknob, such as at a big box store or a supermarket, was spreading whatever virus made them sneeze. The next customer would walk into the building, grab the same doorknob, then scratch their eye, then the next customer, and the next.

The same scenario existed at the checkout counters. Everyone touched the same credit card terminal screen with their fingers, the same fingers they just sneezed into. Any virus that was being spread, was being spread through touch. The person checking out your food at the grocery store touched every single item you bought. But they had their faces covered — for your safety.

The purpose of the masking was mostly psychological. With everyone walking around with their faces covered in full view of each other so only their eyes were visible, the concerned and frightened looks in their eyes reminded everyone to be afraid. The masked faces could also signal to each other how virtuous they were by keeping their faces covered "to protect others," while people who didn't cover their faces were immediately identifiable and viewed with contempt and disgust by the boiled frogs.

And so it went. The idiocy was only outdone by the gullibility of the brainwashed public. Now that everything was shut down, the public were locked in their homes where they would "be safe." And there they sat cowering, with their faces covered, waiting on the edges of their seats for the next instructions from their brainwashing machines. The TV-watchers had literally been driven into a mass insanity. STAY THE FUCK HOME! people posted on their social media platforms.

Nosy neighbors called the police if they saw a service truck next door providing, for example, plumbing or roofing services at a nearby house. The state police would show up and force the contractor to stop working and leave the area or be arrested, even if it meant no running water or a leaking roof for an elderly couple in the house. A contractor working alone on top of a roof was deemed a public health hazard and threatened by democrat politicians with the cancellation of their contractor's licenses. Not only were you not allowed to work, but you weren't even permitted to leave your own home. It was just too dangerous, or so we were

Border Patrol's Twitter Account Deactivated Over 'Inappropriate' Posts Criticizing Biden's Border Policies

Jury finds former Milwaukee election official guilty of obtaining fake absentee ballots

The search engine manipulation effect (SEME) and its possible impact on the outcomes of elections

Judge rules Pilsen mom can't see her son because she's not vaccinated against COVID-19

In what many say is the first ruling of its kind, a divorced Pilsen mother has had her child visitation revoked by a Cook County judge because she is not vaccinated against COVID-19.

Facebook, White House Colluding on Censorship

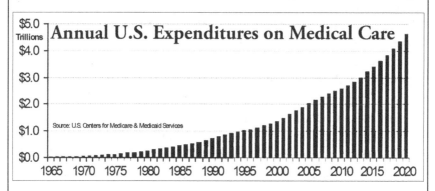

Study Finds 'Significant Increase' in Cancer Mortality After Mass Vaccination With 3rd COVID Dose

Democratic-led House authorizes $3.5 trillion of spending as national debt climbs to $29 trillion

The Democratic-led House on Tuesday authorized $3.5 trillion of spending in a party-line vote, as the national debt climbs to a record $29 trillion. [2021]

told. And people believed it.

In the seventies, it was "the Reds are coming!" In the eighties and nineties, it was the commies and socialists. In the 2000s, it was the terrorists. Now it was an invisible, non-human, electron-microscopic threat that was so deadly and horrible that normal life for everyone had to suddenly grind to a stop nationwide as well as in much of the TV-watching world. The virus was coming! And, like the reds, the commies, and the terrorist threats, the boiled frogs responded in unison with frenzied croaks of fear. The frogs were now corralled like sheep, ready and waiting to be fleeced. And fleeced they were.

The book you're now reading is not George Orwell's *1984* — that was fiction. The book you're now reading is nonfiction. It all really happened, and very well may happen again if people don't wake up out of their media-imposed lunacy.

2020 Election

Let's get back to the 2020 election. Virus released, pandemic declared, media frenzy follows, stock market crashes, weak-minded and/or unhealthy people are scared to death, the economy is destroyed for everyone but the billionaires who are raking in record profits. Millions of people are suddenly unemployed. And because it's too scary to be outside in the fresh air and sunshine, nobody has to show up at an election site to cast their vote for the president in 2020. Everyone can use paper ballots "to be safe." No matter that paper ballots were the least secure and most likely to be fraudulent method of casting votes during an election. Or was it planned that way? Of course it was.

On the evening of the election, Trump was winning in most states by a landslide. He was, for example, hundreds of thousands of votes ahead of Joe Biden at the end of election day in Pennsylvania, a crucial swing state, with a seemingly insurmountable lead. But suddenly and without precedent, democrat election officials called a halt to the counting of votes in Pennsylvania and other swing states simultaneously, late on election night. Everyone went to bed believing Trump had won. But in the middle of the night, hundreds of thousands of paper ballots showed up, virtually

> # The Party told you to reject the evidence of your eyes and ears.
> # It was their final, most essential command.
>
> GEORGE ORWELL, 1984

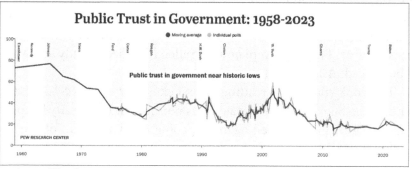

Public Trust in Government: 1958-2023

Public trust in government near historic lows

PEW RESEARCH CENTER

James Woods

As an objective political observation I think the Trump situation is a huge risk for the Democrats. After an exhausting two years of a foul and completely debunked Democrat scam (RussiaGate), for them to launch this legal jihad is a monster gamble. It is an absolute cluster bomb against one man, and boy, they better be right.

For one thing many of these charges are flimsy, some specious, and others truly ridiculous. If they stick, even temporarily, they will make a martyr out of Trump. His supporters and many independents will see him as one individual against a massive political machine, an armada of dirty tricks, and historically the lone warrior is a sympathetic scenario.

If Trump is ultimately acquitted, however, he will be the David who beat Goliath, and the Democrat Party will never recover. They will be forever seen as venal, nasty, mendacious charlatans and cheats, whose latest charade failed miserably.

Even if they convict him of all charges though, millions of Americans will feel deprived of their candidate regardless how hated he is by the other side, and they will be in a civil war frame of mind.

As a merely objective observer, I am guessing this judicially engineered attack on the major candidate of the "other party" feels decidedly un-American. It just reeks of banana republic hijinx, and it's going to backfire.

all for Joe Biden. Biden was loudly declared the winner by all of the billionaire-controlled media outlets the next morning.

The globalists had what they wanted. Trump had been pushed out of the way. Although he was not the sort of person to take this kind of treatment sitting down, and his voters, at least half the country, were angry, to say the least. Joe Biden was now "in power." He was a career politician with a reputation sullied by ethical corruption and incompetence. He had been one of the most influential promoters of the disastrous invasion of Iraq in the Democratic Party. Any politician who supports and encourages any crime against humanity is not qualified to hold public office. Yet, there they were, career politicians entrenched in their political dynasties, like an infection that can't be cured. Biden was the perfect puppet the globalists needed.

Trump put up a fight. In return, the democrats and their billionaire handlers attacked him relentlessly. The democrats immediately impeached him for a second time. After that was unsuccessful, democrat attorneys general began charging Trump with serious, but bogus crimes. The district attorney in Fulton County, Georgia, Fani Willis, charged Trump with election interference for questioning the results of the rigged election. She announced that Trump had committed a racketeering crime, no less, which is frankly insane.

Alvin Bragg, a Manhattan, New York district attorney, charged Trump with a 34-count felony indictment alleging that Trump falsified New York business records. New York attorney general Letitia James charged Trump with fraud for taking out real estate loans and paying them back with interest. The judge in that case, Arthur F. Engoron of the New York State Supreme Court, denied Trump a jury trial, then found Trump guilty before the bench trial even began.

Trump, now facing over 100 years in prison, was running for president again. The criminal charges mushroomed. Letitia James made sure she included Trump's family members in her persecution of Trump, and she made sure the penalties for everyone would be very harsh. Trump's public support increased with every new criminal indictment.

The deep state became very worried. Trump was going to be the republican presidential nominee in 2024 against democrat Joe Biden, a man

MGP

I just went to vote. Half way through the explanation from one of the helpers that their machines have been switching votes all day so I should double check my ballot.... I just held up my hand and explained........ "then I'm not voting on the machine."...I continued...." If you've been paying attention, that's how they have been stealing elections and they're not going to steal my vote today." They prepared my wife and I paper ballots, which we have receipts for to confirm our votes.

I asked if they would like to see my identification and they replied "no that's not necessary". I replied...."That's very disappointing."

Anyone that thinks our elections are secure at this point are fucking morons. This is happening every election...in federal, state and local elections.

The machines belong in the scrap yard. Identification should be required. I could have been voting proxy for someone who isn't voting and they have no way to check it. The process is criminal, corrupt, and commonplace in all elections now.

Our republic was stolen years ago. If we want it back, it's going to be messy.

The Most Expensive Judicial Race in US History Is Raising Questions

Peter Bernegger, a data analyst with Election Watch, filed the complaint. The group's research found that the Protasiewicz campaign has received a myriad of repetitive small contributions purportedly from the same individuals totaling at least $6 million.

According to the complaint, the official reports from the Wisconsin Campaign Finance Information System reveal that 234 of Justice Protasiewicz's 38,169 contributors donated more than 10 times.

Election Watch has dubbed the observed repetition of thousands of small donations being made under the same name as "smurfing." It's occurring nationwide and has been detected down to the municipal election level.

Salty Texan

ICYMI: Connecticut Police have launched an investigation after video evidence was discovered of a Democrat clerk dumping illegal mail-in ballots into a drop box at 5 AM in the morning for the recent Democrat primary election.

Election Integrity Win: Arizona Court Rules Against State's 'Unlawful Signature Matching Process'

whose best days had long ago come and gone. If, under these circumstances, the globalists managed to fraudulently rig another presidential election, humanity would likely sink into a new Dark Age, the foundation could be laid for another American civil war, and the unraveling of cvililzation will have begun.

The communists once faced demented ultra-wealthy elites in the nineteenth century. In response, they created a political movement based on the *Communist Manifesto*. Our founding fathers dealt with an unhinged, tyrannical monarchy in the eighteenth century. They declared independence from the British and wrote the United States Constitution to protect their new nation from the wretched tyranny that it had been the victim of. Their problems were the same. A small minority of people with a lot of wealth were trying to control everyone else. In the 2020s, the curse continues. A group of wealthy elitists were intent upon taking over the world, while creating an underclass of subservient citizens who will "own nothing and be happy." The "useless people" would be slowly eliminated through targeted mass drug injections, intentionally released pathogens (biowarfare), or shooting wars.

Once the globalists and other swamp creatures had gained control of the American presidency in 2020, they immediately pivoted to infect the minds of entire nations with a "Virus Hysteria," a mass psychosis. The Virus Hysteria, in turn, mentally prepared societies for the orchestrated "Worldwide Pandemic," which then lead to the mass injection of billions of people with experimental, poorly tested, gene-altering drugs.

Approximately 80% to 90% of Americans received at least one dose of the COVID drug. The other 10% to 20%, the sceptics who were exercising independent, critical thinking, who were conducting personal research outside the constraints of mainstream propaganda, and who just wanted to remain normal, without unnecessary drugs injected into their bloodstreams, were relentlessly ridiculed and reviled through the propaganda outlets, including TV, radio, print media, and online social media. The boiled frogs, in unison, croaked their disgust at the normal, uninjected people, on cue, led by media talking heads who were being paid handsomely by big pharma to push the mass drug injection narrative.

Remember the communist philosophy whereby nobody owns private

Study Finds 80 Percent of Americans Exposed to Fertility- Lowering Chemicals in Cheerios, Oats

EPA proposed in April last year to allow the use of chlormequat on oats, barley, wheat, and triticale grown in the United States.

Demasculinization and feminization of male gonads by atrazine: Consistent effects across vertebrate classes

Atrazine is the most commonly detected pesticide contaminant of ground water, surface water, and precipitation. Atrazine is also an endocrine disruptor that, among other effects, alters male reproductive tissues when animals are exposed during development.

New Study Confirms Atrazine's Effects Across a Range of Species (Including Us)

Top Professor Testifies: Covid 'Intentionally Released' to Push Vaccines onto Public

A world-renowned professor has given an explosive testimony before the European Parliament in Brussels regarding the origins of the pandemic. Testifying before Europe's top officials at the International Covid Summit, Dr. David Martin asserted that COVID-19 was "intentionally released." According to Martin, the virus was released with the intention of triggering a global pandemic. The goal was to create widespread acceptance of vaccines through fears of the virus, he stated. While providing evidence, Martin specifically links Democrat President Joe Biden's former chief medical adviser Dr. Anthony Fauci and the National Institute of Allergy and Infectious Diseases (NIAID) to the research which he says led to the alleged "intentional release" of the virus.

Democrat Senator Received Huge Payments from Pharma Companies Behind Opioid Crisis

Democrat Senator Sherrod Brown (D-OH) received hundreds of thousands of dollars in payments from pharmaceutical companies behind America's ongoing opioid crisis, financial records have revealed. Brown took massive payouts from three drug firms at the center of the opioid epidemic.

House Considers Federal Ban on Private Money to Run Elections

Eight House Republicans have introduced **a bill to block the use of private money to operate elections and curb the controversial process called ballot harvesting.**

If enacted, the Protect American Election Administration Act would **block what the bill's sponsors call a "private takeover of government election administration."**

AnOmaly

Within the last two years, people were forced out of work and travel for not getting a Big Pharma poke. How is that not even a top 5 issues being debated on for this next election? Wild.

property? Remember Klaus Schwab and the WEF group stating that you will own nothing, and you will be happy? Consider this: According to *Newsweek*, there were 607 *billionaires* in Communist China in 2022, second only to the United States, with 735 billionaires. According to Credit Suisse, the number of *millionaires* residing in China totaled 6.2 million in 2023, second again only to the United States. This doesn't make much sense, considering that one of the basic tenets of communism is the elimination of private property. Is Communist China "communist" in name only? Has communism changed its founding principles to adapt to a capitalist world? If so, why is *anti-communism* still so rampant in the United States? Numerous Chinese entities are major supporters of the WEF and the WHO. Meanwhile, the WHO appeared to have been the biggest promoter of Virus Hysteria worldwide, and the most vocal pusher of the COVID drugs and vaccines in general. Exactly what is going on here?

Gender Confusion

What about the family? The *Communist Manifesto* proclaimed that the state should take the place of the family and be responsible for the education and health decisions of children, a reprehensible thought at best. Government exists to serve the people, period. It's not the other way around and never should be.

Why were American public schools and universities promoting gender confusion in the 2020s? Why would they be allowing children to have gender confusion encouraged by medical professionals without the knowledge of their parents? For that matter, why would state governments allow minor children to be injected with COVID drugs or *any* pharmaceuticals without the knowledge and permission of their parents? What is really going on? Is the pharmaceutical industry and the medical industrial complex so embedded in government agencies, public schools, and universities that the basic rights of parents to control their children's medical decisions are being cast aside by politicians and school administrators for the benefit of personal profit?

The "transgender" issue, touched upon earlier with the mention of Rachel (Richard) Levine, the top Pennsylvania "health" professional,

Mom's Use of Acetaminophen During Pregnancy May Lead to ADHD, Autism in Babies

More than 90 scientists, doctors and public health researchers are calling for new safety reviews of the common painkiller, pointing to mounting evidence fetal exposure to acetaminophen could increase the risk of neurodevelopmental disorders and reproductive system effects.

NIH-funded study suggests acetaminophen exposure in pregnancy linked to higher risk of ADHD, autism

Evidence the U.S. autism epidemic initiated by acetaminophen

(Tylenol) is aggravated by oral antibiotic amoxicillin/clavulanate

(Augmentin) and now exponentially by herbicide glyphosate (Roundup)

PMID: 29460795   DOI: 10.1016/j.clnesp.2017.10.005

Risk of Suicide 12 Times Greater After 'Gender-Affirming' Surgery: Study

The study examined data from nearly 16 million U.S. adult patients between the ages of 18 and 60.

Thousands of Doctors Take Legal Action Against Transgender Mandate

The HHS mandate in May 2021 followed an executive order issued four months earlier by President Joe Biden. The order expanded the interpretation of "sex" beyond a person's biology, to include a person's declared "gender identity" or "sexual orientation."

healthline Myth 6: Only women get periods

Not every female who gets a period considers themselves a woman. Transgender men and nonbinary people may get their periods.

Weed Killer and Autism (ASD) or ADHD?

Food type	glyphosate residue detected (%)
Infant cereal	31.7%

We detected glyphosate and AMPA in the majority of pregnant women from this predominantly urban Canadian cohort. Diet was a probable route of exposure.

needs to be revisited. Anyone in government or education or in the media who questioned government policy on gender confusion risked an immediate end to their career. Same for anyone who questioned vaccine policy. There were important questions that could not be broached in public discourse without the very real risk of being censored, deplatformed, fired, defamed, publicly ridiculed and humiliated, or otherwise punished.

Let's look at some of the common environmental pollutants many Americans are exposed to on a regular basis, starting with atrazine, the second-most commonly used herbicide and the most common contaminant of groundwater, surface water, and rainwater in the United States. Atrazine is made in laboratories — it does not occur naturally. It is a white, odorless powder that is used to stop the growth of weeds in crops such as corn, which is grown on about 90 million acres in the United States alone, yielding 15.3 billion bushels in 2023. Atrazine is used on over 54 million acres of the U.S. corn crop. There are more than 60 premix products that have atrazine in them.

Atrazine exposure is linked to consistent reproductive problems in amphibians, fish, reptiles, and mammals, with at least 10 studies showing that such exposure feminizes male frogs, sometimes to the point of reversing their sex. Atrazine exposure can change the expression of genes, inhibit key enzymes that control estrogen and androgen production (female and male sex hormones), skew the sex ratio of wild and laboratory animals, and otherwise disrupt the normal reproductive development and functioning of males and females.

About 40,000 tons of atrazine were used in agricultural and weed control settings in the United States in 2010. The global atrazine market was worth $1.6 billion in 2022 and is expected to be almost double that by 2030. What effect is this chemical having on human reproductive health? Might this be a clue to the increased gender confusion among children, adolescents, and adults? Would atrazine exposure be having an effect on the development of human embryos in the womb, or on infants?

According to the U.S. Department of Health and Human Services, any atrazine that is washed from the soil into streams and other bodies of water will stay there for a long time, because breakdown of the chemical is slow in rivers and lakes. It will also persist for a long time in

100% Voter Turnout: Massive Nursing Home Election Fraud

After investigating several tips that he received, the sheriff of Racine County made a televised, public presentation in which he exposed the evidence that his office was able to collect regarding possible felony violations committed by the Wisconsin Elections Commission. Specifically, the evidence showed that absentee ballots were cast on behalf of nursing home residents who were too cognitively impaired to vote themselves. This was then followed up by a state-wide investigation which found that this practice was widespread, and actually led to many nursing homes (in the most populous counties) having voter turnout rates of 100 percent. And according to video testimony of the actual seniors and their family , it appears that the nursing home residents might've been forced to vote.

'Discrepancies and Irregularities' Still Plague Michigan Election Practices

Thousands of Fraudulent Ballot Registration Requests Found on New York's Voter Rolls

Minnesota's New Election Legislation Criminalizes What Officials Deem Misinformation

Has American Democracy Been a Hallucination for Nearly 60 Years?

Call it a democracy, call it a democratic republic, call it a constitutional republic, call it anything you want—it doesn't really matter what America is if there's truth to what Tucker Carlson was reporting the other night via a source who had "direct knowledge" of still-hidden documents concerning the Kennedy assassination, implicating the CIA.

If indeed the CIA was in any way involved in the assassination of JFK on Nov. 22, 1963, then anything that has happened in the public sphere in our country since that day has basically been a hallucination created by an intelligence agency far deeper than most of us—certainly I, since I was never much given to conspiracy theories—ever imagined.

'Printer Error' Mysteriously Flips One Million Registered Voters to Democrats

groundwater. Little information is available regarding the effects of atrazine on children. Maternal exposure to atrazine in drinking water has been associated with low fetal weight and heart, urinary, and limb defects in humans. Atrazine has been shown to slow down the development of fetuses in animals, and exposure to high levels of atrazine during pregnancy causes reduced survival of fetuses.

Consider the chemical glyphosate, another weed killer: 75% of pregnant Canadian women in the first trimester of their pregnancy had detectable concentrations of glyphosate in their urine. How would this interact with atrazine during the gestation period of human embryos? Has anyone thought about this, or is such research being avoided for fear of what would be discovered?

Or chlormequat, a highly toxic agricultural chemical found in wheat and oat products, including common breakfast cereals. Chlormequat, when applied to oat and grain crops while they're growing, stops the plants from bending over, making the grain easier to harvest. But chlormequat can disrupt fetal growth in animals and damage their reproductive systems. How will it interact with human embryos and babies? Exposure to chlormequat can result in lower fertility and can harm developing fetuses even at doses below levels set by regulators.

Researchers detected chlormequat in 80% of urine samples collected between 2017 and 2023, with "a significant increase in concentrations for samples from 2023." Throw that chemical into the soup that humans are exposed to, especially pregnant mothers, then study what the effect of all three of these chemicals combined, atrazine, glyphosate, and chlormequat, may be having on developing human fetuses.

This is just the tip of the iceberg. Gender confusion is not normal, and it is not natural. People who have this condition may be victims of biochemical aberrations that may have occurred in the womb from exposure to environmental pollutants during pregnancy, potentiated by drinking chemically contaminated water in baby formula and eating contaminated baby food during infancy. People so afflicted don't need to be congratulated, promoted, or held up as examples to society and especially not to children. But gender-confused people do need to be understood, supported, helped, and respected for who they are. We should not hate

'Nothing Has Changed': Lawmaker Fears Loophole in Wisconsin Elections

"Going into the midterms, a person can still register, get a ballot, and vote before his or her identity and address are verified with the Wisconsin Department of Transportation, as required by law," Brandtjen told The Epoch Times. "I saw this going on in the August primary. Nothing has changed since 2020. There is still no instantaneous identity check for the thousands of people utilizing Wisconsin's same-day registration law.

Conservatives Seek to Ban Private Funding of Elections Ahead of 2024 Races

Soros Bucks, Private Jets Found in PA AG Josh Shapiro's Campaign Finance Report

The campaign finance report for Pennsylvania Attorney General Josh Shapiro, Democrat gubernatorial candidate, would take 22 reams of paper to print.

On June 29, George Soros' son, Jonathan Soros, who lives in New York, gave Shapiro $10,000. The next day, June 30, Jennifer Soros, Jonathan Soros' wife, contributed $10,000. On Aug. 8, Andrea Soros, George Soros' daughter, gave Shapiro $100,000. The large number of special interest donations may explain why Shapiro has raised significantly more than state senator and Republican gubernatorial candidate Doug Mastriano.

Shapiro has proved himself as a well-connected Democrat fundraiser, with nearly $39 million raised for his campaign, compared to Mastriano's $3.6 million raised.

Missing Ballots Found in New Jersey County

Mercer County Board of Elections officials Thursday found missing ballots from at least four New Jersey precincts, according to a New Jersey Globe report.

The report noted ballots for three voting districts in Princeton and one in Robbinsville had been at the county facility since Election Day. There were between 13,000 – 15,000 uncounted mail-in ballots remaining at the county office Friday, according to a New Jersey Monitor report.

Group Sues Louisiana for Denying Access to Voter Files

The Public Interest Legal Foundation (PILF) says that Louisiana Secretary of State Kyle Ardoin, a Republican, is violating the National Voter Registration Act (NVRA) by not allowing the foundation to access voter documents.

people for who they are, but we can certainly despise them for what they do. When gender-confused adults, or any adults, try to influence impressionable children to doubt their natural gender, then we have a very serious problem.

In the 2020s, medical professionals were seizing upon gender-confused children and interfering with their sexual development, encouraging them to engage in hormone treatments and surgery to block their natural gender maturation. They were influencing young women to surgically remove their breasts and men to have breast implants (*"chest or 'top' surgery to remove breast tissue for a more masculine appearance or enhance breast size and shape for a more feminine appearance,"* according to the Cleveland Clinic); to have surgical penises attached (*"Phalloplasty: Uses a flap of skin from another part of your body to form an average-sized penis, about 5 to 6 inches. It usually happens alongside scrotoplasty."*).

And, in case you're wondering what scrotoplasty is, according to the Cleveland Clinic, it *"reshapes part of the labia majora (outer lips of the vulva) into a scrotum. Once you heal, you may choose to get silicone gel or saline implants that look and feel like testicles (testicular prosthesis)."*

Oh heck, we may as well throw in *vaginectomy*, which *"removes the vagina. This may be an option if you don't desire bottom surgery, like metoidioplasty or phalloplasty. These procedures often involve using vaginal tissue to reconstruct your genitals."* And *metoidioplasty*, which *"uses the clitoris to form a penis. Before surgery, you'll take testosterone to enlarge the clitoris to the size of a micropenis (a penis that's less than about 2.57 inches long). This procedure usually happens alongside scrotoplasty."*

Young gender-confused males can be encouraged to have their penises removed and replaced with holes, known as *"vaginoplasty,"* or *"feminizing bottom surgery."* According to the Cleveland Clinic, this is *"a procedure to construct or repair your vagina. People . . . have vaginoplasty as part of gender affirmation surgery."* What happens during "feminizing bottom surgery"? Your anesthesiologist will give you anesthesia. Your surgical team will remove your testicles (orchiectomy) and perform a vaginoplasty. They'll remove most of the penis tissue (penectomy) and create a space between your urinary bladder and rectum. They'll then reshape and invert the outer penis skin and insert it into the space they've

Judge Rules New Mexico Officials Violated Federal Law by Restricting Access to Voter Data

Judge said that New Mexico violated the Public Inspection Provision by denying the group's request for voter data.

Man Continues His Fight for Milwaukee's 2020 Election Records

Arizona 2020 Election Results May Have Been Different If 20,000 Invalid Ballots Had Not Been Counted: Report

Fluoride in pregnancy may harm child's brain development: study

A new study suggests a link between greater fluoride intake in pregnancy and toddlers with behavioral problems.

Non-Citizens Have Been Voting Since 2008
Is this why Biden recklessly opened the border to millions of illegal immigrants?

24 States Banned 'Zuckerbucks' Grants After 2020 Election

Watchdog Groups Allege Election Violations in Florida's 2022 and 2020 Elections

A grassroots group presented evidence to Florida election officials and law enforcement last week showing that almost 1,100 mail-in ballots in one county were cast from undeliverable addresses in the state's Aug. 23 primary election.

created, to form a "vagina." Then they will remove a small part of the tip of the penis to create your clitoris (clitoroplasty). They will then perform a labiaplasty, where they'll rearrange the pouch of skin that holds the testicles, into your labia. The surgery takes about five hours. After the surgery, if you want a vagina, your surgeon will place a "conformer" into the hole. A conformer is an object that helps your "vagina" keep its shape as the body tries to heal.

As many as 300 new pediatric gender confusion clinics have opened in the United States over the past few decades, providing an entirely new revenue source for the medical establishment. It's hard to believe that this information can be factually written, but it's the truth.

In Rachel Levine's expert opinion: *"There is no argument among medical professionals — pediatricians, pediatric endocrinologists, adolescent medicine physicians, adolescent psychiatrists, psychologists, etc. — about the value and the importance of gender-affirming care."*

Vaccines

While we're on the topic of children and chemical pollutants, let's briefly touch upon another provocative topic: childhood vaccines and autism. Boiled frogs are taught to repeat the mantra: *"Vaccines do not cause autism!"* There is ample evidence to contradict this claim, evidence that will never be seen on mainstream propaganda outlets but as long as people are met with the mantra "vaccines do not cause autism," usually accompanied with a fiercely indignant and condescending tone, no further discussion is warranted. Case closed. Research has conclusively proven that there is no connection between vaccines and autism, or so we are told, so shut up or they'll label you "anti-science" and give you a tinfoil hat to wear.

But let's ask some perfectly reasonable questions. What about when vaccines are administered to children who are on antibiotics? Both vaccines and antibiotics affect the immune system. What research lab has studied that topic? What about babies on antibiotics, given multiple vaccines at once, then administered Tylenol on top of everything else? Has anyone done research on *that*? Why wouldn't these obvious concerns be

CDC Quietly Admits to Covid Policy Failures

In so many words—and data—CDC has quietly admitted that all of the indignities of the Covid-19 pandemic management have failed: the masks, the distancing, the lockdowns, the closures, and especially the vaccines; all of it failed to control the pandemic.

Election Firm Knew Data Had Been Sent to China, Prosecutors Say

Election Software Firm Used by LA County - and by Counties in Swing States - Gave 'Superadministrator' Privileges to Contractors in China

Shocking Discovery Found on Voting Rolls in Fourth Most-Populous County in the Nation

RFK Jr. Responds to DNC's Plans to Skip Primary Debates: 'The System Is Indeed Rigged'

North Carolina Judges Strike Down Voter ID Law, Claiming It's Racist

Democrat Megadonor Behind Defamation Lawsuit Against Trump

Former President Donald Trump is questioning the "bias and motive" behind a defamation suit against him by a New York writer after learning the lawsuit is funded by a Democrat megadonor, Reid Hoffman, court filings on April 13 indicate.

Millions of Tiny, Suspicious Political Donations Questioned by Watchdog Group

New Report Shows Chinese Company Spends Millions On Lobbying Democrats to Fulfill Their Interests

studied? One reason is because scientific research costs money and consequently research requires funding. Funding sources don't want to expose information that may have a negative impact on product sales, so funding will not be offered if the research doesn't benefit the funding source. What about our government? Why can't we use taxpayer dollars to fund research about these critical and timely issues? Because the government is controlled by Big Pharma. Our representatives depend on Big Pharma handouts to help fund their reelections.

Yet, the two toxins most implicated in the U.S. autism epidemic are in fact Tylenol (acetaminophen) and the oral antibiotic amoxicillin. Recently, the herbicide glyphosate was also "exponentially implicated." Researching the administration of childhood vaccines, combined with childhood exposure to other chemicals in a soup of environmental contaminants, seems to be conspicuously absent from scientific studies.

What happens with the addition of glyphosate, chlormequat, and atrazine exposure to the baby in the womb? Add vaccines administered on the day the baby is born, then inject the baby with several vaccines at once while the baby is on an antibiotic, then give it Tylenol on top of everything else? Add the more than 70 doses of 17 pharmaceutical drugs (vaccines) on the CDC childhood schedule. Most of these vaccines contain the adjuvant aluminum, which is a known neurotoxin. Shall we do some research on this? Does it not seem like this could have something to do with human gender confusion, autism, peanut allergies, and the host of other conditions that children are afflicted with today? These conditions are certainly not hereditary, so there has to be an environmental factor. So far, the strategy has been "don't look, don't find." Don't forget, "all vaccines are safe and effective," and keep repeating, "vaccines don't cause autism!"

What does any of this have to do with direct democracy? When you vote for a representative, you are not exercising your right to vote, you are sacrificing your right to vote. Laws then become written and voted upon by a small group of individuals, members of congress, senators, and other representatives, who require the financial backing of special interests. Those special interests include the medical industrial complex, the military industrial complex, the chemical industry, the vaccine industry,

Judge Orders Biden's DHS to Release Docs Exposing Agents Who 'Helped Censor Election Misinformation'

Documentary Exposes Rise of the Unaccountable Fourth Branch of Government, Rule by Experts

National Debt Reflects a Nation That Has Lost Its Way

How can it be that we have national debt equal to size of our entire economy? And where were we all when this happened? As recently as 2008, debt was 39.2 percent, rather than 100 percent, of our GDP.

Election Integrity Watchdog Finds California Lost 10.9 Million Mail-In Ballots in 2022 Midterms

'Mail voting practices have an insurmountable information gap'

FOIA Requests Reveal There Were No DOJ Investigations on Election Fraud After 2020 Election as Bill Barr Claimed

Florida elections office has no oversight for ballots or chain of custody, whistleblower alleges

With 25,000 Mysterious Votes And Missing Documents Maricopa's 2022 Election Marked By Chaos And Uncertainty

US National Debt Default Is a 'Real Threat' Both Sides Must Take Seriously

Rep. Don Bacon (R-Neb.) has warned that the risk of a U.S. national debt default is a "real threat" that must be taken seriously, as Republicans push for spending cuts while the White House vows not to yield to the GOP in exchange for avoiding a debt ceiling standoff.

and so on. If you are one of the 535 voting members in the U.S. Congress, there's a damn good chance that you'll be voting for the best interests of your financial backers.

On the other hand, if American citizens claimed their true right to vote directly on legislation, and if only 15% of the 162 million registered voters actually took the time to do the research, inform themselves on legislation, and vote on it, then 24,300,000 people would be weighing in on the issues. That's over 24 million people deciding what legislation would pass and what wouldn't.

Of course, if we're talking about 24 million boiled frogs, we're toast. This is why, in the 2020s, there is an insistent effort by the democrats, RINOs, the deep state, and the globalists, to undermine the 1st amendment of the Constitution, blocking free speech, and replacing it with censorship and propaganda. If the minds of the masses can be controlled, they will allow themselves to be happily herded, like sheep, to their own demise. Independent media, free and open Internet, freedom of speech, freedom of assembly, freedom of the press, and the suppression of censorship, have never been more important than they are now.

Add to this the obvious prospect that ordinary citizens would also participate in the *crafting* of legislation. This would entail discussion and debate among the millions of participants at public venues and/or on whatever social media platforms allowed free speech. The result would be legislation tailored to fit the needs *of the people*. Which system do you think best represents democracy? The American people would be voting, by and large, for their best interests, not the interests of Big Pharma, the War Machine, the chemical industry, or any billionaire.

Let's fund research to see what happens to fetuses in the womb who are exposed to various common chemical pollutants. Let's research vaccines in depth, from all angles. Let's release all the data related to the assassination of JFK. Let's release everything our government knows about UFOs. Let's decide how our taxes are going to be spent. Let's have people advance in positions of public service based on meritocracy, not on what family they belong to, who they know, or how much money they have. Let's take the money that is perennially squandered on warfare and invest in things that are important and constructive.

WHO Makes Key Concessions Ahead of Pandemic Treaty Vote

"Ultimately, the goal of these instruments isn't to protect public health. It's to cede authority to the WHO—specifically its director-general—to restrict our citizens' rights to freedom of speech, privacy, movement (especially travel across borders), and informed consent."

This is bigger than COVID: Why are so many Americans dying early?

Life insurers have been consistently sounding the alarm over these unexpected or, "excess," deaths, which claimed 158,000 more Americans in the first nine months of 2023 than in the same period in 2019. That exceeds America's combined losses from every war since Vietnam. Congress should urgently work with insurance experts to investigate this troubling trend.

Increased Age-Adjusted Cancer Mortality After the Third mRNA-Lipid Nanoparticle Vaccine Dose During the COVID-19 Pandemic in Japan

Statistically significant increases in age-adjusted mortality rates of all cancer and some specific types of cancer, namely, ovarian cancer, leukemia, prostate, lip/oral/pharyngeal, pancreatic, and breast cancers, were observed in 2022 after two-thirds of the Japanese population had received the third or later dose of SARS-CoV-2 mRNA-LNP vaccine. These particularly marked increases in mortality rates of these ERα-sensitive cancers may be attributable to several mechanisms of the mRNA-LNP vaccination rather than COVID-19 infection itself or reduced cancer care due to the lockdown. The significance of this possibility warrants further studies. This article was previously posted to the Zenodo repository server on September 18, 2023.

The Tide Turns: Research on COVID Vaccine Harms, Once a Taboo Subject, Now Appearing in Some Medical Journals

A 'PANDEMIC OF VACCINATIONS'
Australian Senator Malcolm Roberts' Wake-Up Call
*This is the **first time they withdrew a proven, safe, effective, affordable, accessible treatment**. Ivermectin. Made it illegal. And then this is the **first time they made a lethal, untested, unproven drug mandatory**. So you could feed your children.*

CDC to drop 'gold standard' COVID test: PCR risks false positives

Let's audit the Department of Defense and find out where the missing trillions have gone. The warmongers in Congress want to funnel billions of our tax dollars to yet another war front? And not account for any of it? That's called money laundering. We can stop it. We can enact whatever legislation we want. Big pharma will not be able to block it, the swamp won't stop us, the political parties will be incapable of controlling legislative outcomes because all concerned citizens will be the ones who vote, not just partisan politicians controlled by one party or another. Career politicians will cease to exist. The swamp will inevitably dry up.

Most current "representatives" are simply puppets. They know who butters their bread and they vote that way. The 2020 election cycle in the United States cost over *$14 billion*! Fourteen billion dollars to elect representatives! Intelligent random selection of representatives would cost very little, almost nothing in comparison. Why haven't we done anything like this already? One reason is because we haven't been capable of it.

The random selection of representatives coupled with direct citizen voting on legislation would never have crossed the minds of the Founding Fathers because no technology had been invented or even imagined that could accomplish such a thing. They didn't even have electricity! Times have changed.

But what about your neighbor? He shouldn't be voting on anything! You don't want some crackhead representing you! You don't trust *yourself* to be able to vote correctly on any legislation. You would rather have a professional make those decisions. Or maybe you just don't have the time or the interest in getting involved in the legislative process. That's okay. It's not for everyone, although every qualified citizen *should* have the right to directly engage in the legislative process if they so choose.

Here's a suggestion: for the next few days or weeks, look around you wherever you happen to be. Look at the floors, the roads, the clothing, the lighting systems. Notice the advanced technology now in automobiles and airplanes. Think about and observe everything positive and constructive that humans have created.

Realize that the person next to you on a bus or in a train quite likely plays a role in maintaining the gears that make society work. There are a lot of level-headed, intelligent, creative, caring, and wise Americans.

Gender-Affirming Care and Young People

Affirming Care	What is it?	When is it used?	Reversible or not
Social Affirmation	Adopting gender-affirming hairstyles, clothing, name, gender pronouns, and restrooms and other facilities	At any age or stage	Reversible
Puberty Blockers	Using certain types of hormones to pause pubertal development	During puberty	Reversible
Hormone Therapy	Testosterone hormones for those who were assigned female at birth Estrogen hormones for those who were assigned male at birth	Early adolescence onward	Partially reversible
Gender-Affirming Surgeries	"Top" surgery – to create male-typical chest shape or enhance breasts "Bottom" surgery – surgery on genitals or reproductive organs Facial feminization or other procedures	Typically used in adulthood or case-by-case in adolescence	Not reversible HHS OFFICE OF POPULATION AFFAIRS

214 Studies, 21 Guidelines: Largest Review on Transgender Youth Medicine Finds Insufficient Evidence for Medicalization

The review stated that there is insufficient evidence to demonstrate the long-term benefits of medicalizing children who want to identify as a different gender.

Cleveland Clinic Feminizing Bottom Surgery

Feminizing bottom surgery is a procedure that allows your physical body to match your gender identity. It reconstructs organs in the male reproductive system into parts of a vulva and possibly a vagina. Recovery can take up to several months.

The Department of Health and Human Services (HHS) provided only a two-page document to support Assistant Secretary Rachel Levine's claim that "gender-affirming care" is "necessary" for transgender youth. This has led to allegations that Levine violated the Dept.'s scientific integrity policies by making unsubstantiated claims.

The Government Accidentally Confirms It Has No Real Evidence To Support So- Called 'Gender Affirming Care' For Minors

In response to a Freedom of Information Act Request, HHS produced a grand total of just one document.

By Matt Walsh, February 7, 2024

How Much Damage Have Vaccines Done to Society?

A long history exists of a wave of severe injuries following new vaccinations being introduced to the market. In most cases, those injuries were swept under the rug to protect the business.

Drive through the countryside and look at the well-kept farms and the small businesses. These represent the best of America. These citizens are not billionaires living on private islands playing with the human race as if we were digital characters in a colossal video game.

Most people work for a living. They have children and homes. They pay their bills and budget their money. They're concerned about their retirement options. They care about the environment. They don't want wars. They care about the future they will be leaving their children and grandchildren. Nothing is more important to them than their health, their homes, their livelihoods, their communities, and their families. Having a healthy young child on your lap reciting the ABCs is so much more precious than a $200 billion fleet of private jets.

Most Americans are perfectly capable of voting directly on legislation. We should trust decisions made by 24 million people working in cooperation, more than decisions made by a few hundred politicians working in back rooms.

The United States debt was over $35 trillion in 2024 and climbing rapidly. Our representatives did that to us. They make the decisions regarding the spending of taxpayer dollars, and they're blowing it. Many of them are incompetent, likely corrupt, and perhaps even deranged.

During the Korean War, it was *our government* that escalated the war, killing millions of Koreans on their own land, in their own homes. It was *our government* that brought us to the brink of WWIII in Korea by threatening to drop two dozen atomic bombs on China, only a few years after the end of WWII. It was *our representatives* who mandated that 18-year-old American boys, fresh out of high school, be forced to invade and occupy Vietnam or be sentenced to a federal penitentiary. It is *our representatives* who budget huge amounts of money for the military, then conveniently ignore how it is spent or where it goes.

In 2024, our representatives are sucking money out of our treasury as fast as they can, siphoning it to war fronts in Ukraine and Palestine. They will never stop until we stop them. It is a cancer, and we must cure it. We have an extra $100 billion in tax revenues to spend? Do we send it to Nazis in Ukraine, or do we use it to clean up our drug-infested inner cities? Let's vote on these things. We the people. All of us.

idiot on the internet

this was the end of my career as a pharmaceutical executive. i was asked to fire a pregnant employee who was declining the vaccine mandate. i refused. i was asked to step down, which i did, and then they fired her anyway. all good, zero regrets. money is never worth your soul.

Pfizer 'Chose Not To' Tell Regulators About SV40 Sequence in COVID Shots: Health Canada Official

Association between simian virus 40 and non- Hodgkin lymphoma

SV40 is significantly associated with some types of non-Hodgkin lymphoma. These results add lymphomas to the types of human cancers associated with SV40.

Wisconsin Voter Roll Transparency Challenged by Public Interest Legal Foundation

A Federal Election Assistance Commission report found that, of the 622,370 address confirmation notices mailed to Wisconsin registrants between Jan. 1, 2021, and Dec. 31, 2022, 299,490 were returned as undeliverable.

'Healthy' 29-Year-Old's Sudden Heart Attack Caused by COVID-19 Vaccine, Cardiologists Confirm

A 29-year-old woman named Florencia Tarque has come forward with a personal health crisis after doctors confirmed her sudden heart attack was caused by her COVID-19 vaccination.

American College of Obstetricians and Gynecologists Still Pushing COVID Shots for Pregnant Women — Could Millions in Government Funding Explain Why?

The Centers for Disease Control and Prevention bankrolled the American College of Obstetricians and Gynecologists to the tune of $11 million to promote COVID-19 vaccination as "safe and effective" for pregnant women, according to an investigation published this week by attorney Maggie Thorp.

People With More COVID-19 Vaccine Doses More Likely to Contract COVID-19: Study

The risk of contracting COVID-19 was 1.5 times higher for those who received two doses, 1.95 times higher for those who received three doses, and 2.5 times higher for those who received more than three doses, the researchers found.

Why the US Debt Is Unsustainable and Is Destroying the Middle Class

Liz Cheney was the daughter of Dick Cheney, one of the architects of the disastrous invasion of Iraq. That invasion was a crime against humanity, executed in response to a group of Saudis attacking the World Trade Center in 2001. Liz Cheney was also a U.S. representative from the state of Wyoming from 2017 to 2023. She was a republican elected to represent the people of Wyoming, a state that voted 70% for republican President Donald Trump in the 2020 election. If 70% of your constituency voted for a particular presidential candidate in an election year, and your responsibility is to represent your constituency, then it stands to reason that you would largely support the candidate that your constituents voted for. That's what *representation* means. Instead, Cheney did exactly the opposite. She devoted her tenure during her time as a representative to undermining and attacking Wyoming's favorite presidential candidate, Donald Trump. She didn't care what her constituency wanted. What mattered to her was what *she* wanted.

This is a perfect example of why one person can't be expected to reliably represent a quarter-million other people. Out of that quarter-million voters in Wyoming, nearly 200,000 voted for Trump. Then why would Cheney devote so many public hours and so many millions of tax dollars trying to *destroy* Trump? When reelection time came around, Cheney was quickly and soundly booted out of office. But she did plenty of damage in the meantime.

Cheney, and all of the members of Congress are entitled to their opinion, which is not more or less important than anyone else's. They are entitled to one vote. The idea that they can take away the votes of their substantial constituency and replace it with their own vote, no matter how petty or emotional, is ridiculous. The population of Wyoming must bypass someone like Cheney and vote directly on legislation. When the people vote, their vote must be binding, regardless of the opinion of their representative. The people of Wyoming would never have permitted Cheney's witch hunt against Trump had they not been blocked from exercising the power they rightfully deserve as citizens in a democratic society.

Cheney provides only one example among hundreds, if not thousands of politicians gone astray. Career politicians pollute Washington, DC, like a plague. They will vote for their own interests, and they will happily, and arrogantly, cut *you* out of the picture. We are being silenced.

We must realize that there are valid alternatives to the political mess we are now in. Then we must start giving those alternatives some serious thought. Then, we must have open, intelligent discussions about creative alternatives and how to make them happen in the real world. Humans are creator beings. We can create our own future. In fact, we always have. First, we must visualize what we want, then we must put energy into that visualization. Then, eventually, it will become reality.

Every idea is a seed planted in the mind of humanity. Some are planted in fertile soil and are nourished. Those ideas can grow rapidly and spread quickly around the world. Other ideas are born before their time has come. These wither, shrivel, die, or go dormant. The grandchildren of the 2020s will be reading this book as adults, years later. The author, already a grandfather, will be gone by then. Grandchildren, you have the gift of hindsight. What happened?

Did the medical-industrial complex continue to force drug injections on humans of all ages, beginning on the day they are born? Did the globalists erase our Bill of Rights and replace it with subjugation and tyranny? Did the Deep State assassinate more presidents, presidential candidates, and political opponents? Did propagandists polarize society to the extent that it sparked a civil war in America? Did gender-confused politicians force their ideology on our vulnerable children? Were parents increasingly stripped of their parental rights, replaced by government control of their offspring? Did incompetent, unwise, and foolish politicians start World War III? Or did they just maintain a low-level simmering global warfare to keep the blood money flowing? Did the citizens get control of their purse, or are they still lining up to be milked like goats, then fleeced like sheep, while pigs gobble up the national treasury like hogs at a slop bucket? Did the people continue their addictions to sugar, processed foods, pharmaceutical drugs, and to their brainwashing machines? Did the natural environment continue to be increasingly polluted by chemical poisons while the people became increasingly burdened by physical and mental illness?

Or did things get turned around? If so, how did it happen?

9
What Did Happen?

Reactions to the idea of Direct Democracy are predictable. Simply stated, naysayers will declare, *"It will never happen. It can't be done!"* The reasoning can be summed up succinctly in three points:

1. The elite will never let the legislative process be controlled by the citizens. The oligarchs have all the power; they control the police and the military, the DOJ, the FBI, the CIA, the IRS, the FDA, the CDC, the NIH, the media, the Democrat party, many of the Republicans, and to some extent, the courts. They will happily sacrifice commoners at the drop of a hat. To them, the U.S. Constitution is not a guidebook, it's an obstacle.

2. The common people are too stupid to make decisions. The government is a vast and complicated entity requiring highly trained professionals to run it. Direct democracy would be a disaster for the United States if we put common working-class people in charge of the legislative process.

3. Even if the citizens managed to regain control of the legislative branch of the government, there is still the executive branch and the judicial branch. They will block you.

The executive branch consists of people who are likely to be installed by the wealthy elite through rigged elections. They will do everything in their power to stop the public from "upsetting the apple cart," i.e., shutting off or controlling the money spigot.

The judicial branch consists of people who are largely unelected. Many are appointed by members of the executive branch. The early 2020s have made it clear that the judicial branch at the federal level is rife with corruption in some jurisdictions. There are judges who will decide cases in a manner that blatantly favors one political party over another.

Canadian Government Plans 'Stalinist Show Trial' of Heroic Doctor
Legal Trickery Would Silence Dr. Charles Hoffe

Prominent Canadian physician Dr. Charles Hoffe has spoken out courageously to warn people of the very serious dangers of the Covid mRNA genetic "vaccines." He now faces trial from the Canadian health authorities aiming to silence him and effectively destroy his medical practice. The government's objective, he says, is "to try to make an example of me and make sure all the other doctors toe the line and keep quiet and just obey." Dr. Hoffe, who is widely regarded as a heroic truth-teller across much of Canada, comes across as a down-to-earth man of great integrity, honesty and humility. An outspoken advocate for patient safety, medical ethics, and the Hippocratic oath ("First, do no harm"), he is accused by the medical authorities of spreading "misinformation," putting people at risk, and encouraging "vaccine hesitancy." After 31 years as an emergency room physician with not a single patient complaint against him, he was fired from his ER position for telling a nurse that somebody who had natural immunity didn't need to get the Covid jab.

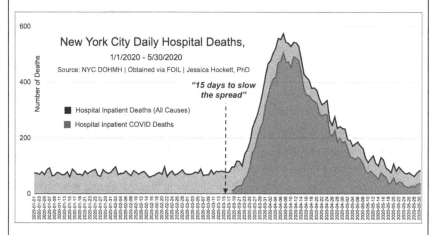

'80% of serious COVID cases are fully vaccinated' says Ichilov hospital director

Israel National News / Feb 3, 2022, 3:12 PM (GMT+2)

Nearly half (48%) of Democratic voters think federal and state governments should be able to fine or imprison individuals who publicly question the efficacy of the existing COVID-19 vaccines on social media, television, radio, or in online or digital publications. Forty-five percent (45%) of Democrats would favor governments requiring citizens to temporarily live in designated facilities or if they refuse a COVID-19 vaccine. RasmussenReports.com

Illinois family credits Ivermectin with saving life of father hospitalized with COVID-19

All these arguments have merit. People who have excess power will not give it up willingly. So, what are we to do?

The Bicycle Repair Shop

Two brothers in Ohio in the late 1800s managed a publishing business where they printed newspapers and manufactured printing presses. Neither of them had attended a university, nor had either married. Perhaps this is why they had the time to expand their mechanical skills into the bicycle trade, eventually owning and operating a bicycle shop.

Profits from their printing and bicycle businesses were eventually used to fund experiments. Between 1899 and 1905, they designed lightweight wood and wire machines and reinforced them with metal tubing, intending to create heavier-than-air contraptions that could fly.

When Wilber and Orville Wright conducted their first historic flight in one of their rickety contraptions on December 17, 1903, the two brothers from Ohio made history. The floodgates to aeronautic science then swung wide open. Incredibly, it was only 63 years later that humans landed on the moon.

In *A Study in Human Incredulity*, by Fred C. Kelly, the Wright brothers' only "authorized" biographer, Kelly explains,

> *"The Wrights' belief that they had achieved something of great scientific importance was not bolstered by the attitude of the general public. Not only were there no receptions, brass bands, or parades in their honor, but the neighbors paid less attention to the history-making feat than if the "boys" had simply been on vacation and caught a big fish or shot a bear.*
>
> *One neighbor, Mr. Webbert, father of the man from whom they rented their bicycle shop, did concede: "I know you boys are truthful and if you say you flew through the air in a machine, I believe you. But then," he added, "down there on the Carolina coast you had special conditions to help you. Of course you couldn't do it anywhere else."*
>
> *Other neighbors thought if the thing had been done at all it must have been an accident, because of unusually powerful winds, and at best was just a stunt, not likely to happen again. One had remarked, just before*

Google Searches Favor Democrat Candidates in 2024 Presidential Race

Not a single Republican candidate appeared on the first page of Google results when searching for 'presidential campaign websites.'

Google's search results on 2024 presidential candidates overlook Republicans while promoting Democrats, according to an analysis by media watchdog MRC Free Speech America.

Between Sept. 20 and 25, MRC Free Speech America analyzed Google search results for three terms related to the upcoming elections—"presidential campaign websites," "Republican presidential campaign websites," and "Democrat presidential campaign websites." The searches were made a week prior to the second Republican presidential primary debate on Wednesday.

It found that search results were skewed heavily in favor of Democrats, with no notable Republican figures appearing on the first page. "Google is either the most incompetent search engine on the planet, or it's intentional. This is not a coincidence."

Tulsi Gabbard Sues Google For Silencing Her Campaign

Google inexplicably suspended Gabbard's campaign advertising account for the crucial six hours following the first Democratic primary debate last month, a lawsuit filed by her campaign on Thursday alleges – a period in which hers was the most-searched name of all the candidates on the crowded stage. Google didn't just violate her First Amendment rights by silencing her, the suit charges – it maliciously meddled with the democratic process.

Election report finds Facebook mogul's 'Zuck Bucks' broke law, swayed election outcome in Wisconsin

WEF Demands Powers to Regulate Public's Speech Online

The World Economic Forum (WEF) is demanding that government regulators and tech firms around the world grant the unelected globalist organization the authority to police the public's speech online. The WEF is seeking to regulate speech by defining which language should be censored.

Klaus Schwab and his allies want to dictate to regulators, social media companies, and other tech firms, their definitions for what constitutes "hate speech," "misinformation," or disinformation." Interestingly, the WEF makes no mention of cracking down on speech that could be linked to serious crimes such as terrorism or child abuse, nor does the organization mention targeting false information. Apparently, the WEF is more concerned with cracking down on political speech or information that may undermine its agenda.

Landmark Lawsuit Slaps Legacy Media With Antitrust, First Amendment Claims for Censoring COVID-Related Content

the Wrights went to Kitty Hawk: "People will fly at the same time they hit on perpetual motion." Many of the Wrights' acquaintances made no reference, when they met the inventors, to the reported flight, because it was embarrassing to discuss anything so preposterous.

One reason why nearly everyone in the United States was disinclined to swallow the reports about flying with a machine heavier than air was that important scientists had already explained in the public prints why the thing was impossible. When a man of the profound scientific wisdom of Simon Newcomb, for example, had demonstrated with unassailable logic why man couldn't fly, why should the public be fooled by silly stories about two obscure bicycle repairmen who hadn't even been to college?"

No doubt there are thousands of examples of revolutionary changes initially scoffed at by the general public. How about the idea that the Earth is round and not flat, for example? Or that the earth revolves around the sun and not the other way around? How long did Galileo stay locked up in prison for making that observation? Or that life evolves over time? Or that organisms too small to be seen with the naked eye exist, a discovery made by a self-educated working-class man in Holland? These changes in human consciousness did not happen overnight — they were refined over generations. Hard work and dedication by many intelligent people are needed to advance the human understanding of new ideas.

Can we create a democratic model that is not controlled by oligarchs and instead works for the common citizen? Of course we can. Will it happen overnight? Of course not. Will it require the combined efforts of thousands of intelligent people working toward a better future for humanity for generations to come? Yes, it will.

The Commoners

Common working-class people can't manage the legislative process? Why not? Yes, there are plenty of dumb people on the planet, but there are many more who are intelligent. They may be farmers, mechanics, hospitality workers, roofers, journalists, nurses, filmmakers, teachers, or any of the army of hard-working citizens who make up society. They all con-

Ẁe̔t̑he̔ Ƥeople

HAVE HAD ENOUGH

Twitter Part of Efforts to Interfere With US Elections

The revelations coming from Twitter's new owner Elon Musk about the platform's behind-scenes operation to suppress certain viewpoints has been "pretty horrifying," and shows that the platform was part of the efforts to interfere with the 2020 presidential elections, according to former House Speaker Newt Gingrich.

CDC Releases Hidden COVID-19 Vaccine Injury Reports

The agency was forced by a federal judge to disclose the reports.

Twitter Exaggerated Russian Propaganda Claims to Appease Democrats and Media

Twitter deliberately exaggerated claims about Russian propaganda flooding its platform in an effort to appease the Democrats and their allies in the corporate media, the latest installment of the "Twitter Files" has revealed.

A "Seahorse Dad"

A transgender man who had a breast removal surgery and was undergoing sex change procedure in Italy was found to be five months pregnant, reported New York Post. Marco, who is expected to go through with the pregnancy, joins a rare group referred to as "seahorse dads." It is believed to be the first such case in Italy. The transperson had mastectomy (surgical breast removal) and was preparing for uterus removal (hysterectomy) when the pregnancy was discovered at a hospital in Rome, the report said. *La Republica,* which first reported the medical case, stated that Marco will be the child's biological mother, but will be registered legally as the father.

The American College of Obstetricians and Gynecologists (ACOG) strongly recommends that pregnant individuals be vaccinated against COVID-19.

New-onset psychosis following COVID-19 vaccination: a systematic review

Only half of the patients analyzed in the review fully recovered, with the remaining half suffering from 'residual symptoms.'

tain a spark of divinity, and they all have something to contribute. We need to listen to each other and cooperatively craft a society and a future that works for everyone. It's not happening in the 2020s, and if you think it is, go back to page one and start over.

There are innumerable goods and services that we rely on daily. Not only are the commoners, as opposed to the wealthy elite, providing those goods and services, but their ancestors laid the groundwork before them, as had their ancestors, and those before them. We are not lacking in human resources. When a small handful of oligarchs controls the government, and thereby the education system, and the means of communication through the mass media, what we lack as a result is knowledge, open communication, and the wisdom and understanding that comes from sharing ideas without censorship and propaganda.

The Executive and Judicial branches will block us? Yes, they will to some extent and already are. When the democrat governor of Pennsylvania, Tom Wolf, declared a "health emergency" in the early 2020s in response to the Virus Hysteria, what started as a supposedly brief period of lockdowns and mandates stretched into months, with no end in sight. The Pennsylvania legislature, in frustration, then voted to end the declaration of emergency. Every republican voted in favor of ending the state of emergency, but every democrat voted to keep the emergency declaration in place. Two democrats voted with the republicans to end the emergency. The republican majority prevailed. The people had spoken. The ridiculous emergency scenario was voted out. Governor Tom Wolf, member of the executive branch of the government, a democrat, then *vetoed* the will of the people. There weren't enough votes to override the veto. The emergency declaration remained in place.

Why would all the democrats, including the democrat governor, align themselves with big pharma? If there really was a public health emergency, wouldn't *everyone* be concerned, no matter what political party they belonged to? Things started smelling fishy real fast when the medical establishment refused to allow people to stay healthy or to heal themselves by their own manner of choosing, instead imposing stay-at-home lockdowns, masking, and forced injections with experimental drugs as the ONLY permitted response to a flu season.

If you can't join 'em, beat 'em

In 2020, our electoral process was pushed to the breaking point. Inaccurate voter rolls, unconstitutional changes in process, mass mail ballots, unmonitored drop boxes, foreign influence, machine failures, rampant lawlessness, wokeism as a weapon ... all under the watchful eyes of corporate media and uniparty politicos who were quick to stifle any dissenting voices. "It was the most secure election ever." To say otherwise made you an election denier and part of the Big Lie. Since then, thousands of Americans have been indicted, jailed, bankrupted, ostracized, and silenced, all because of what happened in 2020, and the situation is getting worse, not better.

@KariLake

Attorney Kurt Olsen: "We found evidence of malware put on the printers used at 223 vote centers & those printers are what caused the Election Day chaos... There were over 7,000 ballot rejections every 30 minutes, beginning at 6:30 AM all the way through 8:00 PM when the polls, even after the polls closed... That's over 200,000 ballot rejections on a day when there were only 248,000 votes cast."

Biden's No. 3 DOJ Pick Demanded Twitter Censor Undercover Reporting on Illegal Voter Registration in Fulton County

James O'Keefe on Friday revealed Vanita Gupta, Biden's No. 3 pick at the DOJ, demanded Twitter censor Project Veritas's previous reporting on the illegal voter registration operation in Fulton County, Georgia.

Here's How Big Tech Plans To Rig The 2022 Midterms

As the 2022 midterms loom, big tech companies are again announcing their plans to meddle in U.S. elections by censoring news and information. Social media censorship ramped up dramatically following President Donald Trump's 2016 victory, leading to companies such as Twitter and Facebook colluding with Democrat operatives in intelligence agencies to censor and suppress factual stories that harmed then-candidate Joe Biden during his 2020 campaign.

Two years later, following heavy documentation of the meddling, big tech companies are intent on using the same strategy. And they're openly admitting as much.

Facebook took no action against the Democrat-funded and coordinated operation to question the legitimacy of the 2016 election by falsely accusing Donald Trump of being a traitor who stole the election by colluding with Russia. That lie, which led to mass public hysteria and years of investigations, is allowed free rein on its platform. Facebook's so-called "fact-checkers" included journalists who participated in spreading the lie or otherwise allowed it to continue without censorship via fact-checking.

Breaking: Jordan Releases 'Smoking Gun Docs' Confirming Facebook Bowed to White House Censorship Demands

So, what if a flu virus had been genetically modified in a bioweapons lab to readily infect humans and to block their uptake of oxygen? So, what if the pathogen had been intentionally released the world over to create panic and widespread death while the criminals behind it all raked in astronomical piles of money? What the "smartest people in the room" forgot about was the strength of the natural human immune system. People who conscientiously take care of their health have little to worry about when flu season rolls around. The solution is not to give the medical establishment dictatorial rein to run roughshod over humanity and force them to take untested experimental drugs. That is insanity.

If representatives were randomly selected, and they had only one vote like everyone else, political parties would no longer maintain a stranglehold on the throat of American democracy. The people would be free to make common-sense decisions without the unfair interference of an industrial complex, any special interest group, or powerful business lobby.

War Island

So, the question is: "What did happen?" You who are reading this maybe five or 10 years later, maybe a generation later or even a century later, did "We the People" prevail? Or did we succumb to the oligarchs?

Was there another devastating world war, or did we secure a lasting peace? Perhaps we set aside an island in the remote Pacific, named it "War Island," and reserved it for war mongers, war pigs, dogs of war, unrepentant violent criminals, and those who mastermind crimes against humanity. On War Island the weeds of humanity, bellicose politicians, demented billionaires, and others who insist that war is necessary can be banished and let loose to fight each other to the death, leaving the rest of us out of it.

War is not defense, and defense is not war. We are collecting trillions of tax-payer dollars, claiming it's for "defense," and instead of using it to defend ourselves, we're using it to attack others, under the direction and control of corrupt and incompetent politicians. Defense is necessary; war is not. One means of defense is rounding up troublemakers and shipping them off to be confined somewhere where their destructive lunacy won't

Kyle Becker

Judge Scott McAfee, a Fani Willis donor who once worked under the Fulton County DA, just upheld the criminal indictment against former President Donald Trump in Georgia.

McAfee rejected the argument that Trump's efforts to legally challenge the 2020 election were protected under the First Amendment.

"The defense has not presented, nor is the Court able to find, any authority that the speech and conduct alleged is protected political speech," McAfee wrote in his order.

The Democratic Party has sought to "overturn" the results of presidential elections in 2000, 2004, and 2016.

Democrats argued both Bush and Trump were "illegitimate" presidents and claimed the elections were "stolen."

The radical left's incendiary rhetoric about Trump led to interruptions of the electoral college proceedings in 2017 and incited violent riots on J20 during Trump's inauguration.

A Secret Service whistleblower warned Monday of another assassination attempt against former President Trump ahead of November's election.

Secret Service counter-sniper warned in an email there would be another assassination attempt, citing the agency's inability to protect leaders after a shooter wounded former President Donald Trump, two of his supporters, and killed another at a rally.

"We all SHOULD expect another [assassination] attempt to happen before November."

Utah Election Official Hit with Felony Charges for Illegally Shredding, Mishandling Ballots

Trump Asks Court to Block Michigan Secretary of State from Banning Him in the 2024 Race

Trump's opponents across the country are actively trying to prevent him from running in 2024 using the 14th amendment clause.

Trump Supporters Targeted by FBI as 2024 Election Nears

Man with health issues arrested by Buckhannon Police for not wearing a mask in Walmart

harm innocent men, women, and children.

Another means of defense is intelligently researching what harms or threatens us, listing the threats in the order of their severity, then using our "defense budget" to neutralize the threats. What would those threats be? Vietnamese peasants? Afghan goat herders? Russians? Chinese? Communists? Socialists?

The three leading causes of deaths in the United States in 2023 were as follows:

1. Heart disease: 681,621 annual deaths

2. Cancer: 570,347 annual deaths

3. Influenza and Pneumonia: 366,963 annual deaths

However, for some inscrutable reason, medical statisticians leave out what many consider to be one of the top-three leading causes of deaths. A 2023 CNN article by Deidre McPhillips stated, *"Misdiagnosis of disease or other medical conditions leads to hundreds of thousands of deaths and permanent disabilities each year in the United States. About 371,000 people die and 424,000 sustain permanent disabilities — such as brain damage, blindness, loss of limbs or organs, or metastasized cancer — each year as a result."*

The 2023 report she refers to (BMJ Journals, Volume 33, Issue 2, *"Burden of serious harms from diagnostic error in the USA"*) states: *"An estimated 795,000 Americans become permanently disabled or die annually across care settings because dangerous diseases are misdiagnosed."*

Looks like the third leading cause of death is debatable, depending on whom you ask.

According to the CDC, in 2021, *"Cigarette smoking remains the leading cause of preventable disease, disability, and death in the United States, accounting for more than 480,000 deaths every year, or about 1 in 5 deaths."* In comparison, the CDC listed the number of COVID-19 deaths in 2021 as 416,893. Sixty-three thousand more people died in 2021 from cigarettes than from COVID.

That's odd, because the CDC, in concert with U.S. government and

The Deep State Prepares for a Trump Victory

There are more than 2 million permanent bureaucrats, ensconced in 430 agencies, who imagine themselves to live outside the democratic system and the U.S. Constitution itself. They believe they are the state and the elected leaders are mere decoration.

The Politicians Who Forced Grandmas To Die Scared & Alone During Covid Are Still In Office

"health" professionals, shut down gyms, beaches, parks, restaurants, barbershops, nail salons, hairdressers, and the like, and rudely arrested barbers, gym owners, beachgoers, paddle boarders, and parents who had children on swing sets during the scamdemic, because COVID-19 was so utterly dangerous, as they repeatedly and even hysterically told us.

But they allowed people to buy cigarettes, soda pop, and junk food at the gas station, on one condition: they cover their faces when entering the store — to protect their health! And these edicts were coming from the "smartest people in the room"?

The insanity should be obvious here. And it should also be obvious why many people were not interested in following the strict mandates of medical professionals. Their expertise is in medicine, and their suggestions are welcome. But their priorities often seem to be off, and they have no right to force drugs on the public or to block the public from making their own decisions about how to take care of their own health. These are the same people who blocked everyone from getting fresh air, sunshine, exercise, and prepared food, while forcing masking, anti-social distancing, and experimental, untested drugs on people as young as six months, even on pregnant women, even on healthy people, even on people who had the virus and had natural immunity. In the meantime, *they themselves are our third leading cause of injury and death* at nearly 800,000 a year, eclipsing cigarettes at about 500,000 a year, and COVID at 417,000!

Doctors of Health

Maybe we should spend some of that defense budget to protect ourselves from these and other obvious threats. For example, medical training seems like it could use some help. But here's a better idea: Let's train *Doctors of Health* as well as Doctors of Medicine. Doctors of health would be trained in *health*. They would focus on the dietary and lifestyle foundations of health rather than drug therapies. They would work in concert with Doctors of Medicine as needed, although they would almost certainly reduce the number of patients who seek medical care. Imagine someone with an MD degree also having an HD degree. That would totally change the face of medicine and public health as we know it today.

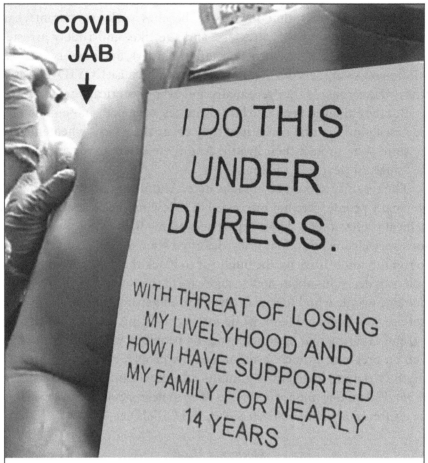

Coronavirus Cases Plummet When PCR Tests Are Adjusted

PCR tests cannot be used for any diagnose or virus detection

As a fundamental precept, let us underline that **Dr. Kary B. Mullis who received the Nobel Prize in chemistry in 1993 for inventing the PCR technique,** witnessed in many videos that he never developed this technique to detect viruses and serve as a disease diagnostics.

Before his death in 2019, he declared publicly in several occasions that **the PCR technique is an invention for in vitro research in the laboratory. He emphasized it is not intended nor reliable as a test for the public or as a medical diagnostic tool for physicians because it is inaccurate to detect any virus**.

Statement Non validity of "PCR test" and consequences for Mika Vauhkala by Dr Astrid Stückelberger PD PhD

The latest versions of the navy's anti-ship cruise missiles cost approximately $3 million each. Theoretically, the cost of only one "defense" missile could easily cover the educational costs for several people wanting to practice as Doctors of Health. Considering that a missile has an expected life of only 30 years, training competent Doctors of Health seems like a good way to spend defense money, especially when one considers the value such professionals would provide toward protecting our country from the real threats that we're faced with daily.

Incidentally, since missiles expire in 30 years, you may begin to understand why war dogs salivate for yet more wars. The expiring hardware needs to be used up and, of course, replacing it is very expensive. Taxpayers will pick up the tab. These may be good reasons for people who want forever wars, but these are also people without a conscience who would fall into the "greedy bastards" category of humanity. We should have a remote island for them to go to and we should give them a one-way ticket, free of charge.

What would a "Doctor of Health" (HD) do anyway? Let's look at some examples. A highschooler on the volleyball team comes home late from school several days a week because of practice. The team frequently stops for pizza and other fast food after the practice sessions. Eventually, the teenager becomes constipated. Not knowing what to do, her parents take her to a doctor, who prescribes a laxative. However, pharmaceutical drugs often come with side effects. Some laxatives are associated with increased colorectal cancer. Colon cancer rates have more than tripled in teens ages 15 to 19 in the past 20 years. Factors influencing gut health include not only laxatives but also antibiotics, which can damage the gut microbiota, and, of course, bad diets high in refined foods such as box pizza. Both the parents and the child need to learn about natural health and dietary nutrition. They need a *health* professional.

This is a very long and detailed topic. However, let's look at a couple more examples. One recent headline stated, *"Disturbances in Gut Flora Linked to Autism, ADHD Development."* Gut flora (microorganisms) are killed by antibiotics. Doctors will say that they're killed by infections, but it's not the infection that kills them, it's the treatment. Another recent headline reads, *"How What You Eat May Change Your Unborn Chil-*

Biden Administration Pushes Social Media Companies to Combat COVID-19 'Misinformation'

Surgeon General Vivek Murthy told reporters in Washington that he targeted social media misinformation with his first advisory because it "poses an imminent and insidious threat to our nation's health."

Biden is sued by state AGs for colluding with Big Tech on censorship

President Joe Biden and multiple top officials in his administration have been sued by two Republican-led states for pressuring and collusion with Big Tech to suppress free speech. The suit cites the Hunter Biden laptop story, the lab-leak theory, the security of mail-in voting, and the effectiveness of cloth masks.

Condemning Twitter's Censorship

As an independent news organization dedicated to reporting the truth, The Epoch Times has been subjected to excessive censorship by Big Tech. In the latest such incident, Twitter on July 28 censored all of our content by putting up a blockade to our website, describing it as "unsafe," and encouraging users not to proceed. Twitter's actions—just like those by other tech giants such as Facebook and YouTube specifically targeted the reach of our independent news and video content.

585 Million Now Killed or Injured by Covid Shots

"Best estimates are 585 million global citizens killed or injured from the COVID-19 'vaccines' and you have inflicted massive harm to pregnant women, pre-borns, and newborns on a global scale." In a bold move to protect patient health, Dr. James Thorp, a prominent Obstetrician and Maternal Fetal Medicine specialist, has issued a stark warning to leading medical organisations regarding the administration of COVID-19 vaccines to pregnant women.

Lawyers File Major Lawsuit Against Facebook, Twitter, Zuckerberg, and Dorsey

Attorneys John Pierce and former U.S. Rep. Bob Barr (R-Ga.) filed in May a federal civil RICO (racketeer influenced and corrupt organizations act) lawsuit seeking over $10 billion in damages against Facebook, Twitter, Mark Zuckerberg, and Jack Dorsey on behalf of Laura Loomer, a Republican who is running for Florida's 11th congressional district.

dren's Genes — and Affect Their Health." Clearly, we should value health professionals who are educated in how "what you eat" impacts your physical state of health.

Here's another, *"The Contentious Role of Food Dyes in Children's Diets."* There is an ongoing debate over whether synthetic food dyes (e.g., red candy, blue candy) disrupt young minds.

Or *"It Was Scientifically Proven Years Ago That a Diet High in Sugar Harms Your Brain."* The average American consumes over 40 pounds of high fructose corn syrup per year when eating the standard American diet. Rats fed on diets with high ructose corn syrup clearly became cognitively impaired. *"A diet steadily high in fructose slows the brain, hampering memory and learning."* A century ago, diabetes in this country was almost unheard of. Now, it's everywhere. You are what you eat.

Next headline: *"Researchers Discover New Mechanism Linking Diet and Cancer Risk."* A recent discovery suggests that a chemical, methylglyoxal (MGO), released whenever the body breaks down glucose, can temporarily switch off cancer-protecting mechanisms. Sugar feeds cancer cells, and this evidence supports that contention.

Another new study suggests a link between greater fluoride intake during pregnancy and toddlers with behavioral problems. Children whose mothers had higher levels of fluoride were 83% more likely to become affected.

How about we spend some of our "defense" budget to train health professionals to gain practical insight about these sorts of things. This is only the tip of the iceberg. Imagine how much healthier we would be as a society if we were educated, guided, and encouraged to pursue actual health rather than to ask for medical intervention when our bodies and minds are damaged by what we have put into them.

Neocommunism

And what about the basic building block of society, the family? Did the globalists and their oligarch masters manage to destroy it, much like the *The Communist Manifesto* had promoted? Did the WEF, the WHO, the UN, and the combined corporatist empires unite to form a Neocom-

Johns Hopkins University, in partnership with the World Economic Forum and the Bill & Melinda Gates Foundation, created a notable tabletop exercise known as "Event 201" in October 2019. This exercise was designed to simulate an outbreak of a novel zoonotic coronavirus that could be transmitted from bats to pigs to people, eventually leading to a severe pandemic. As we now know, the primary objective of "Event 201" was to brainwash the already mindless governmental apparatchiks to act in lockstep when COVID-19 trigger words and images get plastered all over media. To induce and maintain the level of fear of the "virus" with 99.8% survival rate necessary for the high degree of public acquiescence to illegal tyrannical measures, Johns Hopkins University developed the COVID-19 Dashboard. It was launched on January 22, 2020.

Court Hears Arguments Against Facebook, Zuckerberg and 'Fact Checkers'

Judge Susan Illston of the Northern District of California Wednesday heard arguments for and against the defendants' motion to dismiss in the Children's Health Defense (CHD) lawsuit, which claims that Facebook, Mark Zuckerberg and three fact-checking operations censor truthful public health posts and engage in racketeering activities against CHD. According to CHD's complaint, Facebook has insidious conflicts with the pharmaceutical industry and its captive health agencies, and has economic stakes in vaccines, telecom and 5G.

Court Rules Against Social Media Companies in Free Speech Censorship Fight

'We reject the idea that corporations have a freewheeling First Amendment right to censor what people say'

Over 50 Biden Administration Employees, 12 US Agencies Involved in Social Media Censorship Push: Documents

Moms for Liberty

Gender dysphoria is a mental health disorder that is being normalized by predators across the USA. California kids are at extreme risk from predatory adults. Now they want to "liberate" children all over the country. Does a double mastectomy on a preteen sound like progress?

munist juggernaut? Neocommunism is where private property ceases to exist, as Marx and Engels had insisted, *except for the wealthy elite minority.* They will keep their treasure and rake in what would have been yours to add to their pile of riches.

Under neocommunism, the family as the foundation of civilization would cease to exist. It would be replaced with gender confusion, mental depravity, biochemically mutated humans, and a blurring of the balance between male and female human beings. Children would be educated by the government, injected with medical drugs from birth, told what to think, rewarded for being obedient and conformist, punished for free thought or for independently questioning the status quo. Wait, that's already happening.

The medical experts who orchestrated the COVID scamdemic brought upon our nation the highest death count attributed to COVID anywhere in the world, by far. That single sentence should be repeated over and over, broadcast far and wide, and hammered into the minds of American citizens until they wake out of their brainwashed slumber. This same professional group is also the third leading cause of death in the United States. Yet, our big-pharma-controlled government will permit them to take children from loving, responsible parents because the mothers and fathers choose non-medical approaches to health care over drug injections for their children. What happened? Did the rights of children and families prevail, or were they trampled under the feet of big pharma's rush for profit? Was the family, as the foundation of civilization, protected and fortified, or did neocommunism wipe it out?

Fundamental Human Rights

Now would be a good time to review the *Fundamental Declaration of Human Rights.* Here are the points summarized:

1. Governments exist to serve the people.
2. The will of the people authorizes the government.
3. The killing of innocent people is prohibited.
4. Everyone has the right to a place on this Earth.

PayPal Demonetises Parents Campaign Group UsForThem That Took on School COVID-19 Closures

Set up in May 2020, UsForThem campaigned for the UK government to discontinue the use of masks for children and adults in school settings and evidenced the harm of lockdowns on kids.

PayPal Shuts Down Free Speech Union and The Daily Sceptic Accounts

He said he suspected the closure of the accounts could be down to a number of reasons including questioning transgender ideology, raising questions about COVID-19 vaccines, and articles critical of the mainstream narrative about the Ukraine war.

Tucker Carlson

This show learned that we were suspended from Twitter last night. What was our crime? We dared to highlight two accounts that Twitter has banned, Charlie Kirk and the Babylon Bee. There was a nothing hateful about either one. Both had noted that biological sex is fixed at birth, as has been universally acknowledged by Homo sapiens for at least 300,000 years.

Coroner: State included a murder-suicide in Grand's COVID deaths

In disputing the numbers, Bock explained that a couple who died of gunshot wounds late last month have been included in the state's numbers. The state told Bock those deaths are included in the count because the two tested positive for COVID-19 within 30 days before their death.

Twitter Censored Dr. Baric's CV and Its Documentation of Gain-of-Function Research and Me for Accurately Reporting the Story

The Intercept's recent Freedom of Information Act (FOIA) results added abundant documentation of Dr. Anthony Fauci's funding, using U.S. tax dollars, for dangerous gain-of-function research at the Wuhan lab–funding that Fauci had denied in testimony to Sen. Rand Paul (R-Ky.)–funding, indeed, that I had tried to share with the public on Twitter in early June, the day before Twitter deplatformed me permanently.

Fact check: Reports of adverse events due to COVID-19 vaccines are unverified
The claim: 1 million 'COVID-vaccine injuries' are reported in a CDC database
As hundreds of thousands of Americans test positive for COVID-19 each day, public health officials are encouraging booster shots to prevent the spread of the highly contagious omicron variant.

5. Everyone has the right to freedom of speech.

6. Everyone has the right to freedom of religion.

7. Everyone has the right to freedom of assembly.

8. Everyone has the right to freedom to publish.

9. Everyone has the right to own property.

10. The family is the basic unit of society and must be protected.

11. Parents have the right to choose their children's form of education.

12. Everyone has the right to medical informed consent.

13. Everyone has the right to choose their form of health care.

14. Everyone has the right to privacy.

15. Everyone has the right to be secure in their homes.

16. No one shall be subjected to arbitrary arrest.

17. Everyone is entitled to a fair trial.

18. Everyone has the right to self-defense.

What happened? Did these rights vanish under neocommunism, or did they flourish under direct democracy?

Pay close attention to Fundamental Right #3. Thou shalt not kill. Although this is also a Christian commandment, it is one that is repeatedly ignored. It has never been a fundamental right proclaimed and established by a government. Yes, killing one person is a crime called murder, which can put an individual in prison for life. But slaughtering hundreds of thousands of men, women, and children, at the command of civilian politicians who control the military, is not a crime. It's an act for which you will be bestowed the title of "hero," and for which medals will be placed upon your chest. You will likely get a promotion in rank.

Notable examples include the firebombing of the civilian city of Dresden, Germany, in February 1945, which killed tens of thousands of men, women, and children. Dresden was over 700 years old when the Americans and their allies bombed it. It was considered one of Europe's great art and architectural treasures. Nearly 30 generations had passed since the city had been founded. Craftsmen and women had developed extremely advanced skills in design and construction over those centuries and had built a magnificent city. What took centuries to achieve was destroyed in a matter of hours on the orders of civilian politicians, some of

Twitter Censors All Content From The Epoch Times

YouTube Bans Forced-Vaccination, Big Tech Critic Naomi Wolf

Wolf, a co-founder of the DailyClout website, is a widely published journalist and bestselling author of books such as "The Beauty Myth: How Images of Beauty Are Used Against Women" (1990) and "The End of America: Letter of Warning to a Young Patriot" (2007). She was an adviser to then-President Bill Clinton's 1996 reelection campaign and to then-Vice President Al Gore, both Democrats.

Twitter banned Wolf, who has been critical of vaccine passports and media coverage of the COVID-19 pandemic, earlier this summer, as The Epoch Times reported at the time. Twitter said Wolf had disseminated vaccine misinformation in violation of the microblogging website's policies, a claim she denies. Wolf said she can't state with certainty why YouTube suppressed the DailyClout channel.

People don't realize how hard it is to speak the truth, to a world full of people that don't realize they're living a lie -Edward Snowden

"FACT CHECKERS" DIDN'T EXIST UNTIL THE TRUTH STARTED GETTING OUT.

'Compared to influenza vaccines given over 34 years, COVID-19 vaccines in 36 months of use had over 1000-fold increased risk of most blood clot events, and compared to all vaccines combined administered over 34 years, this risk remained at over 200-times greater with COVID-19 vaccination.'

Excellent scholarship substack by McCullough et al.

The third-leading cause of death in US most doctors don't want you to know about

whom no doubt never even worked with their hands enough to develop callouses. While destroying the monumental accomplishments of generations of working-class people, the warmongers also guaranteed the deaths of tens of thousands of innocent civilians.

The bombing of the civilian cities of Hiroshima and Nagasaki in Japan in August of 1945 killed hundreds of thousands of men, women, and children, with many more dying of radiation poisoning afterward. Japan was over 2,000 years old when it was bombed. It also had highly developed cities and magnificent architecture. The 12-man crew on the Enola Gay, the B-29 that dropped the atomic bomb on Hiroshima, were mostly in their 20s. The captain, Theodore "Dutch" Van Kirk, was 24. The bombardier who pushed the button to drop the bomb, Thomas Ferebee, was 26. These men turned an ancient city the size of Dallas into ashes in a matter of minutes, then flew home and were congratulated for what they did.

The nation of Vietnam was well over 3,000 years old when American B52 bombers flew over the rice patties and villages in the 1960s and 1970s, "carpet bombing" the people who lived there. Here was a nation that was as close to "sustainable" as we can imagine. Their agricultural system was completely organic and dated back thousands of years. The villagers made their clothing by hand, pumped water from wells using foot power, crafted their own furniture from the surrounding jungle trees, and lived in harmony with nature in a manner that we can't comprehend in America today. Our politicians, our representatives, small-minded, fearful, ignorant, greedy, corrupt, and pathetic individuals, had convinced the American population, at least the TV-watchers, that the Vietnamese people needed to be violently assailed, invaded, and, if they resisted, destroyed.

There is no need to review the atrocities against innocent populations that have occurred worldwide, paid for by American taxpayers. We have already touched upon them throughout this book. But let's not forget one very important point: War is failure. War is insanity. War is caused by human individuals, primarily by politicians. We cannot allow them to continue. They must be stopped. Let's sacrifice an island somewhere and ship the warmongers off to a permanent vacation so we can all live in peace. This idea is not as frivolous as it may seem. War is the enemy. We only fight each other because of failures in leadership. Let's pull the weeds out of the garden of humanity, and start a compost heap with them somewhere far away. Very far away.

Who Pockets the Interest Payments on our National Debt?

It became clear in the early 2020s that a vast, international, dark, quasi-government could not only control international policy throughout the TV-watching world, but it could, and would, cast aside all of the rights listed above. How? By creating a new disease vector and releasing it into the world, then engaging in a massive psychological operation to scare the hell out of everyone who watches TV and other media platforms under its control. Then, inform the huddling masses that the only means for their survival is in the cure *they* provide — a series of drug injections that appear to have been designed for something other than a respiratory virus. This is what they did. This is what happened in the early 2020s.

Before viruses were added to the public list of enemies, to the list of things that were threatening to destroy us, it wasn't heart disease, cancer, or medical error on the list; it was the Koreans, the Vietnamese, the Communists, the Terrorists, the Iraqis, the Afghans, the socialists, and a government lineup of dictators, scoundrels, or criminals warranting American bomb attacks and military interventions. These included Manuel Noriega, Saddam Hussein, Muammar Gaddafi, Bashar al-Assad, Kim Jong-Il, Joseph Stalin, Osama bin Laden, and many others whose personalities were used to justify huge military buildups in the United States as well as wars and interventions, some of which we have already mentioned.

Not specifically mentioned is the even longer list of dictators, scoundrels, and criminals who were supported and/or financed by the American taxpayer, no matter how authoritative, repressive, or murderous they may have been. All of this is the result of our government, or, more specifically, the people who control it, intended to siphon money from the taxpayer, funnel it into a military budget account, then use it to convert our natural resources into bullets, bombs, tanks, missiles, and other weapons. Not to mention financing proxy armies intended to overthrow democratically elected leaders who were unfortunate enough to consider themselves socialists and to be caught in the crosshairs of American fear, rage, and greed. Our converted natural resources are then blown up, along with millions of people, many, if not most of whom, are innocent, including our own military soldiers, who are forced to follow the orders of leaders, however deficient in wisdom they may be.

In the process, huge profits are raked in by the political factions lurking in the swamp. All that is required is a scared American population, a poorly educated citizenry, and a boiled frog culture. In 2024, it was estimated that our national debt, then at 35 trillion dollars, would climb to 55 trillion dollars within ten years. We were already paying a trillion dollars a year in interest payments. Every night while Americans sleep, tens of billions of dollars of interest payments disappear from their treasury and slide into someone's pockets. Who were the people raking in this windfall? Could they also be the ones who were most vociferously pushing for wars, pulling the strings of the government to run up the already obscene debt? Why was this question not being asked anywhere? What was the answer?

What happened next? Did we put an end to the forever wars? Did we root out the individuals behind them and bring them to justice Nuremberg-style? Did we the people rise up, affirm our rights, strengthen our democracy, hunt down and prosecute the dark, quasi-government, shine a light on the cockroaches, clean up the deep state, and drain the swamp? Or did we continue to stand aside and watch the rats clustering around our unguarded treasury unhindered, like pigs feeding at a trough, gobbling up our tax dollars like a locust plague wiping out our amber waves of grain? If we were stupid enough to allow the thievery to continue, it could be argued that we deserved it. But our children do not deserve it, nor do our grandchildren. They rely on us to leave them a world of beauty, prosperity, and hope. It is our responsibility. What did we do?

Meritocracy

Assuming random selection became implemented and direct democracy prevailed, then, among other things, the entire process became a popular feature of TV and social media. Eyes would be glued on the random selection process. The final round of candidates would be interviewed and showcased, with the final selection of representatives treated like celebrities. The showcasing of democracy would provide a new and unique entertainment niche in the media world. Citizen engagement and participation would be at an all-time high.

The focus on meritocracy as a means of advancement in government would allow legislative representatives to become preferred candidates for executive branch positions after their legislative terms have been completed. Successful, respected representatives could then become candidates for governorships and/or other elected government roles. We the people would eventually create processes to even the playing field in general elections so that working-class people would be able to mount serious candidacies and not be at a disadvantage compared with the ultra-wealthy or to people who are financed by the oligarchs.

One good thing about the scamdemic was that it exposed the people who want to trample on the Constitution and replace it with tyranny. All anyone had to do was to post a comment on any social media about a "vaccine injury," and any media that was aligned with big pharma would censor it, block it, or label it "misinformation." Why would they want to block important information about people who are injured by an experimental drug? The Vaccine Adverse Event Reporting System, (VAERS) had 1.6 million reports of adverse events associated with the COVID drugs and rising. The 1.6 million is estimated to be 1% to 10% of the actual total.

Who would block information about drug side effects and adverse reactions then force more and more people to get the drug injections? Why would anyone do this? Is it because the forcing of experimental, untested, DNA-altering drugs on billions of people under conditions of rigid coercion, intense propaganda, unwavering censorship, and threats of violence is a crime against humanity, and therefore any mention of the harms done by these crimes has to be blocked by the people who committed them?

All anyone had to do was to mention election fraud in the 2020 presidential election, and the same cabal of ultrawealthy elitists would block, censor, smear, defame, and destroy anyone who opened their mouths. Why? Is it because they knew that election fraud of this scale constitutes the crime of treason and that they were complicit in that crime?

Anyone who speaks out against the never-ending warfare, the "forever wars," is branded a traitor, a tool of Putin, and a Russian asset. If they're a member of Congress, they're attacked by the media and by the mainstream propaganda outlets, then they're driven out of power.

Ironically, the boiled frogs know little or nothing about any of this. They only see and hear what the propaganda platforms allow them to see and hear. What happened? Did the boiled frogs wake up, cast aside the propaganda devices, abandon the brainwashing machines, open their eyes, think for themselves, engage in independent research, and move civilization constructively forward? No doubt many have. Did the rest follow?

It didn't start with gas chambers. It started with one party controlling the media. One party controlling the message. One party deciding what is truth. One party censoring speech and silencing opposition. One party dividing citizens into "us" and "them" and calling on their supporters to harass "them." It started when good people turned a blind eye and let it happen.

REFERENCES

ARIZONA

'They're Trying to Run Out the Clock': Kari Lake Files 1st Lawsuit Aft... Zachary Stieber, 11/24/2022. theepochtimes.com

A major Arizona county ran out of ballots during primary voting. Republicans are now demanding the election director resign. Katie Anthony, Aug 3, 2022. MSN.com

Arizona County Refuses to Certify Election Results, Threatening A GOP House Win - PRICKLY PEAR. Arjun Singh. MSN.com

Angry Maricopa Residents Deliver Blunt Election Comments During B... Allan Stein, 1/18/2022. https://www.theepochtimes.com

Arizona Certifies 2022 Midterm Election Results. Zachary Stieber, 12/5/2022. theepochtimes.com

Arizona Democrat Katie Hobbs Colluded with Twitter to Censor Americans for 'Election Misinformation,' Leaked Email Shows. Frank Bergman. slaynews.com

Arizona Democrat Sentenced to 30 Days in Jail for Ballot Harvesting. Bill Pan, 10/16/2022. https://www.theepochtimes.com

Arizona GOP Offers $50,000 Reward for Evidence of Vote Buying. Allan Stein, 7/21/2022. https://www.theepochtimes.com

Arizona Gov Katie Hobbs Demanded Twitter Censor Her Critics, Emails Show - Slay News. Frank Bergman. slaynews.com

Arizona Mohave County Board of Supervisors to Discuss Litigation Against Maricopa County for Fraudulent Election. Jim Hoft, 12/8/2022. thegatewaypundit.com

Arizona Official Demands Investigation of Kari Lake on Potential Felony Charges. Tom Ozimek, 1/31/2023. theepochtimes.com

Arizona Protesters Demand Election Redo Amid Claims of 'Serious Voter Suppression.' Tom Ozimek, 11/26/2022. theepochtimes.com

AZ Secretary of State Says Resolution Banning the Use of Voting Machines Will Not Be Enforced. Shane Trejo. thepricklypear.org

Arizona Senator Files Lawsuit, Seeks to 'Nullify the Results' of Maricopa County's Election. Jack Phillips, 12/13/2022. https://www.theepochtimes.com

Arizona Set to Certify the Lake-Hobbs Race; Here Are 3 Key Takeaways. Patricia Tolson, 12/3/2022. theepochtimes.com

Arizona Supreme Court Orders Hearing on Kari Lake's Signature Verification Case. Jack Phillips, 5/5/2023. theepochtimes.com

Arizona's Law to Confirm Who Mails in Election Ballots (Signature Verification) is Ignored to Steal Elections. Joe Hoft, 12/26/2022. thegatewaypundit.com

Ballots Cast Without Proof of Citizenship 'Exploded' After Lawfare Crippled Arizona Election Laws. Prickly Pear. M.D. Kittle. https://thepricklypear.org

Behind Closed Doors: More on Runbeck Election Services in Maricopa County and the Scanning of Ballot Envelopes. Jim Hoft. thegatewaypundit.com

Gateway Pundit Was Right! -- AZ Media PR Company Find Impossible Variant in Election Day Data - 25% of GOP Voters Flipped their Votes on Top GOP Candidates. Jim Hoft. thegatewaypundit.com

Maricopa County Files Response to Kari Lake - Claims Tabulators Were Working as Intended When 60% FAILED on Election Day. Jordan Conradson. thegatewaypundit.com

Brnovich Ignoring Credible Concerns About Ballots Cast Through Arizona's Overseas Internet Portal. arizonadailyindependent.com

Close Arizona Gubernatorial Race Could Be Headed to Recount. Zachary Stieber, 11/25/2022. https://www.theepochtimes.com

CORRUPT Maricopa County Supervisors Ask Judge To Sanction Trump- Endorsed Mark Finchem and Kari Lake Over Lawsuit To Ban Voting Machines. Jordan Conradson. thegatewaypundit.com

CORRUPTION: Arizona GOP head Jeff DeWit Stepping Down After Leaked Audio Tapes - The Editors. thepricklypear.org

Court of Appeals Agrees to Expedite Kari Lake's 2022 Election Case. Jack Phillips, 1/1322023. https://www.theepochtimes.com

Court rules Arizona's ballot signature verification guidance doesn't have force of law. Charlotte Hazard. https://justthenews.com/

Governor Hobbs Thumbs Nose at Election Integrity and American Manufacturing. https://arizonadailyindependent.com/2023/05/17

Group Releases Analysis of Pinal County's 2022 Election, Finds 'Deliberate Malfeasance,' Concludes Election Should Not Have Been Certified. Rachel Alexander. https://thepricklypear.org

Investigation finds printers and ballot size responsible for 2022 election troubles in Arizona. Emily Jacobs. https://www.washingtonexaminer.com

Judge Denies Katie Hobbs Request to Sanction Kari Lake Over Arizona Election Lawsuit. Jack Phillips, 12/27/2022. https://www.theepochtimes.com

Judge Dismisses Bid to Quash Jan. 6 Panel Subpoena of Arizona GOP Party Chair's Phone Records. Caden Pearson, 9/24/2022. https://www.theepochtimes.com/mkt_app/judge-dismisses-bid-to-quash-...

Judge Makes Massive Decision in Arizona Election Case. Carmine Sabia. conservativebrief.com

Judge Orders Arizona's Cochise County to Certify Election Results. Caden Pearson, 12/2/2022. https://www.theepochtimes.com

Judge Orders Kari Lake and Katie Hobbs to Appear at Emergency Court Hearing Over Election Lawsuit. Jack Phillips, 12/13/2022. https://www.theepochtimes.com

Judge Rules on Kari Lake's Latest Legal Challenge. Tom Ozimek, 5/23/2023. theepochtimes.com/

AZ Senate Elections Committee Chair Senator Wendy Rogers Fires Off Public Records Request to Inspect Maricopa County 2022 Ballot Signatures. Apr. 3, 2023. thegatewaypundit.com

Kari Lake Calls for Arizona GOP Chair to Resign After Leaked Audio. Caden Pearson, 9124/2024. https://www.theepochtimes.com

Kari Lake Files Lawsuit in Arizona Challenging Gubernatorial Results. Carmine Sabia. https://conservativebrief.com

Kari Lake Files Opening Brief with Arizona Court of Appeals in Election Lawsuit Containing New Evidence and Alleging Crimes. The Arizona Sun Times. Rachel Alexander. arizonasuntimes.com

Kari Lake Issues Warning as Her Lawyers Face Discipline. Jack Phillips. theepochtimes.com

Kari Lake Says She 'Will Become Governor' After Attorney General's Letter. Jack Phillips, 11/20/2022. theepochtimes.com

Kari Lake Says She Is Still 'Laser-Focused' on Arizona Election Lawsuit. Jack Phillips, 4/18/2023. https://www.theepochtimes.com

Kari Lake Uncovers Bombshell New Evidence to Support Cybersecurity Expert's Findings in Maricopa County. Frank Bergman. https://slaynews.com

Katie Hobbs Lawyer Moves to Dismiss Kari Lake's Lawsuit. Jack Phillips, 12/15/2022. https://www.theepochtimes.com

Lake Issues 1st Major Update in Arizona Since Hobbs Declared Victory. Zachary Stieber, 11/17/2022. theepochtimes.com

Lake v Hobbs Case in Arizona *DISMISSED*. We're Sure You Can Guess Why. Brian Lupo, 8/27/2022. thegatewaypundit.com

Maricopa County Recorder Furious after Judge Rules Maricopa County's Election Procedures Are Unlawful - News Addicts. Hunter Fielding. https://newsaddicts.com

Maricopa County Should 'Delay Certification' of 2022 Election: GOP. ack Phillips, 11/27/2022. https://www.theepochtimes.com

Maricopa County Superior Court Judge Refuses to Grant Access to Ballot Envelopes for Kari Lake in Third Election Trial. Hunter Fielding. https://newsaddicts.com

Mohave County Delays Certifying Arizona Election Results in Protest. Caden Pearson, 11/22/2022. https://www.theepochtimes.com

New Testimony Confirms Ballot Tampering in Maricopa's 2022 Election. Wendi Strauch Mahoney. https://www.uncoverdc.com

Predetermined Algorithms Source of Widespread Election Fraud in Arizona. uncoverdc.com.

SCOTUS Filing Contains Three 'Bombshell' Developments That Show How Elections Can Be Rigged. Melinda Davies, March 21, 2024. newsaddicts. com

Supreme Court Justice Kagan Temporarily Blocks Jan. 6 Committee Subpoena for Phone Records... Mimi Nguyen Ly, 10/26/2022. theepochtimes.com

Thousands of Ballots Cast in Arizona 2020 Election without Proof of US Citizenship - News Addicts. Melinda Davies. https://newsaddicts.com

Trump Alleges Voter Fraud in Arizona Senate Race, Demands Do-Over. Tom Ozimek, 11/12/2022. https://www.theepochtimes.com

We're Suing Adrian Fontes for His Illegal Elections Procedures Manual. Arizona Free Enterprise Club. thepricklypear.org

Were They Told to Stand Down? The DOJ's Arizona Election Fraud Investigators Go AWOL Following 2020 and 2022 Elections – Where Are They Today? thegatewaypundit.com

BIDEN

Biden Just Got a Huge "Secret" Boost - Big Money Comes Flowing to Joe from Concerning Source. Mick Farthing. https://pjnewsletter.com

Biden Pick for Intelligence Board Signed Infamous Hunter Biden Laptop Letter. Zachary Stieber, 8/29/2022. theepochtimes.com/

Biden Scores Big Win in Censorship Case as Appeals Court Lifts Block on Contacting Big Tech. Frank Bergman. slaynews.com

Biden Will Win Democratic Nomination Hands Down, Says Prominent Presidential Historian. Alice Giordano, 5/1/2023. https://www.theepochtimes.com

Biden 'Won' 2020 Election with Mail-in Ballot Fraud, Study Confirms - News Addicts. Hunter Fielding. https://newsaddicts.com

DOJ Conceals Records About Biden's Use of Federal Agencies To Influence Elections. 2022/09/12. thefederalist.com.

DOJ Is Hiding How It's Complying with Biden's Voter Registration Drive. Frank Wang/Eva Fu. 10/18/2022. theepochtimes.com

GOP Senators Hunter Biden Prosecutor Be Made Special Counsel. Tristan Justice. https://thefederalist.com

Hunter Biden Laptop Repairman Reveals 'Chilling' Warning from FBI Agent. Jack Phillips. 11/21/2022. theepochtimes.com

President Biden Sued Over Executive Order Interfering in State Elections. Melinda Davies. https://newsaddicts.com

Wall Street and Hollywood Titans Team Up to Back Biden. Austin Alonzo. 2/13/2024. https://www.theepochtimes.com

CENSORSHIP

Alert: Ex-Wikipedia Co-Founder Says Site Hijacked by US Intelligence for 'Info Warfare.' The Western Journal. https://www.thegatewaypundit.com/

Breaking: Jordan Releases 'Smoking Gun Docs' Confirming Facebook Bowed to White House Censorship Demands. John-Michael Dumais. 7/27/2023. https://childrenshealthdefense.org

Breaking: Landmark Lawsuit Slaps Legacy Media with Antitrust, First Amendment Claims for Censoring COVID. Michael Nevradakis Ph.D. 1/10/2023. https://childrenshealthdefense.org

CISA Was Behind the Attempt to Control Your Thoughts, Speech, and Life. Brownstone Institute. https://thepricklypear.org/

Citing 'Orwellian' Tactics, Federal Judge Orders White House to Stop Censoring Social Media Posts. Michael Nevradakis Ph.D. 7/05/2023. https://childrenshealthdefense.org

The Weaponization of "Disinformation" Pseudo-Experts and Bureaucrats: How the Federal Government Partnered with Universities to Censor Americans' Political Speech. Interim Staff Report of the Committee on the Judiciary and the Select Subcommittee on the Weaponization of the Federal Government. U.S. House of Representatives. November 6, 2023

Elon Musk Reveals Extent of Old Twitter Regime's Censorship. WLT Report. Vince Quill. 9/14/2023. https://wltreport.com

Facebook 'Fact Checker' Caught Running Political Censorship Operation to Manipulate Voters. Frank Bergman. slaynews.com

Enemies list? Fed-backed censorship machine targeted 20 news sites. Greg Piper. 10/1/2022. justthenews.com

State of Missouri; State of Louisiana; Aaron Kheriaty; Martin Kulldorff; Jim Hoft; Jayanta Bhattacharya; Jill Hines, Plaintiffs—Appellees, versus Joseph R. Biden, Jr.; Vivek H. Murthy; Xavier Becerra; Department of Health & Human Services; Anthony Fauci; Et al., Defendants. Appeal from the United States District Court for the Western District of Louisiana USDC No. 3:22-CV-1213. FILED September 8, 2023

Government-Backed Censors Who Rigged the 2020 Election Are Now Stealing 2024. thepricklypear.org. John Daniel Davidson.

Here's How Big Tech Plans to Rig The 2022 Midterms. Victoria Marshall. 9/14/2022. thefederalist.com

House Republicans Shine a Light On The Feds' Egregious Censorship-Industrial Complex. Shawn Fleetwood. thepricklypear.org

How they program your mind… Who is Robert Malone (Substack)

Incoming DOJ Official Pressured Twitter to Remove Tweets About GA Election Irregularities, Emails Show Article Reports. evol.news

O'Keefe: Biden's No. 3 DOJ Pick Demanded Twitter Censor Project Veritas's Undercover Reporting on Illegal Voter Registration in Fulton County. https://evol.news/

Propaganda and The US Government. Who is Robert Malone (Substack)

The Weaponization of the National Science Foundation: How NSF is Funding the Development of Automated Tools to Censor Online Speech "At Scale" and Trying to Cover Up Its Actions. Interim Staff Report of the Committee on the Judiciary and the Select Subcommittee on the Weaponization of the Federal Government U.S. House of Representatives.

Deep State Censorship Exposed. Who is Robert Malone (Substack)

"How a 'Cybersecurity' Agency Colluded with Big Tech and 'Disinformation' Partners to Censor Americans": The Weaponization of CISA - Interim staff report for the Committee on the Judiciary and the Select Subcommittee.

The Perversion of FISA and FISC. Who is Robert Malone (Substack)

The White House's 'Misinformation' Pressure Campaign Was Unconstitutional. Aaron Kheriaty, 9/30/2023. brownstone.org.

Tulsi Gabbard Sues Google for Silencing Her Campaign. The People's Voice. thepeoplesvoice.tv

Users Outraged by Instagram and Threads Limiting Political Content Ahead of Election. Jen Krausz. 3/24/2024. theepochtimes.com

CONSTITUTION

Constitution of the United States. https://constitution.congress.gov

Declaration of Independence: A Transcription. archives.gov/founding-docs/ declaration-transcript

Constitution Annotated. https://Constitution.Congress.gov/constitution

The 'Unexploded Bomb' in the Constitution That's Threatening the 2024 Election. By Petr Svab. 1/20/2024. theepochtimes.com

What If the President Ignores the Supreme Court? Jeffrey A. Tucker. 3/14/2024. theepochtimes.com

The Declaration of the Rights of Man and of the Citizen, 1789. National Assembly of France.

Black Dems & NPR Trashed the Declaration of Independence Yesterday. zerohedge.com

Constitution 101 Module 15: The Constitution as Amended: Article V and a Walking Tour of America's 27 Constitutional Amendments. 15.3 Info Brief. National Constitution Center. ConstitutionCenter.org.

15th Amendment - Definition, Date & Summary. history.com

A Declaration of Independence. Who is Robert Malone (Substack).

COVID

Nicolas Hulscher, Paul E. Alexander, Richard Amerling, Heather Gessling, Roger Hodkinson, William Makis, Harvey A. Risch, Mark Trozzi and Peter A. McCullough, A Systematic REVIEW of Autopsy findings in deaths after COVID-19 vaccination, Forensic Science International, (2024) doi:https://doi.org/10.1016/j.forsciint.2024.112115

How public health's ideological capture by left-wing ideology systematically undermined the public health response to the COVID-19 pandemic. Kevin Bass. 4/21/2024. https://kevinbass.substack.com

Safety signals for 770 different serious adverse events in VAERS were ignored by the CDC. Steve Kirsch. KirschSubstack.com

28 Types of Kidney Complications Reported Following COVID-19 Vaccination. Marina Zhang. 3/15/2024. theepochtimes.com

Pfizer Scientist Admits Deadly Vax Side Effects Were Planned. NewsAddicts.com. Hunter Fielding.

Doctors Warn COVID-19 mRNA Jabs Can Cause Primary Cutaneous CD4 Small/Medium T-Cell Lymphoproliferative Disorders and Cutaneous Lymphomas! Mar 18, 2024. ThailandMedical.news

Japanese Researchers Warn About Risks Associated with Blood Transfusions From COVID-19 mRNA Vaccinated Individuals. ThailandMedicalNews.com

Never Forget, Never Forgive, Never Again. The presidency of Donald J. Trump ended on a bleak day in February 2020 when he ceded control of the United States of America to a malevolent midget with a medical degree named Anthony Fauci. Michael Walsh. the-pipeline.org

9 New 'Vaccine Billionaires' Amass Combined Net Worth of $19.3 Billion During Pandemic. 05/25/21. childrenshealthdefense.org

$3 Billion of Taxpayer Money to Be Used on Ad Campaign to Increase Vaccine Uptake. Dr. Joseph Mercola. 5/25/2021. childrenshealthdefense.org

Late-Night Host Ghoulishly Mocks Sick and Unvaccinated: 'Rest in Peace, Wheezy.' Grant Atkinson. WesternJournal.com

Breakthrough COVID infections show 'the unvaccinated are now putting the vaccinated at risk.' PBS.org

Indian Study on AstraZeneca COVID-19 Vaccine: Troubling Atypical Adverse Event Rate — 9.7% of Boosted Population Injured. Staff at TrialSite, May. 21, 2024. trialsitenews.com

Israel Didn't Check Most Reports of COVID Vaccine Side Effects: Watchdog. Zachary Stieber. 5/29/2024. theepochtimes.com

Masks Found to Be Ineffective After First Omicron Wave: New Study. Megan Redshaw J.D. 5/29/2024. theepochtimes.com.

Government Stockpiling Vaccines ahead of Pre-Election Pandemic. Hunter Fielding. NewsAddicts.com.

Billions of Copies of Residual DNA in a Single Dose of COVID-19 mRNA Vaccine. Marina Zhang 11/7/2023. theepochtimes.com

OpenSAFELY: Effectiveness of COVID-19 vaccination in children and adolescents. Colm D Andrews, Edward P K Parker, Elsie Horne, Venexia Walker, Tom Palmer, Andrea L Schaffer, Amelia CA Green, Helen J Curtis, Alex J Walker, Lucy Bridges, Christopher Wood, Victoria Spee, Christopher Bates, Jonathan Cockburn, John Parry, Amir Mehrkar, Brian MacKenna, Sebastian CJ Bacon, Ben Goldacre, Miguel A Hernan, Jonathan AC Sterne, The OpenSAFELY Collaborative, and William J Hulme.

Classen JB. COVID-19 RNA Based Vaccines and the Risk of Prion Disease. Microbiology of Infectious Disease. 2021; 5(1): 1-3.

Could COVID Shots Trigger 'Avalanche' of a Contagious Form of Dementia? Dr. Joseph Mercola. ChildrensHealthDefense.org

Drugmakers' Secret Royalty Payments to Fauci's NIAID Exploded After Inquiry: Report. Mark Tapscott. 6/3/2024. theepochtimes.com

Swine flu 'could kill up to 120m.' 4/26/2009. Metro.co.uk.

Facing Inquiry, WHO Strikes Back at "Fake Pandemic" Swine Flu Criticism. 1/14/2010. Martin Enserink. ScienceInsider. Health

COVID-19 Vaccine Linked to Sudden Onset Tinnitus; Metabolic Disease Increases Risk: Study. Marina Zhang. 6/3/2024. theepochtimes.com

The Pharmaceutical Conspiracy to Silence Online Dissent is Bigger Than You Think. 4/16/2024. By vnninfluencers. Originally appeared on The Forgotten Side of Medicine. Guest post by A Midwestern Doctor.

Possible toxicity of chronic carbon dioxide exposure associated with face mask use, particularly in pregnant women, children and adolescents – A scoping review. Kai Kisielinski, Susanne Wagner, Oliver Hirsch, Bernd Klosterhalfen, Andreas Prescher. 3/3/2023. https://doi.org/10.1016/j.heliyon.2023.e14117

Non validity of "PCR test" and consequences for Mika Vauhkala by Dr Astrid Stückelberger. astrid.stuckelberger@gmail.com

Physical interventions to interrupt or reduce the spread of respiratory viruses. Cochrane Database of Systematic Reviews, 2023, Issue 1. Art. No.: CD006207. DOI: 10.1002/14651858.CD006207.pub6. Jeerson T, Dooley L, Ferroni, Al-Ansary, van Driel ML, Bawazeer GA, Jones MA, Homann, TC, Clark J, Beller EM, Glasziou PP, Conly JM. cochranelibrary.com

Haiti has lower coronavirus death counts with more restrictions. Why? Jacqueline Charles. 12/16/2020. Miami Herald

Africa Is Starkly Unvaccinated, And Starkly Unvanquished by COVID. Tyler Durden. zerohedge.com

Proposed Brazil Laws to Imprison Anti-vaxxers for up to a Decade! Critical of the Vaccine? Jail Time, Too. TrialSite Staff. 1/31/2023. trialsitenews.com

Mostert S, Hoogland M, Huibers M, et al. Excess mortality across countries in the Western World since the COVID-19 pandemic: 'Our World in Data' estimates of Jan. 2020 to Dec. 2022. BMJ Public Health 2024;2:e000282. doi:10.1136/bmjph-2023-000282

Double Digits: Biden Admin Tells

Americans It's Almost Time for Their 10th COVID Shot. June 14, 2024. By vnninfluencers. Originally appeared on The Dossier. Guest post by Jordan Schachtel

Very large Cleveland Clinic study shows more vaccines make you more likely to get COVID. Steve Kirsch. kirschsubstack.com

Risk of Coronavirus Disease 2019 (COVID-19) among Those Up-to-Date and Not Up-to-Date on COVID-19 Vaccination by US CDC Criteria. Nabin K. Shrestha, Patrick C. Burke, Amy S. Nowacki, Steven M. Gordon. 9/14/2023. Department of Infectious Diseases, Cleveland Clinic, Cleveland, Ohio.

A summary of the evidence against the COVID vaccines. Steve Kirsch. 1/07/2024. kirschsubstack.com

New Zealand data leaked by Barry Young has a smoking gun: a 27% increase in all-cause mortality over 12 months if you got the jab. Steve Kirsch. 6/20/2024. https://kirschsubstack.com

Apple Valley Village Health Care Center saw 7X higher COVID death rates after COVID vax rollout. Wasn't it supposed to decrease rates? Steve Kirsch. 8/15/2023. https://kirschsubstack.com

The COVID "vaccine" had no benefit. Zero. Zip. Nada. Steve Kirsch. 6/19/2024. https://kirschsubstack.com

Vaccine-Induced Immune Response to Omicron Wanes Substantially Over Time. 7/19/2022. https://www.nih.gov

California makes face coverings mandatory outside the home. Ray Sanchez. 6/19/2020. CNN.com

Blood clots to the brain (devastating) following Malone Bourla Bancel Sahin Weissman et al. (Pfizer, Moderna, BioN...). Substack by McCullough et al. COVID-19 Vaccines: A Risk Factor for Cerebral Thrombotic Syndromes[v2]. Preprints.org

Widow of scientist who invented PCR test hits out at COVID denier conspiracists who claim he was murdered... Alex Diaz. The-Sun.com

Kary Mullis, inventor of the PCR test, died of "pneumonia" on August 7, 2019, just 3 days before Epstein's "death." Mullis was very critical of Dr. Fauci and his cohorts in the past. DeadEndFred. reddit.com/r/conspiracy/comments/hwb3bl/kary_mullis_in ...

In New York's largest hospital system, many coronavirus patients on ventilators didn't make it. Ariana Eunjung Cha. WashingtonPost.com

Do COVID-19 Vent Protocols Need a Second Look? John Whyte, MD, MPH; Cameron Kyle-Sidell, MD. Medscape.com

Why Remdesivir Failed: Preclinical Assumptions Overestimate the Clinical Efficacy of Remdesivir for COVID-19 and Ebola. Victoria C. Yan, Florian L. Muller. 9/17/21. Amer. Society for Microbiology.

Exclusive: Fired ICU Nurse Speaks Out on COVID Protocols, Vaccine Injuries. John-Michael Dumais. ChildrensHealthDefense.org

Many Pregnant Women Were Forced to Get COVID Shots. Here's What Happened to Them. Dr. Joseph Mercola. ChildrensHealthDefense.org

'I Knew They Were Killing People': Whistleblower Says COVID Hospital Protocols Led to Patient Deaths. John-Michael Dumais. ChildrensHealthDefense.org

A Randomized, Controlled Trial of Ebola Virus Disease Therapeutics. Authors: Sabue Mulangu, M.D., Lori E. Dodd, Ph.D., Richard T. Davey, Jr., M.D., Olivier Tshiani Mbaya, M.D., Michael Proschan, Ph.D., Daniel Mukadi, M.D., Mariano Lusakibanza Manzo, Ph.D., +10 , Didier Nzolo, M.D. https://orcid.org/0000-0002-1297-9581, Antoine Tshomba Oloma, M.D., Augustin Ibanda, B.S., Rosine Ali, M.S., Sinaré Coulibaly, M.D., Adam C. Levine, M.D. https://orcid.org/0000-0003-3982-3824, Rebecca Grais, Ph.D., Janet Diaz, M.D., H. Clifford Lane, M.D. https://orcid.org/0000-0001-9509-1045, and Jean-Jacques Muyembe-Tamfum, M.D., for the PALM Consortium Study Team-10. Published 11/27/2019. N Engl J Med 2019;381:2293-2303. DOI: 10.1056/NEJMoa1910993

A Critical Analysis of All-Cause Deaths during COVID-19 Vaccination in an Italian Province. Peter A. McCullough, MD, MPH. [Alessandria, M.; Malatesta, G.M.;

Berrino, F.; Donzelli, A. A, Critical Analysis of All-Cause Deaths during COVID-19 Vaccination in an Italian Province. Microorganisms 2024, 12, 1343. https://doi.org/10.3390/microorganisms12071343]

A Systematic REVIEW of Autopsy findings in deaths after COVID-19 vaccination. Nicolas Hulscher, Paul E. Alexander, Richard Amerling, Heather Gessling, Roger Hodkinson, William Makis, Harvey A. Risch, Mark Trozzi, Peter A. McCullough. PII: S0379-0738(24)00196-8. DOI: https://doi.org/10.1016/j.forsciint.2024.112115. Reference: FSI112115. Forensic Science International

Pfizer Buys Up Companies That Profit from Treating Vaccine Injuries. Hunter Fielding. NewsAddicts.com.

Pfizer CEO Albert Bourla Refused to Take COVID Vaccine. Kate Stephenson. NewsAddicts.com

Population Mortality Worsens Over Pandemic Years, Peter A. McCullough, MD, MPH.

German Bombshell? Respected Researchers' Investigation Demonstrates COVID-19 Vaccination Correlates with Excess German Deaths Across Federal States. 6/28/2024. trialsitenews.com

Are COVID-19 Vaccines in Pregnancy as Safe and Effective as the U.S. Government, Medical Organizations, and Pharmaceutical Industry Claim? Part II. James A Thorp, Albert Benavides, Maggie M Thorp, Daniel C McDyer, Kimberly O Biss, Julie A Threet, Peter A McCullough. 7/1/2024. doi:10.20944/preprints202407.0069.v1

Differential Increases in Excess Mortality in the German Federal States During the COVID-19 Pandemic. Christof Kuhbandner and Matthias Reitzner. researchgate.net/publication/378124684

U.S. buys additional 200 million doses of Pfizer vaccine. 7/23/2021. Axios.com.

Former Pfizer VP warns child-bearing-age women: 'Do not accept these vaccines.' 8/5/2021. https://www.lifesitenews.com

The WHO's Pandemic Treaty: The End of National Sovereignty and Freedom. Birsen Filip. 6/7/2022. theepochtimes.com

1 Million Vaccinated Brits Died Suddenly in Past Year, Government Admits. Hunter Fielding. NewsAddicts.com.

The Fauci/COVID-19 Dossier. This document is prepared for humanity by Dr. David E. Martin. https://archive.org/details/the-fauci-COVID-19-dossier_202109

CDC-Funded Study of Nearly 100 Million COVID-19 Vaccine Recipients Reveals a Host of Adverse Events. Naveen Athrappully. 2/19/2024. theepochtimes.com

Russia Releases 2,000 Page Report Proving Deep State & Big Pharma Manufactured COVID Pandemic. https://twitter. com/JimFerguson UK/ status/176165 22129445 7 6946

75% of congressmen and woman in the United States have investments in Big Pharma. A Pfizer executive stated that a a senator could be bought for $10k. twitter.com/JimFergusonUK/thread/1761393940874293335

A Host of Notable COVID-19 Vaccine Adverse Events, Backed by Evidence. Marina Zhang. 2/23/2024. theepochtimes.com.

COVID-19 A "Novel" Approach to Pandemic. FreedomRising.info Coordinated Contradictions: COVID Care Overturns Accepted Science and Medical Protocols. FreedomRising.info

What Do Crazy Changing COVID Orders from Govt Have to Do With Chinese Coercion Techniques? FreedomRising.info

WHO Pandemic Declaration (developed during the 2009-2010 H1N1 pandemic). Centers for Disease Control and Prevention, 1600 Clifton Road Atlanta, GA 30329-4027, USA. 800-CDC-INFO (800-232-4636).

Former NIH Director's Jaw-Dropping Testimony Released to Public for First Time. 5/16/2024. VigilantNews.com.

'The Power of Natural Immunity': COVID Challenge Trials Struggle to Infect Participants, Even at High Doses. Brenda Baletti, Ph.D. childrenshealthdefense.org.

6-Foot Social Distancing Rule During COVID Not Based On Scientific Evidence, Ex-NIH Director Testifies. Tom Ozimek. 5/16/2024. theepochtimes.com

CDC HEALTH ADVISORY. Distributed via the CDC Health Alert Network. September 29, 2021, 12:00 PM ET. CDCHAN-00453

Doctor Fined for Prescribing Ivermectin Against COVID-19. Zachary Stieber. 5/17/2024. theepochtimes.com

Since ... the vaccine rollout, we have 1.1 million excessive Americans dying, 4.0 million disabled- we estimate another 28.6 million injured ... So, it's about 33 million Americans have been injured, disabled, or died from this vaccine. https://twitter.com/SenseReceptor/thread/1789561485229953084. 5/12/2024

Vitamin D Insufficiency May Account for Almost Nine of Ten COVID-19 Deaths: Time to Act. Comment on: "Vitamin D Deficiency and Outcome of COVID-19 Patients". Nutrients 2020, 12, 2757. Hermann Brenner, and Ben Schöttker, Division of Clinical Epidemiology and Aging Research, German Cancer Research Center, 69120 Heidelberg, Germany; b.schoettker@dkfz.de. Network Aging Research, University of Heidelberg, 69120 Heidelberg, Germany. Published: 11/27/2020. Nutrients 2020, 12, 3642.

Virologist Predicts Imminent 'Tsunami of Death' Among COVID Vaccinated. April 2, 2024. Jamie White. VigilantNews.com

Vaccinated People Show Long COVID-Like Symptoms with Detectable Spike Proteins: Preprint Study. Marina Zhang. 3/29/2024. https://www.theepochtimes.com

Vaccinated People Are Immune Imprinted, Has Unusual Response to COVID-19 mRNA Boosters. Marina Zhang. 3/24/2024. https://www.theepochtimes.com

This Is Not an April Fool's Gag. James Howard Kunstler. Clusterfuck Nation. https://jameshowardkunstler.substack.com

The average American believed in 2020 that they had a 25% risk of dying from COVID-19. 4/4/2024. Forbidden Science (Substack).

Systematic Review Reveals Many COVID-19 Vaccine Recipients Experienced New-Onset Psychosis. Naveen Athrappully. 5/4/2024. https://www.theepochtimes.com

Study Finds 'Significant Increase' in Cancer Mortality After Mass Vaccination With 3rd COVID Dose. Megan Redshaw, J.D. 4/18/2024. theepochtimes.com

Rutgers will still require COVID vaccine. Elizabeth Prann. Aug 25, 2023. newsnationnow.com

Dr. Mattias Desmet: Technocratic Totalitarianism. Speech at the Fourth International COVID/Crisis Summit, 11/2023. Bucharest Romania.

Report Criticizes 'Catastrophic Errors' of COVID Lockdowns, Warns of Repeat. Kevin Stocklin. 3/17/2024. theepochtimes.com

American College of Obstetricians and Gynecologists Still Pushing COVID Shots for Pregnant Women - Could Millions in Government Funding Explain Why? Brenda Baletti, Ph.D. 05/02/24. childrenshealthdefense.org

Hidden Conflicts? Pharma payments to FDA advisors after drug approvals spark ethical concerns. Charles Piller, Jia You. 7/5/2018. Science Fund for Investigative Reporting. doi:10.1126/science.aau6842

Pfizer Admits Cover-up: 'mRNA' COVID Shots 'Modify' DNA. Hunter Fielding. newsaddicts.com

Pfizer 'Chose Not To' Tell Regulators About SV 40 Sequence in COVID Shots: Health Canada Official. Noe Chartier and Matthew Horwood. 4/23/2024. https://www.theepochtimes.com

People With More COVID-19 Vaccine Doses More Likely to Contract COVID-19: Study. Zachary Stieber. 5/3/2024. theepochtimes.com

Of Cancers, Cures, and LNPs. Dr. Jessica Rose. 5/4/2024. brownstone.org

Expert Statement. Hanna Nohynek, MD, Chief Physician. At Helsinki 8/30/2023

New York City to mandate vaccines for indoor restaurants, gyms, performances. Amanda Eisenberg. 08/03/2021. politico.com

Millions of Americans Were Assigned 'COVID-19 Violation'

Scores Based on Cellphone Data Collected During Lockdowns. By Michael Nevradakis, Ph.D. https://childrenshealthdefense.org

Judge rules Pilsen mom can't see her son because she's not vaccinated against COVID-19. Bob Chiarito. The Sun-Times

Jessica Rose Breaks Down 1.6 Million Adverse Event Reports in VAERS, Definitive Evidence of Causality. 3/7/2024. theepochtimes.corn

Japan Bans COVID Shots over Soaring Sudden Deaths. NewsAddicts.com. Hunter Fielding

Ivermectin for COVID-19: real-time meta analysis of 102 studies @COVIDAnalysis, 4/18/2024, Version 228 — GidMK response. https://c19ivm.org/meta.html.

Ivermectin: Australian regulator bans drug as COVID treatment after sharp rise in prescriptions. Josh Taylor. 9/10/2021. TheGuardian.com

How the authorities systematically lied to the public about the threat of COVID-19 in 2020. Forbidden Science (Substack)

Nirmatrelvir for Vaccinated or Unvaccinated Adult Outpatients with COVID-19. Authors: Jennifer Hammond, Ph.D., Robert J. Fountaine, Pharm.D., Carla Yunis, M.D., M.P.H., Dona Fleishaker, B.S.N., Mary Almas, M.S., Weihang Bao, Ph.D., Wayne Wisemandle, M.A., +5 , and James M. Rusnak, M.D., Ph.D. Author Info & Affiliations. Published April 3, 2024. I N Engl J Med 2024;390:1186-1195 I DOI: 10.1056/NEJMoa2309003 VOL. 390 NO. 13

'Healthy' 29-Year-Old's Sudden Heart Attack Caused by COVID-19 Vaccine, Cardiologists Confirm. Kate Stephenson. NewsAddicts.com.

Healthcare is Turning Texas Blue. Mary Talley Bowden MD. https://maloneinstitute.org

Government Ordered Doctors to Kill Patients to Boost COVID Fears. Hunter Fielding. NewsAddicts.com

Further evidence supports controversial claim that SARS-CoV-2 genes can integrate with human DNA. Jon Cohen. Science.org

From beer to Tinder boosts: The bribes for people to get jabbed. Jack Hunter. 5/21/2021. https://www.bbc.com

New-onset psychosis following COVID-19 vaccination: a systematic review. Marija Lazareva1, Lubova Renemane1, Jelena Vrublevska, and Elmars Rancans. Dept. of Psychiatry and Narcology, Riga Stradins Univ. Riga, Latvia: The emergence of a new coronavirus strain caused the COVID-19. 4/12/2024. DOI10.3389/fpsyt.2024.1360338. Frontiers in Psychiatry.

Fact check: Reports of adverse events due to COVID-19 vaccines are unverified. 5/1/2022. USA Today.

COVID-19 mRNA Vaccines: Lessons Learned from the Registrational Trials and Global Vaccination Campaign. Mead M, Seneff S, Wolfinger R, et al. (1/24/2024) COVID-19 mRNA. Cureus 16(1): e52876. doi:10.7759

COVID-19 injections neither safe nor effective. Canadian National Citizens Inquiry: Live Press Conference. 9/14/2023. Unacceptable Jessica (Substack)

COVID-19 'Vaccines' Are Gene Therapy. Joseph Mercola, 6/26/2022. theepochtimes.com

COVID Vaccine Gene Could Integrate into Human Cancer Cells: Researcher. Marina Zhang. 3/11/2024. theepochtimes.com

Couple's deaths ruled murder-suicide. McKenna Harford. skyhinews.com

Coroner: State included a murder-suicide in Grand's COVID deaths. Amy Golden. skyhinews.com

Chevron Deference and the Administrative State. Who is Robert Malone (Substack).

CDC: Fully Vaccinated People Should Wear Masks Indoors in Some Areas. Zachary Stieber. 7/27/2021. theepochtimes.com

CDC to drop 'gold standard' COVID test: PCR risks false positives. justthenews.com

CDC Releases Hidden COVID-19 Vaccine Injury Reports. Zachary Stieber. 4/3/2024. theepochtimes.com

CDC Quietly Admits to COVID Policy Failures. brownstone.org Bribing America to Get the COVID Vaccine. 5/19/2021. USAToday.com

A 'Pandemic of Vaccinations.' Australian Senator Malcolm Roberts' Fierce Wake-Up Call to the World. https://twitter.com/aussie17/thread/1789464240715427976

Egyptian Physician Asks Why Were COVID-19 Death Rates So Much Higher in the West vs. Africa? He Believes He Has the Answer. 4/19/2024. trialsitenews.com

The Real Reason They're Pushing Vaccines So Hard is Both Ludicrous and Terrifying. JD Rucker. July 3, 2021. NOQ Report

Top Professor Testifies: COVID 'Intentionally Released' to Push Vaccines onto Public. Frank Bergman. https://slaynews.com

The Great Cloud of Disrepute. brownstone.org

WEF Declare 'We Are Gods, If You Stand In Our Way, You Will Die' - The People's Voice. Baxter Dmitry. thepeoplesvoice.tv.

COVID-19 Vaccine Protection Among Children Plummets: CDC. Zachary Stieber. 4/23/2024. theepochtimes.com

Moderna Admits COVID mRNA Shots Cause Deadly 'Turbo Cancers.' Hunter Fielding. News Addicts.

DNA fragments detected in monovalent and bivalent Pfizer/BioNTech and Moderna modRNA COVID-19 vaccines from Ontario, Canada: Exploratory dose response relationship with serious adverse events. David J. Speicher, Jessica Rose, L. Maria Gutschi, David Wiseman, Kevin McKernan. osf.io/xv3nz/

The Pharmaceutical Conspiracy to Silence Online Dissent is Bigger Than You Think. 4/26/2024. Originally appeared on The Forgotten Side of Medicine. Guest post on X by A Midwestern Doctor

Pa. Health Secretary issues new order, makes mask wearing required indoors even if you are physically distant. Adrianne Burke. WPXI.com

PA sharpens mask mandate, orders virus testing. Michael Rubikam. 11/17/2020. APNews.com

Pennsylvania officials tell residents to wear masks in their homes when guests are over. Joseph Choi. TheHill.com

PA Health Details. Media Contact: Nate Wardle, ra-dhpressoffice@pa.gov. media.pa.gov

The number of Americans who say they won't get a COVID shot hasn't budged in a year. John Burnett/NPR. May/2022

Woman seen in viral Galveston mask refusal video sentenced to 12 days in jail. Ronnie Marley. 12/9/2021. Fox26Houston.com

Not wearing a mask during COVID-19 health emergency isn't a free speech right, appeals court says. Mike Catalini. 2/6/24. ap-news.com

Wyoming teenager arrested after refusing to wear mask on schoolgrounds, family says. Stephen Sorace. FoxNews.com

Woman tasered after refusing to wear face mask at Ohio school football game. Yasmine Salam. NBC News Investigative Unit

Cancer 'is our new COVID' – Pfizer CEO. rt.com

US Won't Investigate Governors Who Ordered Nursing Homes to Accept COVID-Positive Residents. Zachary Stieber. Twitter: @zackstieber. theepochtimes.com

Autopsy Histopathologic Cardiac Findings in 2 Adolescents Following the Second COVID-19 Vaccine Dose; James R. Gill, MD; Randy Tashjian, MD; Emily Duncanson, MD; Arch Pathol Lab Med (2022) 146 (8): 925–929.

Exclusive: Health Canada Not Concerned About Scientists' Finding of Plasmid DNA Contamination in COVID Shots; Matthew Horwood and Noe Chartier. 8/25/2023. theepochtimes.com

Association between simian virus 40 and non-Hodgkin lymphoma; Lancet. 2002 Mar 9; 359(9309):817-23. doi: 10.1016/S0140-6736(02)07950-3.

COVID- 19 vaccine boosters for young adults: a risk benefit assessment and ethical analysis of mandate policies at universities. Bardosh K, Krug A, Jamrozik E, et al. J Med Ethics 2024;50:126–138.

The Mask Debacle — How partisan warfare over mandates became a central feature of the pandemic. Jacob Hale Russell and Dennis Patterson, 2/16/2022. Science.org

Disease experts call for nationwide closure of U.S. schools and businesses to slow coronavirus. Jocelyn Kaiser. Science.org

Walsh S, Chowdhury A, Braithwaite V, et al. Do school closures and school reopenings affect community transmission of COVID-19? A systematic review of observational studies. BMJ Open 2021;11:e053371. doi:10.1136/bmjopen-2021-053371

https://www.science.org/content/article/having-sars-cov-2-once-confers-much-greater-immunity-vac ... Meredith Wadman

My op-ed from Newsweek January 30, 2023. Kevin Bass

Security guard arrested after not wearing mask on bus dies. Lisa Fernandez and Cristina Rendon. Updated 11/19/2021. ktvu.com

CDC Found Evidence COVID-19 Vaccines Caused Deaths. Zachary Stieber. 5/01/2024. theepochtimes.com

ELECTION

WEF Plotting Cyber Attack to Block 2024 Election. Hunter Fielding. NewsAddicts.com

Judge Denies Sidney Powell's Motion to Dismiss Charges in Georgia Election Case. Jack Phillips. 10/5/2023. theepochtimes.com

House Passes Election Bill That Makes It Harder to Decertify Presidential Results. Joseph Lord. 9/21/2022. theepochtimes.com

MGP on X: "I just went to vote. Halfway through . . ." https://twitter.com/MGPalmer2/status/1722044336202752228

Foreign Country Bans Smartmatic Voting Machines Firm to 'Safeguard Integrity of Elections.' Jack Davis. westernjournal.com/

Supreme Court Refuses to Hear Trump's Last Remaining Election Challenge. Matthew Vadum. 3/8/2021. theepochtimes.com

Texas GOP Passes Resolution Declaring Biden 'Not Legitimately Elected.' Gary Bai. 6/19/2022.

https://www.theepochtimes.com Supreme Court Allows GOP Legal Defense of North Carolina's Embattled Voter ID Law. Matthew Vadum. 6/23/2022. https://www.theepochtimes.com

Jerry Nadler Gets Desperate as Primary Challenger Takes Commanding Lead: "I'm the son of a chicken farmer, no fortune over here." David Hawkins. 7/18/2022. https://slaynews.com

9 Senate Republicans Join Democrats in Unveiling, Backing Election Law Reform Bills. Joseph Lord. 7/21/2022. https://www.theepochtimes.com

Legal Foundation Sues New York City to Keep Non-Citizens from Voting in Municipal Elections. Steven Kovac. 8/30/2022. https://www.theepochtimes.com

Fate of Wisconsin's Use of Private Vendor to Maintain Voter Roll on the Line After Citizens File Complaint. Steven Kovac. 9/18/2022. https://www.theepochtimes.com

Depleting America's Emergency Oil Supply to Elect Democrats. Thomas McArdle. 9/17/2022. https://www.theepochtimes.com

Wisconsin Voter Roll Contains 350,000 Errors, Watchdog Group Alleges. Steven Kovac. September 22, 2022. theepochtimes.com

Report Critical of Group Managing Voter Rolls in 33 States. Beth Brelje. August 21, 2022. theepochtimes.com

Grassroot Election Integrity Movement Sweeps Battleground States. Gary Bai. 9/21/2022. theepochtimes.com

Over 50 Percent of Americans Fear Midterm Elections Could Result in Divided Government, Gridlock: Poll. Katabella Roberts. 10/3/2022. theepochtimes.com

Election Integrity Advocates Cheer Independent State Legislature Case Before Supreme Court. John Haughey. 10/5/2022. https://www.theepochtimes.com

FBI Issues Update on US Elections Ahead of 2022 Midterms. Jack Phillips. 10/5/2022. theepochtimes.com

Wisconsin Judge Orders Officials to Stop Allowing Voters to 'Spoil' Ballots and Cast New Ones. Zachary Stieber. 10/8/2022.

https://www.theepochtimes.com 'Nothing Has Changed': Lawmaker Fears Loophole in Wisconsin Elections Will Make Midterms a Rerun of 2020. Steven Kovac. 10/4/2022. theepochtimes.com

GOP Candidates Surge in Governors' Races While Raising Less Money than Democrats. Dan M. Berger. 10/31/2022. https://www.theepochtimes.com

Plaintiffs Ask Judge to Find Benson in Contempt of Court for Failing to Correct Election Guidance Manual. Steven Kovac. 11/3/2022. https://www.theepochtimes.com

Wisconsin Court Shoots Down Attempt to Change Rules for Absentee Ballots before Midterms. Katabella Roberts. 11/3/2022. https://www.theepochtimes.com

Decisions on Wisconsin Election Integrity Lawsuits Revealed as Election Day Nears. Jeff Louderback. 11/4/2022. theepochtimes.com

Judge Orders Voting Machines to Be Opened Following Mistake by Poll Worker. Jon Dougherty. conservativebrief.com

You've Been Gaslighted - Democrats Just Stole Another Election. Wayne Allyn Root. TheGatewayPundit.com

Poll Pads Caught Adding Hundreds of Voters in Real Time as Poll is Being Closed. Brian Lupo. TheGatewayPundit.com

Republican Wins Idaho House Seat After a Computer Glitch Is Corrected. Jon Dougherty. conservativebrief.com

Multiple Errors Found in Virginia's 2022 Election Scanner. Electoral Process Education Corporation (EPEC.info) is a Virginia-based, non-profit, 501c (3) corporation.

Uncounted Votes on Overlooked Memory Card Flip Election in Georgia. Jack Phillips. 11/20/2022. https://www.theepochtimes.com

Brunson v. Alma S. Adams; et al., (Biden, Harris, Pence & 385 Members of Congress). http://ralandbrunson.com/

2022 Pennsylvania Gubernatorial Election: After Action Review. Doug Mastriano. 1/18/2023. https://www.theepochtimes.com

'No Labels' Political Party Qualifies for Arizona 2024 Election Ballot. Katabella Roberts. 3/8/2023. theepochtimes.com

9 Solutions to Secure America's Elections. AmericanProgress.org

Catastrophic "Loss of Control" Data Breach in NY Elections. UncoverDC. Wendi Strauch Mahoney. 5/25/2023. uncoverdc.com

Congressional Leaders Clash Over DC Election Reform, Statehood. Steven Kovac, 6/9/2023. theepochtimes.com

North Carolina Governor Vetoes GOP Election Bill, Setting Up Override Clash. Samantha Flom. 8/24/2023. theepochtimes.com

America's Dangerous Election Cycle. Malcom Kyeyune. https://compactmag.com

An Inconvenient Trump: Republicans Are Living an Enormous Lie. Melissa Mackenzie. https://spectator.org/

WEF Adviser Calls for Elections to Be Scrapped: 'Bad for Democracy.' Frank Bergman. SlayNews.com.

Georgia election indictment highlights wider attempts to illegally access voting equipment. ABC News. https://abcnews.go.com/

Week Four of the Disbarment Trial of Trump's Attorney John Eastman Brings Out Reasons Judges Dismissed Election Cases. The Arizona Sun Times. Rachel Alexander. arizonasuntimes.com

Explosive Testimony from Former Wisconsin Supreme Court Justice at Disbarment Trial of Trump's Attorney John Eastman. Rachel Alexander. 2023. TheStarNewsNetwork.com

Robert F. Kennedy Jr. About to Run as Independent? daniel_g. 9/8/2023. wltreport.com

Election report finds Facebook mogul's 'Zuck Bucks' broke law, swayed election outcome in Wisconsin. Susan Ferrechio. 3/2022. www.washingtontimes.com

Wisconsin Election Chief Hit with Articles of Impeachment. David Lindfield. SlayNews.com.

America's New Politics of Nothing. Ryan Zickgraf. compactmag.com

Wisconsin Voter Alliance Says State Violates Federal Election Law. Beth Brelje. theepochtimes.com

Judge Orders Redo Of 2022 Judicial Race In Texas After More Than 1,400 Illegal Votes Cast. Brianna Lyman. PricklyPear.news

Kennedy Assassination Threat: Armed Man Pretending to Be Federal Agent Arrested at RFK Jr. Event in LA. Slay News. David Hawkins. https://slaynews.com

Zuckerberg Suffers Defeat as Yet Another State Bans His Election Funding. News Addicts. Melinda Davies. https://newsaddicts.com/

The Most Expensive Judicial Race in US History Is Raising Questions. Steven Kovac. https://www.theepochtimes.com

Georgia Republican Says He Received Death Threats After Voting Against Jordan. Frank Fang. https://www.theepochtimes.com

Voter Turnout Effort Leads to Prosecution Threat, Lawsuit. Janice Hisle. theepochtimes.com

No Labels Party Sues Arizona Over Ballot Line. Caden Pearson. 10/20/2023. theepochtimes.com

Huge Win for Election Integrity: North Carolina Republicans Override Democratic Governor's Veto. Warner Todd Huston. https://www.westernjournal.com

Democrats Want to Criminalize Republican Election Challenges. Shawn Fleetwood, staff writer for The Federalist.

Ranked-Choice Voting Is the Monster Under the Bed Of American Elections. Shawn Fleetwood. https://thepricklypear.org.

Party Calling For GOP Chairwoman's Removal After Devastating Defeat In Key State. Graham. https://wltreport.com

Closely-Watched Kentucky Gov. Race Called. Martin Walsh. https://conservativebrief.com/

Conservative Group Files FEC Complaint Alleging Coordinated Election Influence for Biden. Savannah Hulsey Pointer. 11/10/2023. theepochtimes.com

Citizens Urged to Prepare as 2024 Election Riot Season Draws Near. David Lindfield. slaynews.com

Wisconsin Supreme Court Overturns 'Rigged' Election Maps. Melinda Davies. newsaddicts.com

Federal Appeals Court Upholds Texas Law Requiring Pen-on-Paper Voter Signature. Tom Ozimek. 12/29/2023. theepochtimes.com

North Carolina Snubs Biden's Challengers for Democrat Primary Ballot. Frank Bergman. slaynews.com

Investigation Reveals How CCP Interfered in US Election. Andrew Thornebrooke. 1/25/2024. https://www.theepochtimes.com

RFK Seeks Path to Victory by Forcing House to Elect President. Jeff Louderback. 1/19/2024. https://www.theepochtimes.com

Colorado Supreme Court Ruling: No. 23-719. In the Supreme Court of the United States, Donald J. Trump Petitioner, v. Norma Anderson, et al., Respondents. On Writ of Certiorari to the Supreme Court of Colorado Brief for Retired State Supreme Court Justices as Amici Curiae Supporting Respondents

Court Strikes Down Law That Let Noncitizens Vote in New York Elections. Tom Ozimek. 2/22/2024. theepochtimes.com

RITE Spots Irregularities with Clark County Election Records Retention, Recommends Steps to Reach Compliance. RiteUSA.org

RNC Files Election Integrity Lawsuit Against Nevada Secretary of State. Tom Ozimek. 3/18/2024. https://www.theepochtimes.com

Media Research Center Finds Google Engaged In Election Interference. Neland Nobel. thePricklyPear.org

Judge Rules NM Officials Violated Federal Law by Restricting Access to Voter Data. Aldgra Fredly. 4/3/2024. theepochtimes.com

Group Sues LA for Denying Access to Voter Files After State Rebukes Democrat-Dominated Data Service. Matthew Vadum. 2/8/2022. theepochtimes.com

24 States Banned 'Zuckerbucks' Grants After 2020 Election. John Haughey. 1/26/2023. https://www.theepochtimes.com

Ohio Orders Purge of Ineligible Voters from State Voter Rolls After Finding 137 'Non-Citizens' Registered to Vote. Tom Ozimek. 5/15/2024. theepochtimes.com

Study: 10% to 27% of Non-Citizens Are Illegally Registered to Vote. James D. Agresti. https://pricklypear.news

Judge Blocks Illinois Law That Changed Ballot Access Rules After Primary. Bill Pan. 5/23/2024. https://www.theepochtimes.com

Eastman Arrested in Arizona 2020 Case.... 5/25/2024. Luis Cornelio. https://pricklypear.news

Noncitizens caught voting in U.S. elections — here's how they did it. By Stephen Dinan. 5/3/2024. The Washington Times

Florida Election Crimes Chief Dies, Issued Dire Warning Weeks Before Death. Jacob Engels. 9/24/2022. thegatewaypundit.com

Florida Court Overturns Ruling on DeSantis Redistricting Map. Caden Pearson. 5/21/2022. https://www.theepochtimes.com

Florida County Supervisor of Elections Placed Under State Oversight for Main-In Ballot Violations. Steven Kovac. 10/30/2023. https://www.theepochtimes.com

DeSantis' election police charged 20 with voter fraud. 9/3/2022. Adam Edelman. nbcnews.com

Appeals Court Upholds Election Integrity Law in Florida. Gary Bai. 4/30/23. theepochtimes.com

Oregon Republicans' walkouts trigger a new state law on reelection. NPR.org. 5/15/2023

Judge Tosses Challenge, Upholds Law Allowing 'Noncitizens' to Vote in DC. Caden Pearson. 3/22/2024. theepochtimes.com

D.C. Forced to Purge Over 100,000 Ineligible Names from Voter Rolls: 'VICTORY.' Melinda Davies. https://newsaddicts.com

Colorado Secretary of State's Office Admits It Mailed Over 31,000 Voter Registration Cards to Non-Citizens. Steven Kovac. 1/8/2023. https://www.theepochtimes.com

Colorado secretary of state calls Trump a 'liar,' vows to see ballot lawsuit through. Julia Shapero. https://news.yahoo.com

California Voters Report Ballot Mix-Ups, Share Concerns About Election Integrity. Travis Gillmore 3/10/2024. theepochtimes.com

Election Software CEO Surrenders to LA Authorities; Prosecutors Allege "Massive Data Breech." Eva Fu and Joyce Kuo, 10/14/2022. theepochtimes.com

States Have Tightened Election Integrity Laws, But Conservative Groups Say More Remains to Be Done. Dan M. Berger, 10/11/2022. https://www.theepochtimes.com

It's been two years since 51 intelligence agents interfered with an election - they still won't apologize. Miranda Devine. 10/19/2022. https://nypost.com

Over 20 Million Have Voted So Far Ahead of 2022 Midterms. Jack Phillips, 10/30/2022. https://www.theepochtimes.com

TX Sup. Court Rules Harris County Should Count Over 2,000 Votes Cast Late. Katabella Roberts, 11/23/2022. theepochtimes.com

The 2022 AZ Midterm Election — A Disaster and Glaring Example of a Broken and Rigged Electoral System. thepricklypear.org

Maricopa County Made Arizona's Elections Even More of A Disaster Than People Realize. Shawn Fleetwood, 11/23/2022. thefederalist.com

Down Ballot AZ GOP US House Races Received Thousands More Votes than... Joe Hoft, 11/23/2022. thegatewaypundit.com

'They're Trying to Run Out the Clock': Kari Lake Files 1st Lawsuit After Election. Zachary Stieber, 1/24/2022. https://www.theepochtimes.com

Kari Lake Responds to Judge Who Sanctioned Her Legal Team in Lawsuit. theepochtimes.com

Trump Forces Shadowy Election-Rigging Cabal Out into the Open. Brian Cates. uncoverdc.com

Supreme Court Set to Hear 'Single Most Important Case' on American Elections. westernjournal.com

People Need to Defend Right to Vote or Lose Freedoms: True the Vote. Ella Kietlinska and Joshua Philipp, 11/22/2022. https://www.theepochtimes.com

FBI Sent Posts to Big Tech Firms for Action Ahead of Election: Agent. Zachary Stieber, 12/6/2022. https://www.theepochtimes.com

Vote Recount Flips Massachusetts Midterm Race from Republican to... theepochtimes.com

Twitter Part of Efforts to Interfere with US Elections: Gingrich. https://www.theepochtimes.com

Judge Sanctions 9 Trump Campaign Attorneys Over Election Lawsuit. Ivan Pentchoukov. 8/25/2021. theepochtimes.com

Jan. 6 Panel Votes to Refer Trump for Criminal Charges. Zachary Stieber, 12/19/2022. https://www.theepochtimes.com

Delaware Supreme Court Strikes Down Voting by Mail, and Same-Day... Matthew Vadum. 12/22/2022. theepochtimes.com

Judge Dismisses State Senator's Lawsuit Against Katie Hobbs and Mar... Jack Phillips, 12/20/2022. https://www.theepochtimes.com

The Dismissal of Kari Lake's Election Lawsuit Shows Voter Disenfranc... Rachel Alexander. 12/26/2022. townhall.com

Leaked Email Alleges Contact Between Hobbs, Twitter Staff to Censor 'Election Related Misinformation'. Jon Dougherty. https://conservativebrief.com

Last Failsafe to Fix 2020 Election at Supreme Court — Brunson v. Adams. Greg Hunter. 12/31/2022. https://usawatchdog.com

Hunter Biden's laptop: Voters lacked 'critical' information in 2020 election, survey shows. James Reinl. dailymail.co.uk

Lawmakers Propose Changes to State Election and Voting Laws Followi... theepochtimes.com

Maricopa County Attorney Argues That Voters Who Wait Until Election Day to Vote Then Encounter Problems Reap What They Sow. Jennifer Van Laar. thepricklypear.org

Jan. 6 Panel's Decision to Refer Trump for Criminal Charges May Work... theepochtimes.com
Supreme Court Rejects Case Seeking to Overturn 2020 Election. https://www.theepochtimes.com

Tennessee Denies Voting Rights to 450,000 Citizens. The Sentencing Project (2022). https://www.jstor.org/stable/resrep40611

New York Bars 30,000 Citizens from Voting. The Sentencing Project (2022). https://www.jstor.org/stable/resrep40608

Voting Rights in the Era of Mass Incarceration: A Primer. Jean Chung and Kevin Muhitch. The Sentencing Project (2021). https://www.jstor.org/stable/resrep35148

Connecticut Bars 5,400 Citizens from Voting. The Sentencing Project (2022). www.jstor.org

Former New York Elections Official Pleads Guilty in Ballot Fraud Scheme. David Hawkins. https://slaynews.com

Former New York Election Official Admits to Vote Fraud Scheme. 1/11/2023. nytimes.com

Maricopa's Election Had 25,000 Mysterious Votes, Missing Docs. 1/18/2023. thefederalist.com.

Election service company and Maricopa's Stephen Richer face scrutiny amid Kari Lake's fiery appeal. Summer Lane. rsbnetwork.com

Florida elections office has no oversight for ballots or chain of custody, whistleblower alleges. Natalia Mittelstadt. https://justthenews.com

More Evidence: FOIA Requests Reveal There Were No DOJ Invest... thegatewaypundit.com

Voting System Error in New Jersey Could Flip the Outcome of School... theepochtimes.com

Election Integrity Watchdog Finds California Lost 10.9 Million Mail-In... theepochtimes.com

Katie Hobbs Asks Court to Toss Kari Lake's Election Challenge. https://www.theepochtimes.com

Judge Orders Biden's DHS to Release Docs Exposing Agents Who 'Helped Censor Election Misinformation.' Frank Bergman. slaynews.com

Testimony to Arizona Senate Election Committee Reveals Thousands of Misdemeanors Allegedly

Committed by Maricopa County in 2022 Election. The Arizona Sun Times. Rachel Alexander.

SHOCKING: AZ Senate/House Elections Presenter Claims That Sinalo... thegatewaypundit.com. 2023

Election Reformers Get New Tool to Pressure States to Clean Up Voter Rolls. theepochtimes.com

'No Labels' Political Party Qualifies for Arizona 2024 Election Ballot. theepochtimes.com How to Transform US Politics — and How Not To. Michael Lind. compactmag.com

Millions of Tiny, Suspicious Political Donations Questioned by Watchdog . . . theepochtimes.com

New 'Late Exit' Poll Finds Eight Percent More Arizona Voters Said They Voted for Lake over Hobbs. The Arizona Sun Times. Rachel Alexander.

SCOTUS to Hear Case That Could Give State Legislatures, Not Judges... theepochtimes.com

Problems in Maricopa County Election Linked to Changes in Ballot Paper. theepochtimes.com

Provisional Ballot Analysis May Reverse Outcome of Attorney General Race. April 2023. azfreenews.com

Maricopa Makes SHOCKING Admission In 2022 Election "Root Cause Analysis." Nick Moseder. https://nickmoseder.substack.com

North Carolina Judges Strike Down Voter ID Law, Claiming It's Racist. theepochtimes.com

Judge Rejects Arizona AG's Attempt to Revoke Elections Agreement. theepochtimes.com

President Biden Officially Announces 2024 Campaign. https://www.theepochtimes.com

RFK Jr. Responds to DNC's Plans to Skip Primary Debates: The Syste... theepochtimes.com

DNC Refuses to Hold Democrat Debates for 2024, Biden's Challengers Outraged. Frank Bergman. https://slaynews.com

Shocking Discovery Found on Voting Rolls in Fourth Most-Populous County in the Nation. Jack Davis. westernjournal.com

Video Shows Fraudulent Mail-In Ballot Signatures Accepted by Maricopa County — Kari Lake Attorneys to EXPOSE Fraudulent 2022 Signatures in Trial Court. Jordan Conradson. thegatewaypundit.com

The Curious Case of the US Dept. of Defense Contract Signed During Obama Presidency, Konnech and Overseas Voters. Patrice Johnson. 100percentfedup.com

Prosecutors: U.S. election firm gave Chinese workers 'super administration' access to election data. justthenews.com

Election Software Firm Used by LA County — and by Counties in Swing... 10/1/2022. redstate.com

Election Firm Knew Data Had Been Sent to China, Prosecutors Say. Stuart A. Thompson. 10/13/2022. nytimes.com

Longtime Democrat Campaign Strategist Charged with Election Fraud. David Hawkins. https://slaynews.com

Elon Musk Weighs in on 'Strange' Ballot Irregularities Exposed in Maricopa County. Frank Bergman. https://slaynews.com

House Considers Federal Ban on Private Money to Run Elections. Fred Lucas. thepricklypear.org

Lawsuit Against True the Vote Dropped as Election Fraud Evidence Published. Catherine Salgado. https://thepricklypear.org

NY Voter Roll's Hidden Algorithms Revealed In Peer-Reviewed Study. Andrew Paquette. https://www.redvoicemedia.com

The Courts v. The Truth — A Huge Week Looms in Arizona. Capt. Seth Keshel. SKeshel.substack.com

Elizabeth Warren Wants to Replace Every Single Voting Machine to Make Elections 'As Secure As Fort Knox.' Abby Vesoulis. Time.com

Election Infrastructure: Vulnerabilities and Solutions. Fact Sheet 9/11/2017. AmericanProgress.org

U.S. intel: Russia compromised seven states prior to 2016 election. Cynthia McFadden, William M. Arkin, Kevin Monahan, and Ken Dilanian. NBCNews.com

U.S. Officials: Putin Personally Involved in U.S. Election Hack. 12/14/2016. William M. Arkin, Ken Dilanian, and Cynthia McFadden. nbcnews.com

'Our House Is on Fire.' Elections Officials Worry About Midterms Security. By Eric Lichtblau. 9/5/2018. Time.com.

My Plan to Strengthen Our Democracy. Medium. Elizabeth Warren. 6/25/2019. Medium.com

Supreme Court Inches Closer to Decision in Major Redistricting Case. theepochtimes.com

'Printer Error' Mysteriously Flips One Million Registered Voters to Democrats. Frank Bergman. 5/22/2023. slaynews.com

Minnesota's New Election Legislation Criminalizes What Officials D... theepochtimes.com

Peter Navarro 'The Immaculate Deception' Report News Conference Transcript. rev.com

The Secret History of the Shadow Campaign That Saved the 2020 Election. Molly Ball. Time.com

New Video Evidence: Maricopa County Elections Officials Illegally Break into Sealed Election Machines after they were Certified and Before the Election – Inserting Reprogrammed Memory Cards. 5/28/2023. thegatewaypundit.com

Thousands of Fraudulent Ballot Registration Requests Found on New York's Voter Rolls. David Lindfield. https://slaynews.com

Election Integrity Project California — EIPCa Every Lawfully Cast Vote... https://eip-ca.com

Election Watchdogs Discover $200M Laundering Scheme Using 'Smurfs.' Facts Matter. Roman Balmakov. theepochtimes.com

Judge Rejects Hobbs, Maricopa County's Demand That Kari Lake Be Santioned for Election Lawsuit. evol.news

The genesis of America's corrupted computerized election system. Jennifer Cohn. https://jennycohn1.medium.com

How Flipping Colorado Blue Has Become Democrats' Blueprint for the... theepochtimes.com

Vote With Your Wallet! https://www.theepochtimes.com

Hobbs Sued by Election Integrity Group For Hiding Election-Related... 5/30/2023. arizonadailyindependent.com

Instagram Bans Robert F. Kennedy Jr's Account. Frank Bergman. https://slaynews.com

'Discrepancies and Irregularities' Still Plague Michigan Election Practices. theepochtimes.com Jesse Morgan and the 200k Missing Ballots. Joe Fried. 6/2/2023. americanthinker.com

Democrat Mayor Arrested on Voter Fraud Charges in Florida. Frank Bergman. slaynews.com

WaPo Accidentally Admits 'Zuckbucks' Were Used to Turn Out Likely-Democrat Voters In 2020. Shawn Fleetwood. https://thepricklypear.org

Florida Democrat Mayor Suspended by DeSantis after He Was Arrested for Illegal Voting Charges. Hunter Fielding. https://newsaddicts.com

Supreme Court Strikes Down Republican-Drawn Election Map for Alabama. theepochtimes.com

100% Voter Turnout: Massive Nursing Home Election Fraud. Facts Matter. Roman Balmakov. https://www.theepochtimes.com

Trump Can Run for President While Being Indicted: Here's the Main R... theepochtimes.com

Pollsters Shift Five House Seats Toward Dems After Supreme Court Ruling. Jon Dougherty. https://conservativebrief.com

Hundreds of absentee ballots found in a storage unit in Genesee County. Courtney Bennett. https://midmichigannow.com

Justice Thomas Issues Critical 50-Page Dissent in Key Supreme Court Case. theepochtimes.com

Virginia Department of Elections Corrects Same-Day Registration Voter... theepochtimes.com

Russiagate Redux: Grassley Calls Out FBI For Leaking False Narratives To Obstruct Biden Investigation. Mollie Hemingway. https://thepricklypear.org

Special Counsel's Indictment Raises Questions of Election Interference. theepochtimes.com

North Carolina Lawmakers Move to Eliminate Gov. Roy Cooper's Power. theepochtimes.com

Halderman Report Reveals Georgia's Dominion Voting Machines Can be Hacked, Votes Can be Changed, Elections Can Be Altered! by Jim Hoft. thegatewaypundit.com

Poll Shows RFK Jr. With Highest Favorability Rating of All Presidentia... theepochtimes.com

Raffensperger Knowingly Ran Vulnerable Voting Machines during His 2022 Reelection, Covered It Up. Frank Bergman. https://slaynews.com.

Supreme Court Throws Out Louisiana's Appeal, Making Way for New... theepochtimes.com

O'Keefe Media Group Uncovers Disturbing Allegations of Money Laundering in Political Campaigns. 6/29/2023. Dallas Ludlum. https://dailyclout.io

YouTube Removes Another RFK Jr. Interview. theepochtimes.com

Voting machine printer company says Maricopa Election Day report 'inaccurate,' seeks correction. Natalia Mittelstadt. justthenews.com

State Senate Republicans Try to Force Vote on Election Chief's Appoi... theepochtimes.com

Investigation Exposes 'Critical Vulnerabilities' in 2020 Election Voting Machines. Frank Bergman. https://slaynews.com

Maryland Republican Dan Cox Says Someone Committed Fraud By Fil... theepochtimes.com

The Crucifixion of Donald Trump. Lee Siegel. compactmag.com

They Can't Let Him Back In. Michael Anton. compactmag.com

How Pfizer Fixed the Election. compactmag.com

Trump's Real Crime Is Opposing Empire. Christian Parenti. https://compactmag.com

Michigan AG Brings Felony Charges Against 16 'False Electors' in 2020 Presidential Election. https://www.ntd.com

Obama Judge Orders Kari Lake's Legal Team to Pay $122,200 in Sanctions to Maricopa County. David Lindfield. slaynews.com

Ruby Freeman Body Cam Admi... 12/25/2022. georgiarecord.com Why the Media Hate RFK. Lee Siegel. compactmag.com

Trump Indicted Over Efforts to Challenge 2020 Election Results. https://www.theepochtimes.com

Supreme Court rejects Trump election challenge cases. Jessica Gresko. apnews.com

Rudy Giuliani Says Jack Smith Indictment Eviscerates First Amendment and Criminalizes Questioning Election Results. https://evol.news

Pelosi Says 2nd Trump Term 'Cannot Happen,' Calls Indictments Again... theepochtimes.com

The Konnech Election Systems Bombshell: A Thread. 10/3/2022. RasmussenPoll/status/1578483416 286101504

Major 2020 Election Voter Fraud Scheme Exposed in Michigan. Frank Bergman. slaynews.com.

Pennsylvania Judge Rules That Trump Has Presidential Immunity on Elections Claims. David Hawkins. slaynews.com

Kari Lake Calls for Decertifying 2020 Election: 'Illegitimate' Biden Is NOT the 'True President.' Frank Bergman. Slay News.

RFK Jr Files Lawsuit against Google over Repeated Censorship on YouTube. Frank Bergman. slaynews.com.

Guns, Burner Phones and Fake Registrations — The Buried Michigan Voter Fraud Scandal: GBI Strategies Director Gar Bell Had 70 Organizations Operating in 20 States in 2020 — TIED TO JOE BIDEN CAMPAIGN. 8/2023. thegatewaypundit.com

Special Counsel Jack Smith Admits Another Error in a Trump Case. theepochtimes.com

Jim Jordan Smells A Rat: "Something's not right, whitewash the Biden family's corruption, stonewall congressional oversight. Article Reports. https://evol.news Judge to Hold Emergency Hearing on RFK Jr.'s Google Censorship Law... theepochtimes.com

Georgia DA Charges Trump, Rudy Giuliani, Jenna Ellis, John Eastman, Sidney Powell, Jeffrey Clark. David Hawkins. slaynews.com

Trump and 18 Co-defendants Will Be Booked at Fulton County Jail: Sheriff. theepochtimes.com

Dershowitz Predicts 'Bad' and 'Fast' Convictions for Trump. theepochtimes.com

Judge Claimed Trump Might Flee If He Learned of Secret Order. https://www.theepochtimes.com

What We Know About Fani Willis, the Prosecutor Leading the Georgia Election Case Against Donald Trump. Katabella Roberts 8/16/2023. theepochtimes.com

The Ten Irrefutable Points of 2020. Capt. Seth Keshel. https://skeshel.substack.com.

What Is the Plan, Republicans? National Review. Charles C. W. Cooke. nationalreview.com

Tom Fitton Sues CIA over Role in Intel Letter Attacking Hunter Biden Laptop Story Just before Election. David Hawkins. https://slaynews.com

Matt Gaetz Calls on Congress to Investigate Political Bias of Trump Judge Tanya Chutkan. Frank Bergman. 8/2023. slaynews.com

The Questions That Tucker Carlson Must Ask Donald Trump. Jeffrey A. Tucker. 8/21/2023. theepochtimes.com

Mississippi Democrat Accuses Fellow Dems of Election Fraud in Primary Race. Frank Bergman. https://slaynews.com

Election Integrity Win: Arizona Court Rules Against State's 'Unlawful Signature Matching Process.' Randy DeSoto. https://www.westernjournal.com/

How Can Mail-In Voting Be 'Secure' When Postal Theft Is Rampant. Shawn Fleetwood. https://thepricklypear.org

Suspended, De-Banked, But Not Sorry: John Eastman 'Tenfold' More Convinced of Illegalities in 2020. Brad Jones. 4/24/2024. theepochtimes.com

Facebook Has Interfered in U.S. Elections 39 Times Since 2008. Hunter Fielding. NewsAddicts.com

RED ALERT: Facebook Caught Interfering In DOZENS Of Elections. Trent Walker. NewsAddicts.com

Supreme Court Rejects Attempt to Expand No-Excuse Mail-in Ballots in Texas. Hunter Fielding. NewsAddicts.com

Manhattan DA Accused of Politically Motivated Prosecution in Trump Trial: House Report. Tom Ozimek. 4/25/2024. TheEpochTimes.com

Audit Finds OK Officials Mismanaged Millions in COVID-19 Relief Funds. Michael Clements. 4/27/2024. TheEpochTimes.com

Arizona State Senator Indicted Over 2020 Election 'Scheme' Secures RNC Position. Jacob Burg. 4/29/2024. TheEpochTimes.com

Records: Michigan voting machines exchanged at mall, 'manipulated' in hotels. bridgemi.com

Muskegon fake voter applications probed in 2020, referred to FBI, Nessel says. bridgemi.com

Michigan police memos raised concern about possible nationwide voter registration fraud scheme. Natalia Mittelstadt. JusttheNews.com

FBI refuses to release documents in probe into possible nationwide voter registration fraud. Natalia Mittelstadt. JusttheNews.com

Georgia Election Board Admits Hand Recount and Machine Audit Violated State Law in 2020 Election. Hunter Fielding. NewsAddicts.com

RNC, Pennsylvania GOP Seek to Intervene in Mail-In Ballot Case. Austin Alonzo. 5/7/2024. theepochtimes.com

Biden Admin Officials Subpoenaed Amid Allegations of Taxpayer Money Used to Help Biden Win Key Battleground State. Tom Ozimek. 5/7/2024. theepochtimes.com

North Carolina Voter ID Trial Begins Ahead of Pivotal Election, By Samantha Flom, 5/7/2024. theepochtimes.com

Wisconsin Voter Roll Transparency Challenged by Public Interest Legal Foundation. Steven Kovac. 5/3/2024. theepochtimes.com

California D.A. Dropped 'Explosive' Election Fraud Case Because It Might Help Trump. Melinda Davies (2024). NewsAddicts.com

"The Most Secure Election in American History." John Eastman. Published by The Gatestone Institute, 2024.

Federal Government Giving Voter Registration Forms to Non-Citizen Refugees, 4/29/2024. Cristina Laila. thegatewaypundit.com

Michigan Senator Goes Viral After Dire Election Fraud Warning. 5/2/2024. Vigilant News

Associated Press Admits New Indictments Are 'Campaign' To 'Deter' GOP From Questioning Elections. Brianna Lyman. https://thepricklypear.org

FRAUD

Election Fraud Issues Are Not Limited to Swing States. Stu Cvrk. 10/3/2022. theepochtimes.com

In A Federal Court In Atlanta on Friday J. Alex Halderman (@jhalderm) was able To hack a Dominion voting tabulator in front of a Judge using only a pen to change vote totals! 1/20/2024. Twitter.com/JohnBasham/status/1 748840877888441782

Hacking the Vote: It's Easier Than You Think. Professor J. Alex Halderman has made a career studying electronic voting security. Steve Friess. Alumni.Umich.edu

'The Government Is Not Our Friend.' 9/12/2022. https://www.theepochtimes.com

Voters Appeal Dismissal of Lawsuit Over Use of Zuckerberg Millions in Michigan Elections. Steven Kovac. 9/14/2022. https://www.theepochtimes.com

Democrats Run Network of Fake Local News Sites in Battleground States. Bill Pan. 10/7/2022. https://www.theepochtimes.com

Lawmaker Receives 3 Mystery Mail Ballots, Rips 'Loopholes' in Wisconsin Military Ballot Procedure. Steven Kovac. 11/1/2022. https://www.theepochtimes.com

Google Is Influencing Elections by Flipping Votes on 'Massive Scale.' Naveen Athrappully. 11/7/2022. https://www.theepochtimes.com

Google Is Shifting Votes on a Massive Scale, But A Solution Is At Hand. Robert Epstein. 11/06/2022. dailycaller.com.

Mystery Swirls Over Batch of Thousands of 2020 Voter Registration Forms in MI. theepochtimes.com

Zuckerberg Ends Controversial Grants to Election Offices. Matthew Vadum. 4/13/2022. https://www.theepochtimes.com

Why elections run out of ballots. Deborah Hastings, Associated Press. 3/31/2008. SFGate.com

What To Do If Your Polling Station Runs Out of Ballots, Because Every Vote Counts. Romper.com

Watchdog Group Finds 24,896 Questionable Names on North Carolina Voter Rolls. Steven Kovac. 3/30/2022. https://www.theepochtimes.com

Voter Fraud Map: Election Fraud Database. The Heritage Foundation. heritage.org/voterfraud

Voter Fraud Convictions Challenge Narrative of Secure Elections. Steven Kovac. 1/13/2024. https://www.theepochtimes.com

Voter Fraud Comes in All Shapes and Sizes but Can Sometimes Swing Elections. Dan M. Berger. 10/14/2022. theepochtimes.com

Voter Fraud Cases Stemming from Jailhouse Voter Registration Drive in Florida. Darlene McCormick Sanchez. 8/3/2022. https://www.theepochtimes.com

Wall Street Apes on X: Countless Videos Surfaced Showing Voter Fraud. https://twitter.com/WallStreetApes/status/1723853499644191099

Utah Election Official Hit with Felony Charges for Illegally Shredding, Mishandling Ballots. Frank Bergman. slaynews.com

Two Weeks to Flatten Became Eight Months to Change the Election. 4/12/2024 brownstone.org/articles/

Top Democrat Election Official Convicted. Trent Walker. NewsAddicts.com

Thousands of Votes in 2020 Election Misreported, Virginia Officials Say. Zachery Stieber. 1/23/2024. theepochtimes.com

Texas GOP launches probe into 23 precincts that ran out of paper ballots ... all Republican strongholds. 11/11/2022. bizpacreview.com

States Reportedly Run Out of Ballots. 3/15/2016. Yvonne Abraham. Boston Globe

Sheriff Mack Encourages Other Sheriffs to Investigate Evidence of Election Fraud... Ella Kietlinska and Joshua Phillip. 8/3/2022. https://www.theepochtimes.com

Scant Election Reforms Since 2020 Forebode a Repeat in November. Steven Kovac. https://www.theepochtimes.com

Researcher Featured in '2000 Mules' Documentary Explains How Local Election Fraud... John Haughey. 5/1/2022. https://www.theepochtimes.com

Prosecutors: FTX Founder Bankman-Fried Made 'Tens of Millions' in Illegal Campaign Donations. Jack Phillips. 12/13/2022. theepochtimes.com

Polling locations opening late, others reporting they are out of ballots. Marcie Cipriani. 5/17/2022. WTAE.com

Noncitizens do vote in U.S. elections — here's how they do it. Stephen Dinan. WashingtonTimes.com

New York Officials Failed to Remove Hundreds of Thousands of Potentially Ineligible Voters. Zach Stieber. 7/8/22. theepochtimes.com

New Evidence Shows Mark Zuckerberg's $350M Election Spend Overwhelmingly Helped Democrats Win in 2020. ()x. https://slaynews.com

New Evidence Shows Crooked Electronic Voter Registration System ERIC Is Politically Compromised...STUNNING 104% of Voting Aged Population In MI Is Registered To Vote! https://100percentfedup.com

Muskegon Voter Registration Probe: Michigan Election Integrity Group Wants to Know What Happened. Steven Kovac. 2/23/2024. theepochtimes.com

MULTIPLE REPORTS of "Votes Getting Flipped" In Key Swing State, Voting Machines Shut Down. Travis. wltreport.com

More Than 8,000 Double-Registered Voters Found on New Jersey Rolls. Mark Tapscott. 6/6/2022. https://www.theepochtimes.com

Milwaukee Officials Sued in Zuckerberg-Related Election Bribery Case. Matthew Vadum. 3/27/22. https://www.theepochtimes.com

Milwaukee DA Ignores 354 Referrals for Possible Registration Fraud from 2020 election. Steven Kovac. 12/20/2023. https://www.theepochtimes.com

Michigan election precinct runs out of Democratic ballots. 3/8/2016. Matt Vande Bunte. mlive.com

Man Continues His Fight for Milwaukee's 2020 Election Records. Steven Kovac. 7/19/2022. https://www.theepochtimes.com

Majority of American Voters Rightly Concerned About Vote Fraud. John R. Lott Jr. 11/24/2022. https://www.theepochtimes.com

Mail-In Ballot Fraud Study Finds Trump 'Almost Certainly' Won in 2020. Tom Ozimek. 2/9/2024. https://www.theepochtimes.com

Election ballot paper shortage bigger than estimated. Jeremy Rogalski. KHOU.com

Judge Overturns Election after Democrat Voter Fraud Exposed. Hunter Fielding. newsaddicts.com

Is the Electoral Fix Already In? Matt Taibbi. racket.news

Iowa Officials Coordinated with Big Tech to Censor Election Posts: Judicial Watch. Li Hai. 5/3/2021. https://www.theepochtimes.com.

Infamous 'Zuckbucks' Group Tries to Election-Meddle Again — This Time With Federal Tax Dollars. William Doyle. ThePricklyPear.org

Indicted Virginia Election Official 'Altered Election Results': Filing. Zachary Stieber. 11/28/2023. https://www.theepochtimes.com

Illinois Illegally Denied Elections Group Access to Voter Records, Federal Court Rules. Mathew Vadum. 3/10/2022. https://www.theepochtimes.com

How Google Stopped the Red Wave. Robert Epstein. 11/15/2022. https://www.theepochtimes.com

Ghost Donors. https://twitter.com-Nillgecrazylady/thread/176254491 1205724618

Georgia Officials Sued Over Unsent Absentee Ballots. Zachary Stieber. 11/7/2022. https://www.theepochtimes.com

Gableman Report. Office of the Special Counsel Second Interim Investigative Report On the Apparatus & Procedures of the WI Elections System. Delivered to the WI State Assembly on 3/1/2022.

Salty Texan on X: "ICYMI: Connecticut Police have launched an investigation..." https://twitter.com/texanmaga/status/1703839570880586151

Former Philly Democrat Sentenced to Prison for Election Fraud Scheme. 10/3/2022. Madeline Leesman. townhall.com

Former Louisiana Police Chief, City Councilmember Plead Guilty in Federal Vote-Buying Case. Katabella Roberts. 7/22/2022. https://www.theepochtimes.com/

Former Louisiana Police Chief and Current City Councilmember Indicted for Alleged Vote Buying Scheme. https://www.justice.gov. 12/14/2021. U.S. Attorneys, Eastern District of Louisiana

FOIA Documents Reveal Secret 2020 Election Day Meeting. February 13, 2024. vnninfluencers. This article originally appeared on The Gateway Pundit. Guest post by Jim Hoft. VigilantNews.com

Filmmaker: Documentary Proves Rampant Illegal Vote Trafficking in 2020. Steven Kovac. 4/26/2022. https://www.theepochtimes.com/

Federal Judge Issues Temporary Restraining Order Against Group Involved in 2000 Mules Documentary. Juliette Fairley. 9/18/2022. https://www.theepochtimes.com

FBI: Election Officials in Nine States Targeted by Cyberattacks. Jack Phillips. 3/29/2022. https://www.theepochtimes.com

Ex-Democrat Congressman Pleads Guilty to Voter Fraud in Multiple Pennsylvania Elections. ()x. June, 2022. https://slaynews.com

New Report Raises Serious Concerns Over Integrity of Florida Elections. Patricia Tolson. 8/19/2022. theepochtimes.com

Election Watchdog Finds 137,500 Ballots Unlawfully Trafficked in Wisconsin. Steve Kovac. 3/29/2022. theepochtimes.com

Election Rigging Threatens the Left. Doug Lain. 9/2023. compactmag.com

Election Fraud Issues Are Not Limited to Swing States. Stu Cvrk. 10/3/2022. https://www.theepochtimes.com

Election Fraud Happens — In Addition to Widespread Election Rigging. Neland Nobel. https://thepricklypear.org

Election Director Resigns After 'Comprehensive Failure' on Primary Day in AZ County. Gary Bai. 8/5/2022. theepochtimes.com.

Donor Bots. Mel. @VillgeCrazy-Lady. https://twitter.comNill-gecrazylady/thread/1759305508584 882680

Detroit Election Update: GOP and Independent Poll Challengers Claim at Least 50% of Absentee Envelopes Missing Signature Verification Check Mark. Patty McMurray. 8/2/2022. 100percent-fedup.com

Democrats Hit with New Election Fraud Charges over Mail-In Ballots. Frank Bergman. https://slaynews.com

Democrat Election Clerk Admits to Ignoring Mail-In Ballot Law during Bombshell Testimony. Frank Bergman. slaynews.com

Democrat Charged over Voter Fraud Scheme Involving Mail-In Ballots. Frank Bergman. https://slaynews.com

Democracy Lost: A Report on the Fatally Flawed 2016 Democratic Primaries. ElectionJusticeUSA.org

Court Strikes Down Law That Let Noncitizens Vote in New York Elections. Tom Ozimek. 2/22/2024. https://www.theepochtimes.com

Court Orders Release of True the Vote Leaders from Jail. Zachary Stieber. 11/7/2022. https://www.theepochtimes.com

Chicago Board of Elections 'Mistakenly' Left Out Over 9,000 Mail-In Ballots in Primary Election. Tom Ozimek. 3/25/2024. https://www.theepochtimes.com

CA City Council Member Arrested on Voter Fraud Charges: Sheriff. Jack Phillips. https://www.theepochtimes.com

Judge overturns Bridgeport, CT mayoral primary election after Democrat clerk busted for ballot stuffing. https://thepostmillennial.com

Box of 2020 Election Absentee Ballots Found Stashed in MI Storage Unit. Frank Bergman. SlayNews.com

Bombshell Report Exposes Voting Scheme In Michigan, Cover-Up By State Officials. evol.news

Bodycam Footage Shows Texas Man Admitting to Brazen Cash-for-Ballots Scheme. Steven Kovac. 10/6/2022. theepochtimes.com

Biden 'Won' 2020 Election with Mail-in Ballot Fraud, Study Confirms. Hunter Fielding. https://newsaddicts.com

Ballot paper shortage could cause problems on Election Day. ABCNews.go.com

As hundreds waited to vote in Houston, a dozen-plus polling sites ran out of ballot sheets. MSN.com

Arizona 2020 Election Results May Have Been Different If 20,000 Invalid Ballots Had Not Been Counted: Report. Beth Brelje. theepochtimes.com

Alachua County precincts ran out of Republican ballots on election day. WCJB Staff. 8/24/2022. WCJB.com

About The Election Fraud Database. The Heritage Foundation. https://www.heritage.org/article/about-the-election-fraud-database

More Than 8,000 Double Registered Voters... Mark Tapscot. 6/6/2022. theepochtimes.com

2020 Election Rigged 7 Months in Advance, Investigation Finds. Hunter Fielding. newsaddicts.com

'2000 Mules' Investigators Arrested by U.S. Marshals for Refusing to Reveal Source. X. 10/31/22. https://slaynews.com

150,000 Votes in the 2020 Election Not Tied to a Valid Address in Wisconsin. Steven Kovac. 1/4/2023. theepochtimes.com
74 Harvesting and Mule Rings:

Where They Were, How They Did It... Capt. Seth Keshel. 5/14/2022. https://skeshel.substack.com

43,000 Absentee Ballot Votes Counted in DeKalb County 2020 Election Violated Chain Of Custody Rule. 9/29/23. https://www.georgiarecord.com

34,000 Illegal 2020 Election Ballots Found in Michigan during Forensic Study. Frank Bergman. https://slaynews.com

20% of Voters Admit to Mail-In Ballot Fraud in 2020 Election, Poll Shows - Slay News. Frank Bergman. https://slaynews.com

19,000 Dead People Registered to Vote in Virginia, Election Officials Admit. David Lindfield. https://slaynews.com

Democrats Exploit Automatic Voter Registration Systems to Register Non-Citizens. Christopher Arps. 7/12/2023. https://12ft.io

10,000 Uncounted Ballots Found in Texas County. Jack Phillips. 3/8/2022. theepochtimes.com

6 Minnesota Counties Have 515 Duplicate Registrations on Voter Rolls... Steve Kovac. 9/28/2022. https://www.theepochtimes.com

5,000 Duplicate Ballots Sent to California Voters in Riverside County. Caden Pearson. 10/19/2022. theepochtimes.com

4th resident of The Villages admits to voting twice in the 2020 election. Mike DeForest. 2/20/2023. clickorlando.com

"Campaign Finance Mules" Part 2: UNEMPLOYED Missouri Donors Who Made Thousands of Donations... Jim Hoft. 12/08/2022. thegatewaypundit.com

WATCH: Yet Another Ballot Fraudster CAUGHT On Camera? Vince Quill. 11/15/2023. wltreport.com

300,000 Ballots Lacking Chain of Custody. Rachel Alexander. https://twitter.com/Rach_IC/thread/1741302699864518977

GEORGIA

Why a Judge Has Georgia Vote Fraud on His Mind: 'Pristine' Biden Ballots that Looked Zeroxed. RealClearInvestigations. 6/8/2021. theepochtimes.com

Refutation of GA Secretary of State Brad Raffensperger's False Election Claims. Produced for the GA General Assembly. Garland Favorito and Bob Covert. 2/8/2022. https://voterga.org

VoterGA to Hold Press Conference on Monday Disclosing Legal Actions. to Over 100 Counties Missing Dropbox Videos. Joe Hoft. 5/22/2022. thegatewaypundit.com

True the Vote Defeats Fair Fight, Stacy Abrams, Marc Elias, and the Biden Department of Justice in Landmark Election Case in Georgia Federal Court. Fair Fight et al v. True the Vote et al. Case No. 2:20-cv-0302-SCJ. truethevote.org

Tens of Thousands of Votes Cast in Georgia with Ineligible Addresses in 2020 Election. Frank Bergman. slaynews.com/news

REPORT: Testimony From GA Secretary of State Dispels Claims That He Was Told To Fabricate Votes. Cullen McCue. https://trendingpoliticsnews.com

Raffensperger Distorted GA Law After I Uncovered Illegal Votes. Mark Davis. thefederalist.com

Judge Throws Out Lawsuit by Stacey Abrams's PAC Over 2018 Georgia Governor's Election. Caden Pearson. 10/1/2022. https://www.theepochtimes.com

John Eastman on the Georgia election conspiracy case. 60 Minutes. Scott Pelley. cbsnews.com

Huge Implications: Georgia Supreme Court Rules Voters Have the Right to Sue Election Officials. Brian Lupo. 10/27/2022. thegatewaypundit.com

Trouble in Fulton County? High-Powered Defense Attorneys Move to Withdraw Amid Questions About 2020 Ballots. Kyle Becker. https://beckernews.com

Georgia's Record-Breaking Early Voting Turnout Defies Voter Suppression Accusations. Tom Ozimek. 5/21/2022. theepochtimes.com. Georgia Special Collection. Open.Ink. open.ink/georgia

GA Senate Introduces Bill to Remove Brad Raffensperger from Any Serious Role in 2024 Election. Melinda Davies. newsaddicts.com

GA Officials Sued Over Unsent Absentee Ballots. Zachary Stieber. 11/7/2022. theepochtimes.com

GA Investigator's Notes Detail 'Massive' Issues During 2020 Election. Zachary Stieber. 6/18/2021. https://www.theepochtimes.com

Georgia Investigating 17,000 Missing Ballot Images from 2020 Presidential Election. Frank Bergman. https://slaynews.com

Georgia Election Board Admits Rigging 2020 Election to Help Biden 'Stop Trump.' Hunter Fielding. https://newsaddicts.com

Fani Willis Has Evidence Exonerating Georgia's Alternate Electors. Shawn Fleetwood, 9/3/2023. The Federalist. realclearpolitics.com

Did data from GA voting machine breach play role in alleged MI election plot? Clara Hendrickson, Detroit Free Press. yahoo.com

Data Analyst Defends 2020 Georgia Election Rolls Challenges. Dan M. Berger. theepochtimes.com

Court Rules No Evidence Georgia's Voting Law Discriminates Against Black Voters. Jack Phillips. theepochtimes.com

Judge Issues Huge Decision on Georgia Voting Machines. Kyle Becker. trendingpoliticsnews.com

Harrison Floyd Lawyers Claim the State of Georgia Has Proof That Trump Won the State's 2020 Election. Hunter Fielding. https://newsaddicts.com

Bombshell Report Exposes Election Rigging with Voting Machines. Hunter Fielding. https://newsaddicts.com

Georgia election server wiped after suit filed. AP News. Frank Bajak.

Declaration of J. Alex Halderman. Case 1:17-cv-02989-AT Document 1630-25. 2/13/23. Page 2 of 49. Civil Action No. 1:17-CV-2989-AT

"The Most Secure Election in American History." John Eastman. PricklyPear.News

HEALTH

Common Laxatives Linked to Behavioral Issues and Worse in Children, Experts Warn. Sheramy Tsai, 5/8/2024. www.theepochtimes.com

Sperm Samples in French Infertility Clinic Have High Levels of Glyphosate. Marco Caceres. 6/3/2024. Environment

High levels of weedkiller found in more than half of sperm samples; study finds. Tom Perkins. 5/17/2024. TheGuardian.com.

EPA Withdraws Glyphosate Interim Decision Released on September 23, 2022. EPA.gov

Prenatal Exposure to COVID-19 mRNA Vaccine BNT162b2 Induces Autism-Like Behaviors in Male Neonatal Rats: Insights into WNT and BDNF Signaling Perturbations. Mumin Alper Erdogan, Orkun Gurbuz, Mehmet Fatih Bozkurt, Oytun Erbas. 1/10/2024. Neurochemical Research (2024) 49:1034–1048. https://doi.org/10.1007/s11064-023-04089-2

Are environmental, occupational, iatrogenic, biological, and other toxicants contributing factors to the explosive increase in Gender Dysphoria? Dr. Ronald N. Kostoff. 5/30/2024. trialsitenews.com

As children line up at gender clinics, families confront many unknowns. Chad Terhune, Robin Respaut, and Michelle Conlin. Reuters.com

Do hormone-modulating chemicals impact on reproduction and development of wild amphibians? Frances Orton, Charles R Tyler. PMID: 25335651 DOI: 10.1111/brv.12147. Epub 10/22/2014

Effects of endocrine disrupting chemicals on gonad development: Mechanistic insights from fish and mammals. G Delbes, M Blazquez, J I Fernandina, P Grigorova, B F Hales, C Metcalfe, L Navarro-Martin, L Parent, B Robaire, A Rwigemera, G Van Der Kraak, M Wade, V Marlatt. PMID: 34509487 DOI: 10.1016/j.envres.2021.112040

CA Senate Approves Ban on Schools Informing Parents of Student's Gender Identity. Brad Jones. 6/14/2024. theepochtimes.com

Justice Department Announces Largest Health Care Fraud Settlement in Its History. Pfizer to Pay $2.3 Billion for Fraudulent Marketing. https://www.justice.gov

Biden admin official pressured medical experts to nix age limit guidelines for transgender surgery: court doc. Victor Nava. NYPost.com. 6/26/2024

Dr. McCullough Calls Out HHS Assistant Secretary Levine. Peter A. McCullough, MD, MPH. Substack.com

Thousands of Doctors Take Legal Action Against Transgender Mandate. Jacob Burg. 1/20/2023. theepochtimes.com

The Silent Epidemic Eating Away Americans' Minds. Marina Zhang. 1/16/2024. theepochtimes.com

Therapeutic Drug Use Data are for the U.S. https://www.cdc.gov

Health Expenditures, Data are for the U.S. https://www.cdc.gov

Corruption of the WHO is the Biggest Threat to the World's Public Health of Our Time. Rhoda Wilson. 5/19/022. exposenews.com

AL Lawmakers Advance 'What Is a Woman' Bill Defining Male, Female Sex. Katabella Roberts. 5/25/2023. theepochtimes.com

New Study Confirms Atrazine's Effects Across a Range of Species (Including Us). Andrew Wetzler Senior Vice President, Nature. NRDC.org.

Demasculinization and feminization of male gonads by atrazine: Consistent effects across vertebrate classes. The Journal of Steroid Biochemistry and Molecular Biology, Volume 127, Issues 1-2, October 2011, Pages 64-73

When Healthcare Looks Like Genocide. FreedomRising.info

Atrazine reproductive issues reviewed. 1/28/2011. upi.com

U.S. maps of atrazine use and predicted concentrations in groundwater. By Water Resources Mission Area. 2015. us gs. gov

Ingredients Used in Pesticide Products. epa.gov/ingredients-used-pesticide-products/atrazine

Atrazine Production, Import/Export Use, and Disposal. atsdr.cdc.gov/toxprofiles/tp153-c5.pdf

Toxicological Profile for Atrazine. U.S. Dept. of Health and Human Services. Public Health Service Agency for Toxic Substances and Disease Registry. September 2003.

Global Atrazine Market 2023 - 2030. GiiResearch.com

Weed Killer and Autism (ASD) or ADHD? Robert Malone. substack.com/@rwmalonemd

Association between vitamin D supplementation and COVID-19 infection and mortality. Jason B. Gibbons, Edward C. Norton, Jeffrey S. McCullough, David O. Meltzer, Jill Lavigne, Virginia C. Fiedler & Robert D. Gibbons. https://doi.org/10.1038/s41598-022-24053-4

Protective Effect of Vitamin D Supplementation on COVID-19-Related Intensive Care Hospitalization and Mortality: Definitive Evidence from Meta-Analysis and Trial Sequential Analysis. Argano, C.; Mallaci Bocchio, R.; Natoli, G.; Scibetta, S.; Lo Monaco, M.; Corrao, S. Pharmaceuticals 2023, 16, 130. doi.org/10.3390/ph16010130

US Vaccine Injury Compensation Program Has 10-Year Backlog of Claims. Megan Redshaw. 2/20/2024. theepochtimes.com

NIH-funded study suggests acetaminophen exposure in pregnancy linked to higher risk of ADHD, autism Media Advisory. Wednesday, 10/30/2019. www.nih.gov

Evidence the U.S. autism epidemic initiated by acetaminophen (Tylenol) is aggravated by oral antibiotic amoxicillin/clavulanate (Augmentin) and now exponentially by herbicide glyphosate (Roundup). Peter Good. Affiliations PMID: 29460795 DOI: 10.1016/j.clnesp.2017.10.005. https://pubmed.ncbi.nlm.nih.gov/29460795/

More than 100 families of children with autism or attention-deficit/hyperactivity disorder are suing companies that market acetaminophen. https://www.spectrumnews.org

Chlormequat is a highly toxic agricultural chemical the EPA refers to as a pesticide. https://www.ewg.org/news-insights/news/2023/05/chlormequat-what-you-need-know-about-problematic-pesticide

Study Finds 80 Percent of Americans Exposed to FertilityLowering Chemicals in Cheerios, Quaker Oats. Naveen Athrappully. 2/16/2024. https://www.theepochtimes.com/health/study-finds-80-percent-americans-exposed-to-fertility-lowering-chemicals-in-cheerios-quaker-oats-5588728

Physiology, Oxygen Transport. Carl E. Rhodes. https://ncbi.nlm.nih.gov/books/NBK538336

Human Gene Therapy Products Incorporating Human Genome Editing: Guidance for Industry. January 2024. U.S. Department of Health and Human Services, Food and Drug Administration, Center for Biologics Evaluation and Research

Burden of serious harms from diagnostic error in the USA. Newman-Toker DE, Nassery N, Schaffer AC, et al. BMJ Qual Saf 2024;33:109–120.

Current Cigarette Smoking Among Adults in the United States in 2021. cdc.gov

Leading Causes of Death, Data are for the U.S. Source: Mortality in the United States, 2021. https://www.cdc.gov

Geographic Distribution of Clinical Care for Transgender and Gender-Diverse Youth. Tara Weixel, MA, and Beth Wildman, PhD. Department of Psychological Sciences, Kent State University, Kent, Ohio. DOI: https://doi.org/10.1542/peds.2022-057054. Sep 22, 2022

Pediatric Transgender Clinics: Who Is Going to Them and Why? Lewis First, MD, MS, Editor in Chief, Pediatrics. October 24, 2019. publications.aap.org

Number of Pediatric 'Gender Clinics' Exploding Across the Country. The Daily Caller News Foundation. WesternJournal.com

Breakfast Cereals Scrutinized for Pesticide That May Harm Reproduction. Sina McCullough. 4/18/2024. theepochtimes.com

Hyperthermia in Humans Enhances Interferon-γ Synthesis and Alters the Peripheral Lymphocyte Population. J.F. DOWNING, H. MARTINEZ-VALDEZ, R.S. ELIZONDO, E.B. WALKER, and M.W. TAYLOR. Journal of Interferon Research.

doi.org/10.1089/jir.1988.8.143 Interferon-γ and infectious diseases: Lessons and prospects. Carl F. Nathan. Science. 19 Apr 2024. Vol 384, Issue 6693

Interferon γ and Its Important Roles in Promoting and Inhibiting Spontaneous and Therapeutic Cancer Immunity. Elise Alspach, Danielle M. Lussier, and Robert D. Schreiber. Department of Pathology and Immunology, Washington University School of Medicine, St. Louis, Missouri 63110. Correspondence: rdschreiber@wustl.edu

Interferon gamma. en.wikipedia.org Pregnancy & Childbirth: What Not To Eat When You're Pregnant. October 19, 2022. https://health.clevelandclinic.org

Do you know which foods to avoid when you're pregnant? Mayo Clinic Staff. MayoClinic.org

11 Foods and Beverages to Avoid During Pregnancy. HealthLine.com

Toxicological Profile for Atrazine. U.S. Dept. of Health and Human Services. Public Health Service Agency for Toxic Substances and Disease Registry. September 2003

In Vivo Hyperthermia Enhances Plasma Antiviral Activity and Stimulates Peripheral Lymphocytes for Increased Synthesis of Interferon-γ. Authors: JAMES F. DOWNING, MILTON W. TAYLOR, KAI-MIN WEI, and REYNALDO S. ELIZONDO. Journal of Interferon Research. https://doi.org/10.1089/jir.1987.7.185

6 points to remember about atrazine. Gil Gullickson. Agriculture.com

214 Studies, 21 Guidelines: Largest Review on Transgender-Youth Medicine Finds Insufficient Evidence for Medicalization. Marina Zhang. 5/2/2024. https://www.theepochtimes.com

Gender-Affirming Care and Young People. HHS Office of Population Affairs. opa.hhs.gov

Rachel Levine condemns Texas officials targeting care for trans youth. Sarah Jacoby. Today.com

Remarks by HHS Assistant Secretary for Health ADM Rachel Levine for the 2022 Out for Health

Conference. Admiral Rachel L. Levine, MD 4/30/2022. TX Christian University Fort Worth, TX

Biden-Harris Administration Finalizes Rule to Strengthen Protections for Youth in the Child Welfare System. 4/29/2024. https://www.hhs.gov

Rachel Levine: Doctors agree on need for 'gender-affirming care' for trans kids. Selim Algar. 5/2/2022. https://nypost.com

The Government Accidentally Confirms It Has No Real Evidence to Support So-Called 'Gender Affirming Care' For Minors. Matt Walsh. DailyWire.com

How Much Damage Have Vaccines Done to Society? MidwesternDoctor.com

Dept. of Health Says It Has Only Two Pages of Scientific Evidence Backing Its Support For 'Gender-Affirming Care.' Andrew Rodriguez. 2024. https://www.msn.com

What Is Gender Affirmation Surgery? MyClevelandClinic.org

Rachel Levine Was a Disaster in Pennsylvania but Is Now Headed to Washington. Zachary Yost. 1/28/2021. theepochtimes.com

Constitutional Rights Legal Firm Obtains Emails Showing HHS Support for 'Gender-Affirming Care' in Prohibited States. Matt McGregor. 5/3/2024. https://www.theepochtimes.com

Scientists Launch New Bird Flu mRNA Vaccine for Mass Public Vaccinations. Hunter Fielding. NewsAddicts.com

Colorectal cancer is rising in children, teens, and young adults, study finds. Corrie Pelc. MedicalNewsToday.com

Atrazine induces complete feminization and chemical castration in male African clawed frogs (Xenopus laevis). Tyrone B. Hayesa, Vicky Khourya, Anne Narayana, Mariam Nazira, Andrew Parka, Travis Browna, Li lian Adamea, Elton Chana, Daniel Buchholzb, Theresa Stuevea, and Sherrie Gallipeaua. www.pnas.org/cgi/doi/10.1073/pnas.0909519107

Researchers Discover New Mechanism Linking Diet and Cancer Risk. Jennifer Sweenie. 5/18/2024. https://www.theepochtimes.com

Risk of Suicide 12 Times Greater After 'Gender-Affirming' Surgery: Study. Patricia Tolson. 5/22/2024. theepochtimes.com

Maternal Urinary Fluoride and Child Neurobehavior at Age 36 Months. Ashley J. Malin, PhD; Sandrah P. Eckel, PhD; Howard Hu, MD, MPH, ScD; E. Angeles Martinez-Mier, PhD, DDS, MSD; Ixel Hernandez-Castro, PhD; Tingyu Yang, MS; Shohreh F. Farzan, PhD; Rima Habre, ScD; Carrie V. Breton, ScD; Theresa M. Bastain, PhD. JAMANetwork Open | Public Health. May 20, 2024.

Gov't Stockpiling Vaccines ahead of Pre-Election Pandemic. Hunter Fielding. NewsAddicts.com

Scientists Launch New Bird Flu mRNA Vaccine for Mass Public Vaccinations. Hunter Fielding. NewsAddicts.com

Laxative Type in Relation to Colorectal Cancer Risk. Jessica S Citronberg, Sheetal Hardikar, Amanda Phipps, Jane C. Figueiredo, and Polly Newcomb. Department of Epidemiology, University of WA, Seattle, WA. Ann Epidemiol. 2018 October; 28(10): 739–741. doi:10.1016/j.annepidem.2018.06.011

How What You Eat May Change Your Unborn Children's Genes — and Affect Their Health. Nathaniel Johnson, Ph.D., Hasan Khatib, Ph.D., and Thomas D. Crenshaw, Ph.D. 04/24/24. https://childrenshealthdefense.org

The Contentious Role of Food Dyes in Children's Diets. Zena le Roux. 5/6/2024. https://www.theepochtimes.com

It Was Scientifically Proven Years Ago That a Diet High in Sugar Harms Your Brain. 5/13/2024. Vigilant News. Brian Cates.

Fluoride in pregnancy may harm child's brain development. Tracy Swartz. 5/20/2024. NYPost.com

The Secret Healing Power of a Treatment Hidden for 200 Years. Yuhong Dong, M.D., Ph.D. 4/30/2024. theepochtimes.com

The Silent Epidemic Eating Away American Minds. Marina Zhang. 1/16/2024. theepochtimes.com

A "Seahorse Dad," Trudeau tanks, and France Joins the Resistance. Who is Robert Malone (Substack)

Disturbances in Gut Flora Linked to Autism, ADHD Development. Amie Dahnke. 4/25/2024. theepochtimes.com

Infant microbes and metabolites point to childhood neurodevelopmental disorders. Angelica P. Ahrens, Tuulia Hyotylainen, Joseph R. Petrone, Kajsa Igelstrom, Christian D. George, Timothy J. Garrett, Matej Oresic, Eric W. Triplett, Johnny Ludvigsson. Correspondence: ewt@ufl.edu. https://doi.org/10.1016/j.cell.2024.02.035

Sugar makes you stupid: Study shows high-fructose diet sabotages learning, memory. University of California, Los Angeles. 5/15/2012

Dept. of Health Says It Has Only Two Pages of Scientific Evidence Backing Its Support For 'Gender-Affirming Care.' Andrew Rodriguez. 2024. MSN.com

What Is Feminizing Bottom Surgery? ClevelandClinic.org

What Is Vaginoplasty? ClevelandClinic.org

IVERMECTIN

Ivermectin: enigmatic multifaceted 'wonder' drug continues to surprise and exceed expectations. Andy Crump. The Journal of Antibiotics (2017) 70, 495–505 & 2017 Japan Antibiotics Research Assoc. www.nature.com/ja

Top Doctor Confirms Ivermectin Cures Cancer. SlayNews.com. Frank Bergman

Patients Sue Pharmacies for Refusing Hydroxychloroquine, Ivermectin Prescriptions. Joseph L. Fink, BPharm, JD, DSc (Hon), FAPhA. PharmacyTimes.com

Gov Parson signs law shielding doctors prescribing ivermectin, hydroxychloroquine. 6/8/2022. FultonSun.com. The Missouri Independent. Tessa Weinberg

NH governor blocks pharmacists from dispensing ivermectin to treat COVID-19 without prescription. AP. FoxNews.com

Ivermectin: Australian regulator bans drug as COVID treatment after sharp rise in prescriptions. Josh Taylor. 9/10/2021. TheGuardian.com.

Study: Ivermectin can lead to "large reductions" in COVID-19 deaths. 6/20/2021. https://sharylattkisson.com

MAIL-IN VOTING

US Postal Service Makes Announcement on Mail-In Ballots Ahead of Midterm Elections. Jack Phillips. 7/31/2022. https://www.theepochtimes.com

Group Monitoring Drop Boxes Sued for Alleged Voter Intimidation. Zachary Stieber. 10/25/2022. https://www.theepochtimes.com

Wisconsin Judge Rules Use of Mobile Vans in Absentee Voting Violates State election Law. Katabella Roberts. 1/11/2024. https://www.theepochtimes.com

Government Suppressed, Censored Concerns Over Mail-In Voting in 2020. Austin Alonzo. 1/25/2024. theepochtimes.com

RNC Files Election Integrity Lawsuit Targeting Michigan's Handling of Absentee Ballots. T.J. Muscaro. 3/28/2024. https://www.theepochtimes.com

Watchdog Groups Allege Election Violations in Florida's 2022 and 2020 Elections. Steven Kovac. 9/8/2022. theepochtimes.com

Warnings of 'Red Mirage' Ignore Real Problem with Mail-in Ballots. Michael Washburn. 11/8/2022. theepochtimes.com

Universal Mail-In Voting Violates Delaware Constitution: Delaware Supreme Court. Zachary Stieber. 10/7/2022. https://www.theepochtimes.com

Supreme Court Denies Bid to Expand No-Excuse Mail-In Ballots in Texas. Tom Ozimek. 4/22/2024. https://www.theepochtimes.com

Missing Ballots Found in New Jersey County. Tony Gray. ResisttheMainstream.org

Judge Rejects Challenge to Mail-in Ballots in N. Dakota. Tom Ozimek. 2/3/2024. theepochtimes.com

The States That Changed Mail-In Voting Rules for 2022. Petr Svab 11/4/2022. theepochtimes.com How Mass Mail-In Voting Changes Everything. William Doyle. https://thepricklypear.org

Forensic Investigators Find 34,000 Illegal 2020 Election Ballots in

Michigan. Hunter Fielding. NewsAddicts.com

Elections Department Sends Out Wrong Ballots to 'Undetermined Number' of People. Jack Phillips. https://www.theepochtimes.com

Delaware Court Strikes Down State's Voting-by-Mail Law. Matthew Vadum. 915/2022. https://www.theepochtimes.com

Court Finds that Texas Law Requiring the Rejection of Mail Ballots and Applications Violates the Civil Rights Act. justice.gov

Election Centers Were Sent Fentanyl-Laced Letters with Antifa Symbols. Matthew Holloway. https://trendingpoliticsnews.com

Absentee Voting from Abroad Presents Myriad of Fraud Vulnerabilities in U.S. Elections. 4/14/2023. theepochtimes.com

MISC

Supreme Court Could Set Landmark Precedent in Trump Jan. 6 Case. Sam Dorman. 2/18/2024. https://www.theepochtimes.com

Sidney Powell Pleads Guilty in Trump GA Election Case. Catherine Yang. theepochtimes.com

Sidney Powell Offers Apology in Georgia Election Case. Zachary Stieber. theepochtimes.com

Republicans Respond After Top FBI Agent Reportedly Resigns. Jack Phillips. 8/30/2022. https://www.theepochtimes.com

Sean Davis on X: "According to a new investigative report by @JudiciaryGOP..." https://twitter.com/seanmdav/status/1721734484922450147

What Did The W.E.F Mean By: "You Will Own Nothing and Be Happy, By 2030"? 11/20/2023. https://teslatelegraph.com.

WEF Demands Powers to Regulate Public's Speech Online. SlayNews.com. Frank Bergman

Schwab Tells World Leaders 'End of Capitalism' Is Here. Hunter Fielding. NewsAddicts.com

Klaus Schwab Calls for Governments to 'Merge' with Unelected Corporate Elite. Frank Bergman. SlayNews.com.

'You'll Own Nothing'— and Like It. Or Will You? David Solway. The-Pipeline.org.

Twitter Suspends 2020 Maricopa County Election Audit Accounts. Jack Phillips. 7/27/2021. https://www.theepochtimes.com

Department of Justice Warns States Against Violating Federal Law with Audits. Zachary Stieber. 7/28/2021. theepochtimes.com

National Police Association: Congress Should Investigate 2020 Riots, Not Jan. 6 Capitol Breach. Jack Phillips. 7/28/2021. https://www.theepochtimes.com

Trump Criticizes Pulitzer for Rejecting Call to Revoke Awards to NYTimes, Washington Post. Frank Fang. 7/19/2022. https://www.theepochtimes.com

It's Worse Than Anyone Wants to Admit. Jeffrey A. Tucker. 7/29/2022. theepochtimes.com

Why Is Election Day a Tuesday in November? The answer lies with America's 19th-century farmers. Evan Andrews. 12/2/2019. History.com

These US Elections Saw the Highest Voter Turnout Rates. Voter turnout rates peaked in the 1870s and decreased in the 20th century. Becky Little. 11/2/2020. History.com

Elections in Colonial America Were Huge, Booze-Fueled Parties. Erin Blakemore. 11/25/2019. History.com

How We Used to Vote. The New Yorker. Jill Lepore. 10/6/2008. newyorker.com/magazine

How Power Grabs in the South Erased Reforms After Reconstruction. Becky Little. 12/20/2018. History.com

Dred Scott Case - Decision, Definition & Impact. history.com

Supreme Court rules in Dred Scott case. March 6. history.com

Weekend Read: The Six Things Americans Should Know About the Second Amendment. Richard W. Stevens. thepricklypear.org

Democratic Party Moved from Uncomfortable to Intolerable for Members: #WalkAway Founder. Beth Berlje. 10/13/022. https://www.theepochtimes.com

Alaska Republicans Vote to Censure GOP Leader Mitch McConnell. Jack Phillips. 10/25/2022. https://www.theepochtimes.com

Former AG Barr: There Will Be No FBI Accountability After Russiagate Controversy. Jack Phillips. 11/3/2022. theepochtimes.com

Brazil's Anti-Globalist Refounding. Ernesto Araújo. 11/17/2022. https://www.theepochtimes.com

German court orders do-over of Berlin elections, citing 'serious systemic flaws' in process. https://justthenews.com

Brazil Freezes Bank Accounts of Citizens Protesting Election Results. ()x. https://slaynews.com

65 Project. https://www.influencewatch.org/. The 65 Project was launched to punish lawyers who supported President Trump.

Break Up America's Elite. Darel E. Paul. https://compactmag.com

America Needs a New JFK. David P. Goldman. compactmag.com

How Long Has Election Corruption Been Going On? Behind the Blue Wall. 7/12/2023. https://skeshel.substack.com

Banning Parties to 'Save Democracy.' Malcom Kyeyune. 8/16/2023. https://compactmag.com

Robert F. Kennedy Jr. to Tucker Carlson: I've Talked to CIA and Mob Hitmen Who Were Assigned to JFK Assassination. 8/16/2023. thegatewaypundit.com

A Defeat for Guatemala's Elites. Juan D. Rojas. compactmag.com The BRICS Plot Against America. Malcom Kyeyune. https://compactmag.com

Judge Denies RFK Jr.'s Request for Restraining Order Against Google. 8/24/2023. childrenshealthdefense.org

America's Shadow Government (Behind the Facade). Ronin. https://roninhardjan.substack.com

The Best kind of "ism" is Americanism. Robert Malone Substack.

Google Searches Favor Democrat Candidates in 2024 Presidential Race. Naveen Athrappully. theepochtimes.com

The Crew of the Enola Gay on Dropping the Atomic. Bomb. MentalFloss.com. Miss Cellania. 2010

Children's Health Defense, Robert F. Kennedy, Jr., Trialsite, Inc., Creative Destruction Media, LLC, Erin Elizabeth Finn, Jim Hoft, Dr. Ben Tapper, Ben Swann, Dr. Joseph Mercola, Ty Bollinger & Charlene Bolllinger, Plaintiffs, v. The Washington Post Co., The British Broadcasting Corp., The Associated Press, & Reuters, Defendants. Case 2:23-cv-00004-Z Document 1 Filed 01/10/23. United States District Court Northern District Texas, Amarillo Division [Court case against the "Trusted News Initiative."]

MSM Plot Exposed: 'Trusted News Initiative' Leads Coup Against Pres. Trump. Renee Nal. 11/7/2020. rairfoundation.com

'Trusted News Initiative' Antitrust Litigation. childrenshealthdefense.org

Davos and its danger to Democracy. 1/18/2016. Nick Buxton. Published at Common Dreams. https ://www.tni.org/ en/article/ davos-and-its-danger-to-democracy

Trusted News Initiative to Combat Spread of Harmful Vaccine Disinformation, Press Release. 12/10/2020. https://www.ebu.ch

ABC joins the Trusted News Initiative. 14 Nov 2022. https://www.abc.net.au

An Evolutionary Timeline of Homo Sapiens. 2/2/2021. smithsonianmag.com

Slovakia's Pragmatic Social Democrats. Petr Drulák. https://compactmag.com

Judge Pierces Electronic Registration Information Center's 'Wall of Secrecy.' Steven Kovac. https://www.theepochtimes.com

How to File an Open Records Request. truethevote.org.

Google is Where Democracy is Dying? Bruce Bialosky. https://thepricklypear.org.

Consequences of Government Weaponization. Mimi Nguyen Ly and Rudy Blalock. 9/15/2023. https://substack.com/@rwmalonemd

Why They Fear Jim Jordan as House Speaker. Jeffrey A. Tucker. https://www.theepochtimes.com

Proper Role of USG- Servant or Master? substack.com/@rwmalonemd

Pandemics as a Catalyst for a New World Order. Jill Glasspool Malone, PhD. https://substack.com/@rwmalonemd

Forget the Founding Fathers. Hamilton Craig. https://compactmag.com/

Anarcho-Capitalism and Dr. Javier Milei. substack.com/@rwmalonemd

Former Congressional Investigator Says DOJ Urged Court Not to Notify Him About Subpoena. Katabella Roberts. https://www.theepochtimes.com.

Adam Schiff Sends Anti-First Amendment Letter to Elon Musk Demanding Censorship on X. Frank Bergman. slaynews.com.

History of Influence, Scandal, and Denial. By Paul Thacker. This essay originally appeared as a chapter in "Integrity, Transparency and Corruption in Healthcare & Research on Health."

Elon Musk Says He Is Prepared to 'Go to Prison' to Defend Free Speech on X. Melinda Davies. https://newsaddicts.com.

Why I am No Longer a Democrat. substack.com/@rwmalonemd

The FBI Conducts Domestic Violent Extremism Investigations on TradCatholics: House Report. https://substack.com/@rwmalonemd

Federal Appeals Court Rules in Favor of Pro-Trump Meme Maker Douglas Mackey, Lifts 7-Month Prison Sentence. Hunter Fielding. https://newsaddicts.com

'Finding the Truth' About Government Censorship Not Easy, Journalists Tell Congress. Michael Nevradakis. 12/04/2023. https://childrenshealthdefense.org

The Rise of Propaganda-Dependent Elites and Lonely Masses. 12/26/2023. brownstone.org

Michigan GOP Descends Into Chaos. Anders Anglesey. 1/8/2024. https://www.newsweek.com

The Mainstream Against Democracy. Sohrab Ahmari. https://thepricklypear.org

Big Law's Troubling Sway at the Supreme Court. John G. Malcolm. https://www.theepochtimes.com

A Timeline of Witch Hunts in Europe. Jone Johnson Lewis. 2/20/2020. ThoughtCo.com

A People's History of the United States, 1492 — Present. Howard Zinn

Davos Elites See Potential Return of Trump as Threat to Global Order. Emel Akan. 1/22/2024. theepochtimes.com

A 'Well-Funded Cabal' Influenced the 2020 Election—What Lies Ahead in 2024? Kevin Stocklin. https://www.theepochtimes.com

Google has Usurped Democracy — Across the globe, fair elections no longer exist. Robert W Malone MD, MS. 2/13/2024. https://rwmalonemd.substack.com

How Senegal's Elites Killed Democracy. Mamadou Ndiaye. Translated from the French by Victoria Hartgrove.

Salem Witch Trials. History.com Editors, Updated: 9/29/2023. https://www.history.com

The Role of the Jews in the Russian Revolutionary Movement. Leonard Schapiro. The Slavonic and East European Review. Vol. 40, No. 94 (12/1961), pp. 148-167. Modern Humanities Res. Assoc.

Pfizer 2021 Annual Review. https://www.pfizer.com

Klaus Schwab. WEForum.org/about/klausschwab

Annual Report 2022-2023. World Economic Forum, 91–93 route de la Capite CH-1223 Cologny, Geneva Switzerland. Tel.: +41 (0) 22 869 1212. www.weforum.org contact@weforum.org.

Who We Are. https://www.who.int. WHO Foundation Strategy 2023-2025 Executive Summary.

Biden's Persecution of Political Opponents. Robert Malone. substack.com/@rwmalonemd

Psychological and Cognitive Warfare on Citizens. Robert Malone. substack.com/@rwmalonemd

What If the President Ignores the Supreme Court? Jeffrey A. Tucker. 3/14/2024. theepochtimes.com

How Did American Capitalism Mutate into American Corporatism? Jeffrey A. Tucker. Brownstone Institute

Johns Hopkins HEAT wants to brainwash your school aged children. sashalatypova.substack.com

The West's Descent into Madness. Laura Hollis. 3/21/2024. https://www.theepochtimes.com

41 Times Google Has Interfered in US Elections Since 2008. Gabriela Pariseau & Dan Schneider. https://cdn.mrc.org (PDF)

"The Final Analysis: Forensic Analysis of the JFK Autopsy X-Rays Proves Two Headshots from the Right Front and One from the Rear" by David W. Mantik M.D., Ph.D. and Jerome R. Corsi Ph.D.

Douglass Mackey Prison Sentence Postponed by Appeals Court. Chris Karr. 12/4/2023. SCNR.com

History of Influence, Scandal, and Denial. Brownstone Institute. Paul D. Thacker

The First Black Man Elected to Congress Was Nearly Blocked from Taking His Seat. Becky Little. 1/27/2021. history.com

What was the Population of the US in 1776? Chase. 7/3/2016. https://overflow.solutions

41% of Voters Believe Civil War Will Break Out By 2029. https://bigleaguepolitics.com

Influenza Pandemics of the 20th Century. Edwin D. Kilbourne. Emerging Infectious Diseases. www.cdc.gov/eid. Vol. 12, No. 1, January 2006

Why do millions of Indians defecate in the open? Shannti Dinnoo. BBC.com

Joy Reid Blames GOP 'Death Cult of Disinformation' for COVID Spikes. Samson Amore. TheWrap.com

The White House is Controlled by the Medical-Industrial Complex. Robert Malone. 10/29/2023. https://www.frontline.news

Crop Production, 2023 Summary. January 2024. United States Department of Agriculture National

Agricultural Statistics Service. ISSN: 1057-7823.

USDA 2023/24 U.S. Grains and Oilseed Outlook. 2/24/2023. PowerPoint presented on behalf of the Grains and Oilseeds Interagency Committees by Andrew Sowell, USDA Economic Service

Do You Recognize Discrimination when You See It? FreedomRising.info

10 Principles of Permissible Medical Experiments. FreedomRising.info

The Nuremberg Code 1947. FreedomRising.info

The Taliban: britannica.com

FBI Agents Involved in Facebook's Suppression of Hunter Biden Laptop Story Were Democrat Donors. Mimi Nguyen Ly, 10/12/2022. theepochtimes.com

Louisiana Attorney General Alleges Fauci and Big Tech Part of Push to Censor Americans' Speech. Katie Spence, 12/1/2022. https://www.theepochtimes.com

Former Twitter Executive Who Censored Hunter Biden Laptop Story Admit Mistakes. Bill Pan. 11/30/2022. theepochtimes.com

Elon Musk Fires Twitter's General Counsel and Ex-FBI Official James... Jack Phillips. 12/6/2022. https://www.theepochtimes.com

Top FBI Official Steps Down as Republicans Prepare to Probe into Bureau. Samantha Flom. 12/6/2022. theepochtimes.com

Sen Johnson: FBI's Sabotage of Hunter Biden Laptop Story Was 'Preplanned.' Frank Bergman. https://slaynews.com

In 2018 Jack Dorsey Said "We Certainly Don't Shadow Ban Based on Po..." thegatewaypundit.com

Elon Musk Exposes Twitter's Plotting against Trump in Latest Secret Files Drop. Frank Bergman. https://slaynews.com/

New Set of Twitter Files Detail Events Surrounding Trump's Permanen... theepochtimes.com

Elon Musk Exposes Real Reason Twitter Censored Former President D... theepochtimes.com

Twitter Deviated from Longstanding Policy to Justify Trump Ban, Part ... theepochtimes.com

Kevin McCarthy to Subpoena All 51 Intelligence Agents Who Signed 'Letter That Said Hunter Biden Info Was Wrong.' David Hawkins. https://slaynews.com

How the Left Became What It Once Hated. Jeffrey A. Tucker. 12/23/2022. theepochtimes.com

Twitter Exaggerated Russian Propaganda Claims to Appease Democrats and Media. Frank Bergman. slaynews.com

Why the Brazilian Political Upheaval Looks Like the U.S. theepochtimes.com

Office of the Spec. Counsel. 2nd Interim Investigative Report. On the Apparatus & Procedures of the WI Elections System. Delivered to the WI State Assem. on 3/1/2022.

What Happened in the Brunson Case? Topic: Saving the Republic. Toni Shuppe. 1/18/2023. Substack.

Documentary Exposes Rise of the Unaccountable Fourth Branch of Government, Rule by Experts. Matthew Vadum. 1/27/2023. https://www.theepochtimes.com

House Oversight Hearing on Twitter's Election Interference Validates Loomer RICO Lawsuit. Lauraloomer.substack.com

Rep. Jordan Subpoenas Big Tech CEOs in House 'Weaponization' Probe. Joseph Lord. https://www.theepochtimes.com

High-Stakes Wisconsin Supreme Court Race May Determine Future of... theepochtimes.com

Dominion's Blow to Free Speech. Hal Conte. compactmag.com

Durham's Report Should Outrage the Left. Christian Parenti. https://compactmag.com

List of everyone guilty in the Durham Report. Kash Patel. Kash Foundation

Russian Disinformation? RWMaloneMD.substack.com

CIA Rushed Approval of False Letter Claiming Hunter Biden Laptop Was Russian Disinformation. Cullen McCue. TrendingPoliticsNews.com

Lysander Spooner Quotes (Author of No Treason). https://www.goodreads.com/author/quotes/238917.Lysander_Spooner

'That's My Whole Life's Work.' How Elizabeth Warren Has Become the Policy Engine of the Democratic Party. Haley Sweetland Edwards. Time.com

Has American Democracy Been a Hallucination for Nearly 60 Years? https://www.theepochtimes.com

IN-DEPTH: Durham Report Shows FBI Repeatedly Hamstrung Clinton... theepochtimes.com

Propaganda and Mind Control. RWMaloneMD.substack.com

DHS outsourced censorship to third parties, then tried to cover it up: House Judiciary GOP report By Greg Piper. justthenews.com

"How a 'Cybersecurity' Agency Colluded with Big Tech and 'Disinformation' Partners to Censor Americans." RWMaloneMD.substack.com

Illegal Border Crossers So Far This Year Outnumber the Population of 8 States. Bethany Blankley. https://thepricklypear.org

State of Missouri, et al. Versus Joseph R. Biden Jr., et al. Case 3:22-cv-01213-TAD-KDM Document 293 Filed 07/04/23 Page 1 of 155 PageID #: 26792

'Pretty Stupid': Obama AG Criticizes Court Ban on Biden Admin's Cen... theepochtimes.com

The Pessimistic Case for the Future. Michael Anton. https://compactmag.com

Judge Rejects Biden Administration Bid to Overturn Injunction in Soci... childrenshealthdefense.org

Over 40 Countries Ready to Join BRICS for 'Inclusive and Equitable Global Order,' Top Official Claims. Frank Bergman. https://slaynews.com

The La Cosa Nostra approach to free speech. Originally composed and published by The Brownstone Institute under a creative commons license as "The Censor's Henchmen."

The One Paragraph that Reveals All. August 9, 2023. brownstone.org/articles/the-one-paragraph-that-reveals-all.

Ron DeSantis Suspends Dem State Attorney Monique Worrell For Neglect of Duty and Incompetence. David Hawkins. SlayNews.com

How the CIA Controls the Past. David P. Goldman. compactmag.com

Tremendous Progress in Missouri v. Biden. Brownstone Institute. https://brownstone.org

Facebook Bans Ads for Mark Levin's Anti-Democrat Book before It Goes on Sale. Frank Bergman. SlayNews.com

Public Trust in Government: 1958-2022. Peter Bell. https://www.pewresearch.org

The Movie 'Civil War' Deserves a Viewing. By Jeffrey A. Tucker. 4/24/2024. theepochtimes.com

BRICS Blasts the NWO. BRICS is an acronym for five regional economies: Brazil, Russia, India, China, and South Africa. RWMaloneMD.substack.com

MONEY

US Dept. of the Treasury, Bureau of the Fiscal Service. Monthly Treasury Statement, Receipts and Outlays of the United States Government For Fiscal Year 2024 Through June 30, 2024, and Other Periods. http://www.fiscal.treasury.gov/fsreports/rpt/mthTreasStmt/mthTreasStmt_home.htm

US National Debt Hits $35 Trillion Milestone. Andrew Moran. 7/29/2024. theepochtimes.com

National Debt Reflects a Nation That Has Lost Its Way. Star Parker. 1/25/2023. https://www.theepochtimes.com

New Report Shows Chinese Company Spends Millions on Lobbying Democrats to Fulfill Their Interests. https://dcenquirer.com

Milwaukee Officials Sued in Zuckerberg-Related Election Bribery Case. Matthew Vadum. 3/27/2022. https://www.theepochtimes.com/

New Evidence Shows Mark Zuckerberg's $350M Election Spend Overwhelmingly Helped Democrats Win in 2020. ()x. https://slaynews.com

Zuckerberg Ends Controversial Grants to Election Offices. Matthew Vadum. 4/13/2022. https://www.theepochtimes.com

Fairfax County Virgina Received Over $1.2 Million in Zuckerbucks in 2020 Election — Does This Explain the Three 300,000 Biden Ballot Drops on Election Night? Joe Hoft. 4/16/2022. thegatewaypundit.com

Not Making Headlines... George Soros Dumps $750,000 into Wisconsin Midterms as Democrats Gear Up for the Steal. Jim Hoft. thegatewaypundit.com

George Soros Gave $1 Million to Help Beto O'Rourke Unseat Texas Gov. Greg Abbott. Caden Pearson. 7/20/2022. theepochtimes.com

Cryptocurrency magnate, new GOP megadonor, sunk millions into primaries. David M. Drucker. 9/18/2022. The Washington Examiner

Counterfeit Cash Financed Midterm Democrats. Thomas McArdle. 11/18/22. theepochtimes.com

FTX Poured Millions into Political Campaigns Before Bankruptcy. Emel Akan. 11/23/2022. https://www.theepochtimes.com

Congress Guts Budget Rules and Misses Chance to Cut Spending. Matthew Dickerson. 1/3/2023. thepricklypear.org

Weekend Read: Everything You've Heard About the Debt Limit is Wrong. James D. Agresti. 5/20/2023. thepricklypear.org

George Soros Hands Control to His 37-Year-Old Son: 'I'm More Political.' Gregory Zuckerman. 6/11/2023. https://www.wsj.com

Biden's DOJ Drops Campaign Finance Charge against Democrat Donor FTX CEO Due to 'Procedural Failing.' Frank Bergman. https://slaynews.com

Federal Budget Deficit Suddenly Doubles, Signaling Disaster. theepochtimes.com

Virginia's General Assembly Elections Drawing Intense National Interest, Money. John Haughey. 10/20/2023. theepochtimes.com

Puppet Masters: Billionaire Mega-Donors Behind Biden's Agenda Revealed. David Lindfield. SlayNews.com.

America's Runaway Debt Scenario: $1 Trillion in Interest per Year. Petr Svab. 11/28/2023. https://www.theepochtimes.com

Meet the Mega Donors at Play in the 2024 Election. Patricia Tolson. https://www.theepochtimes.com/

A Crisis Ignored Is a Crisis Fulfilled: A U.S. National Debt Odyssey. Neland Nobel. ThePricklyPear.org

Income in the U.S. 2022. Issued September 2023. Gloria Guzman and Melissa Kollar. Social, Economic, and Housing Statistics Div. of the U.S. Census Bureau

The Richest in 2023. Edited by Rob LaFranco and Chase Peterson-Withorn. Forbes.com

Forbes' 37th Annual World's Billionaires List: Facts And Figures 2023. Chase Peterson-Withorn. Forbes.com

The 25 Richest People In The World 2023. Chase Peterson-Withorn. Forbes.com

The World's Richest Women Billionaires 2023. Gabriela Lopez Gomes. Forbes.com

7 Companies Owned by Google (Alphabet). Matthew Johnston. October 23, 2022. Investopedia.com

Who is Sundar Pichai and what does Alphabet do? BBC News. 12/4/2019. BBC.com

Who Really Owns Google (Alphabet) and Who Controls It. Kamil Franek. KamilFranek.com

Larry Page. By Andy Frye. Forbes.com

Lawrence Page. Larry Page was Google's founding CEO. He continues to share responsibility for Google's day-to-day operations with Eric Schmidt and Sergey Brin. https://research.google

Who are the Biggest Donors? OpenSecrets.org

Here Are The Billionaires Funding The Democratic Presidential Candidates, As Of September 2019. Michela Tindera. Forbes.com

These are the 50 top donors for the 2022 midterm elections. Luis Melgar, Chris Alcantara, Isaac Stanley-Becker, Anu Narayans-

wamy, Chris Zubak-Skees. WashingtonPost.com

Two Million Dollar Checks: Out-of-State Liberals Dominating Donations to Wisconsin Political Parties in 2020. Peter Cameron. 10/23/2020. TheBadgerProject.org.

The Biggest Donors to Wisconsin Political Parties in 2020. Molly Libergall. The Badger Project. 10/23/2020

How to Explain the Fed's Massive Losses? Jeffrey A. Tucker. 1/29/2024. theepochtimes.com

Jamie Dimon Warns of 'Rebellion' as Government Debt Balloons, Economy Heads Towards 'Cliff.' Tom Ozimek 1/31/2024. https://www.theepochtimes.com

'Never Trump' Billionaires Lead Nikki Haley's 2023 Fundraising. Austin Alonzo. 2/9/2024. https://www.theepochtimes.com

FedEx Founder Issues Dire Warning About 'Unsustainable' Government Debt. Tom Ozimek. 2/16/2024. theepochtimes.com

The Money Machine Behind Progressive Election Efforts. Austin Alonzo. theepochtimes.com

Most expensive ever: 2020 election cost $14.4 billion. Karl Evers-Hillstrom. OpenSecrets.org

China's 100 Richest 2023. 11/8/2023. https://www.forbes.com

How Rich Is the Chinese Communist Party? John Feng. Newsweek.com

Chinese millionaires - statistics & facts. C. Textor, Dec 20, 2023. https://www.statista.com

50 Richest Members of Congress. David Sim and Sam Earle. 4/6/18. Newsweek.com

The Price of Power - A deep-dive analysis into how political parties squeeze influential lawmakers to boost campaign coffers. Michael Beckel. issueone.org

The Price of Power Revisited. With control of the House of Representatives comes gavels — and fundraising expectations. Amisa Ratliff, Ariana Rojas, and Michael Beckel. issueone.org

New Congress, Same "Committee Tax." How the parties pressured legislative leaders to raise huge sums of campaign cash during the 116th Congress. Amisa Ratliff. issueone.org

Democrats Commit Vastly More Dark Money Than Republicans for2024. Austin Alonzo. 4/8/2024. theepochtimes.com

Conservatives Seek to Ban Private Funding of Elections Ahead of 2024Races. Steven Kovac. 4/13/2024. theepochtimes.com

Democratic-led House authorizes $3.5 trillion of spending as national debt climbs to $29 trillion. Nicholas Ballasy. 8/24/2021. https://justthenews.com

Fiscal watchdog group urges House not to pass $3.5T budget bill. Nicholas Ballasy. 8/24/2021. https://justthenews.com

RFK Jr's Running Mate Nicole Shanahan Injects $8 Million to Secure Nationwide Ballot Access. Chase Smith. 5/16/2024. https://www.theepochtimes.com

Daily Treasury Statement. Cash and debt operations of the United States Treasury. 6/15/2023. Fiscal-Data. Treasury.gov

Forbes World's Billionaires List 2024: The Top 200. Chase Peterson-Withorn. Forbes.com

The National Debt Crisis Is Coming - WSJ. 6/25/2024. Dow Jones & Company, Inc.

Bill Gates' net worth in 2024 is estimated to be $121.4 billion, making him the eighth richest person in the world. https://parade.com/1204965/jessicasager/bill-gates-net-worth

Bill Gates' House Worth: https://www.velvetropes.com/backstage/bill-gates-house.

Bill Gates' Private Jet Collection: https://simpleflying.com/bill-gates-private-jet-collection

Hillary Clinton Net Worth $120 Million. https://www.celebritynetworth.com/richest-politicians

Donald Rumsfeld Net Worth $200 Million in 2021: https://www.celebritynetworth.com/richest-politicians

Federal Employee Salaries Average $143,643 in Total Compensation. https://www.fedsmith.com

The median annual wage in 2021

in the US was $45,760. https://usafacts.org/data/topics/economy/jobs-and-income/jobs-and-wages/median-annual-wage

Median net worth by all American families in 2022 was $192,700. https://www.federalreserve.gov/econres/scf/dataviz/scf/table

In 2022, there were 22.7 million people with a net worth of over one million U.S. dollars in the United States. https://www.statista.com/statistics/268411/countries-with-the-most-millionaires

The median net worth of members of Congress who filed disclosures last year is just over $1 million. https://www.opensecrets.org/news/2020/04/majority-of-lawmakers-millionaires

Bill Gates Says He Needs to Own 4 Private Jets Because He's 'The Solution' to 'Climate Change' Article Reports. evol.news/news

U.S. Spending on Interest Tops National Defense, Medicare. Brett Rowland. PricklyPear.news

The median net worth of members of Congress who filed disclosures last year is just over $1 million: https://www.opensecrets.org/news/2020/04/majority-of-lawmakers-millionaires

In 2022, there were 22.7 million people with a net worth of over one million U.S. dollars in the United States (6.7% of the population), which put the country on the top of the ranking. China was ranked second in that year, with 6.2 million individuals. https://www.statista.com/statistics/268411/countries-with-the-most-millionaires

Median net worth by all American families in 2022 was $192,700: https://www.federalreserve.gov/econres/scf/dataviz/scf/table/#series: Net_Worth; demographic: all; population: all; units: median; range: 1989, 2019

Median annual wage: https://usafacts.org/data/topics/economy/jobs-and-income/jobs-and-wages/median-annual-wage

Elon Musk: FTX CEO Funneled 'Over $1B' to Democrats. Frank Bergman. https://slaynews.com US National Debt Default Is a 'Real Threat' Both Sides Must Take Seri... theepochtimes.com

Democrat Senator Received Huge Payments from Pharma Companies Behind Opioid Crisis. Frank Bergman. slaynews.com

US National Debt Hits All-Time High of $32 Trillion. https://www.theepochtimes.com/

Goldman CEO Issues Warning as Interest Costs on America's Ballooning Debt Exceed Spending on Defense, Medicare. https://www.theepochtimes.com

Some Unpleasant Federal Reserve Arithmetic. Paul Mueller. https://thepricklypear.org

Revealed: Dark Money Funders Behind 'Disinformation Dozen' Report... childrenshealthdefense.org

Democrat Donor Bought $1.3M of Hunter's 'Art' before Joe Biden Appointed Her to Prestigious Commission. David Hawkins. https://slaynews.com

Fitch Downgrades US Credit Rating, Citing Erosion of Confidence in Fi... theepochtimes.com

Mega Donor Threatens to Cut Off Funding If DeSantis Doesn't Go Moderate. theepochtimes.com

George Soros Bankrolling 'Mysterious' Organization to 'Buy Texas' for 'Progressive' Democrats.' David Lindfield. https://slaynews.com

Retirees Could See $17,400 Reduction in Benefits by 2033. Naveen Athrappully. 8/16/2023. https://www.theepochtimes.com

JPMorgan CEO Issues Dire Warning About Biden Administration's 'Huge' Deficit Spending. Tom Ozimek. 4/25/2024. https://www.theepochtimes.com

Why the US Debt Is Unsustainable and Is Destroying the Middle Class. Daniel Lacalle. https://thepricklypear.org

US Household Debt Surges to Record $17.8 Trillion. Andrew Moran. 8/6/2024. theepochtimes.com

PENNSYLVANIA

Polling places run out of ballots in PA primary. Michael Rubinkam. 5/18/2021. APNews.com

What the %!@- happened in Pennsylvania... AGAIN? Toni Shuppe. From Mom to Patriot.

Voting Machine Company That 'Flipped' Votes in Pennsylvania Admits 'Someone Programmed the Election.' Frank Bergman. SlayNews.com

Voters In Lancaster County Demanding Answers From US Postal Service. WLT Report. Vince Quill. 12/3/2023. https://wltreport.com

The PA Supreme Court Circumvented State Election Law. Bryan E. Leib. 11/12/2020. theepochtimes.com

Supreme Court Lifts Stay, Allows Counting of Questionable Ballots in Pennsylvania Judicial Election. Matthew Vadum. 6/10/2022. https://www.theepochtimes.com

Supreme Court Backs Republican in Pennsylvania Mail-In Ballots Case. Jack Phillips. 10/11/2022. https://www.theepochtimes.com

Supreme Court Allows 3-Day Extension for Mail-In Ballots in Pennsylvania. Mimi Nguyen Ly. 10/19/2020. theepochtimes.com

Soros Bucks, Private Jets Found in Pennsylvania AG Josh Shapiro's 11,000 Page Campaign Finance Report. Beth Brelje. 10/20/2022. https://www.theepochtimes.com

Republicans Sue Pennsylvania Officials Who Said They'll Accept Mail-in Ballots Without Dates. Zachary Stieber. 10/17/2022. https://www.theepochtimes.com

Republicans Score Win in Court Battle Over Pennsylvania Ballot Requirements. Zachary Stieber 3/29/2024. theepochtimes.com

Polling places run out of ballots in Pennsylvania primary. Michael Rubinkam. Associated Press. 5/19/2021. tnonline.com

Philadelphia Imposes Last-Minute Change to How Votes Are Counted. Zachary Stieber. 11/8/2022. theepochtimes.com

PA's Dept. of State Has Sent Out 249k Ballots to Unverified Voters in 2022 Election. Beth Brelje. 10/31/2022. theepochtimes.com

Pennsylvania Voters Request Numerous Precinct Election Recounts. Beth Brelje. 11/22/2022. https://www.theepochtimes.com

Pennsylvania Supreme Court Upholds No-Excuse Mail-In Voting Law. Matthew Vadum. 8/2/2022. https://www.theepochtimes.com

Pennsylvania Supreme Court Orders Undated, Wrongly Dated Ballots to be Counted. Mimi Nguyen Ly. 11/1/2022. theepochtimes.com

Pennsylvania Settles Voter Roll Lawsuit with Judicial Watch. 5/11/2023. judicialwatch.org

Pennsylvania Settles Election Integrity Lawsuit, Deletes 178,000 Names from Voter Rolls. Bill Pan. 5/11/2023. theepochtimes.com

Pennsylvania Set for Messy Election Aftermath, Including Court Challenges. Petr Svab. 11/2/2022. theepochtimes.com

PA Report Recommends 5 Changes to Election Code. Beth Brelje. 1/31/2023. theepochtimes.com

Pennsylvania Patriot Groups Implore Voters to Engage. Beth Brelje. 8/29/2022. theepochtimes.com

Pennsylvania Mail-In Ballot Case Filed by Republicans Dismissed by Democrat Judge. Beth Brelje. 3/24/2023. theepochtimes.com

Pennsylvania House in Turmoil as Political Maneuvers Halt Business. Beth Brelje. 1/13/2023. https://www.theepochtimes.com

Pennsylvania County Sues Dominion Voting Systems Over 'Severe Anomalies' In 2020 Election. Tyler Durden. zerohedge.com

Pennsylvania County Sued Over Illegal Ballot Drop Box Usage Captured on Camera. Bill Pan. 9/16/2022. theepochtimes.com

Pennsylvania Abruptly Cuts Short Contract with Voter Registration Firm. Beth Brelje. 12/18/2023. https://www.theepochtimes.com

More than 100 Lancaster County mail-in ballots tossed after postal service delay. Tom Lisi. 12/1/2023. https://lancasteronline.com

Doug Mastriano on X: @LauraLoomer. To get the endorsement of Vass' PAC for PA governor, I was asked to renounce Trump. https://twitter.com/dougmastriano/status/17679803810414 71691

Mastriano Promises 'New Birth of Freedom' for Pennsylvania on

Campaign Bus Tour. Frank Liang and William Huang. 10/24/2022. https://www.theepochtimes.com.

Left-Wing Group Tries to Disqualify Republican Frontrunner in PA Governor's Race on 'Insurrection' Grounds. Matthew Vadum. 4/17/2022. theepochtimes.com

Incomplete Mail-In Ballots Must Be Counted in PA, Judge Rules. David Lindfield. SlayNews.com

GOP Says Pennsylvania Mail-In Voting Law is Invalid. Rita Li. 7/22/2022. theepochtimes.com

Former Congressman Sentenced to Prison for Stuffing Pennsylvania Ballot Boxes. Beth Brelje. 9/29/2022. theepochtimes.com.

Democrats Win PAs Statewide Judicial Races. Beth Brelje. 11/8/2023. theepochtimes.com

Cancel Culture: The Voter Intimidation Tactic of Pennsylvania Governor's Race. Beth Brelje. 7/22/2022. theepochtimes.com

TRUE THE VOTE

'The Government Is Not Our Friend': Founder of True the Vote Discuss... theepochtimes.com

True the Vote Defeats Fair Fight, Stacy Abrams, Marc... truethevote.org

True the Vote Worked Hard to Follow the Law, Founder Testifies. Dan Berger. theepochtimes.com

Lawsuit Against True the Vote Goes to Judge to Decide. Dan M. Berger. theepochtimes.com

If You Can't Join 'Em, Beat 'Em. Catherine Engelbrecht. truethevote.org

BREAKING: CEO of election company that sued True the Vote was ju... https://therightscoop.com

CEO of election software firm Konnech charged with grand theft by embezzlement. The Center Square Staff. justthenews.com

Appeals Court Clears True the Vote Leaders of Contempt. Zachary Stieber, 11/22/2022. https://www.theepochtimes.com

Court Orders Release of True the Vote Leaders from Jail. Zachary Stieber, 11/7/2022. https://www.theepochtimes.com

True the Vote Founders Jailed for Contempt. Zachary Stieber, 10/31/22. www.theepochtimes.com

'2000 Mules' Investigators Arrested by U.S. Marshals for Refusing to Reveal Source. slaynews.com

NYT 'Right Wing Conspiracy Theory' Comes True In Less Than 24 Hours. Tyler Durden. Zerohedge

Election Software CEO Arrested Over Data Theft, Storing Data on Serve... theepochtimes.com

TRUMP

Democrat Megadonor Behind Defamation Lawsuit Against Trump. https://www.theepochtimes.com

Why Didn't President Trump Start a New Party in 2021? Capt. Seth Keshel. skeshel.substack.com

When They've Come for The Lawyers, It Might Be Too Late. Aspects of the GA RICO case are proof it is a show trial. 8/27/2023. greatamericanmail.substack.com

Voting Firm That Sued Trump Team over 2020 Election Caught in Bribery Scheme. Frank Bergman. SlayNews.com.

Trump's 'LIBERATE' tweets might be both unconstitutional... Mary McCord. 4/17/2020. https://www.washingtonpost.com

Trump: Colorado Supreme Court Decision 'Shame for Our Country.' Catherine Yang. 12/20/2023. https://www.theepochtimes.com

Trump Wants Redo of 2020 Election 'Immediately' Over New FBI Revelations. Jack Phillips. 8/29/2022. theepochtimes.com

Trump Supporters Targeted by FBI as 2024 Election Nears. Kate Stephenson. NewsAddicts.com.

Trump supporters flood N.H. election office with calls after false claims about ballot access. Emma Barnett. nbcnews.com

Trump Sues British Ex-Spy Steele Over Infamous Dossier. NewsAddicts.com. Melinda Davies

Trump Not Immune From Jan. 6 Lawsuits, Appeals Court Rules. Tom Ozimek. 12/29/2023. https://www.theepochtimes.com

Trump Cases for Supreme Court Review Start Piling Up. Catherine Yang. 12/22/2023. theepochtimes.com

Trump Campaign Fires Back After 'Virulent Leftist' Maine S.O.S. Rules 45th President Ineligible to Appear on the State's Primary Ballot. Liam Donovan. NewsAddicts.com

Trump Asks Court to Block Michigan Secretary of State from Banning Him. Naveen Athrappully. 11/1/2023. theepochtimes.com

The Liberal Plot Against Democracy. Alan Dershowitz. https://compactmag.com

Supreme Court Would Rule 9-0 in Favor of Trump in Colorado Case... Aaron Pan. 12/20/2023. https://www.theepochtimes.com

Supreme Court Takes Up Trump Ballot Disqualification Case. Catherine Yang. 1/5/2024. https://www.theepochtimes.com

Special Counsel Obtained trump's DMs... Kyle Cheney. 8/15/2023. politico.com.

Soros Vows to Focus on Defeating Trump in 2024, Warns 'MAGA-Style Victory' Will 'Undermine' Globalism. David Lindfield. SlayNews.com.

Pelosi's J6 Committee Deleted Over 100 Encrypted Files to Keep Them from Republicans. Melinda Davies. NewsAddicts.com.

Mike Pence 'Confident' that President Trump will NOT be GOP Nominee. 8/27/2023. Graham. https://wltreport.com

Maine Secretary of State Claims Politics Played 'No Role' in Booting Trump Off Ballot. Tom Ozimek. 1/2/2024. theepochtimes.com

Legal Review: Majority of 2020 Election Challenges Decided on the Merits Went for Trump or GOP. Melinda Davies. NewsAddicts.com.

Kathy Griffin Says She Moos 'Like a Cow' to Cope with Trump Derangement Syndrome. Frank Bergman. SlayNews.com

Trump Files Motion Calling On Judge Tanya Chutkan To Recuse Herself From Jan 6 Case Over Biased Statements. Cullen McCue. https://trendingpoliticsnews.com

Judge's Dissent in 'Absurd' Colorado Ruling Holds Key to How Decision Should Be Overturned. Melinda Davies. NewsAddicts.com.

Judge Denies Fulton County D.A. Request to Try All 19 Defendants Together in Trump Election Case. Catherine Yang. theepochtimes.com

James Woods on Twitter: "As an objective political observation I think the Trump situation is a huge risk for Democrats..." https://twitter.com/RealJamesWoods/status/168761990203380 1219

In Her Jan. 6 Courtroom, Judge Who Will Hear Trump's Case Is the Pot Calling the Defendant Incendiary. Julie Kelly. https://www.realclearinvestigations.com/articles/2023/08/23/

Former Trump Campaign Attorney Says Fulton County Case Based on Illegal Evidence. Catherine Yang. 9/22/2023. https://www.theepochtimes.com

Federal Judge Tosses 14th Amendment Lawsuit against Trump. David Lindfield. Slay News.com.

Donald Trump Followers Targeted by FBI as 2024 Election Nears. William M. Arkin. 10/13/2023. Newsweek.com

El Salvador President Becomes First Global Leader to Push Back on Colorado's Fascist Move to Remove Trump from Ballot. 12/20/2023. by vnninfluencers. https://vigilantnews.com

Donald Trump Jr is Sent Letter Containing White Powder and Death Threat Against His Father. Melinda Davies. NewsAddicts.com.

DOJ Seeks to Exclude Trump Evidence in Jan. 6 Case After Pause Ordered. Catherine Yang. 12/27/2023. theepochtimes.com

DOJ Says Trump Has No 'Absolute Immunity' in Jan. 6 Case. Catherine Yang. 10/20/2023. https://www.theepochtimes.com

DA Fani Willis Held Exonerating Evidence for Trump Case While Pursuing Charges. Frank Bergman. SlayNews.com.

D.C Watchdog Files Lawsuit to Block Trump from 2024 Ballot. Frank Bergman. SlayNews.com

Cowboys for Trump Co-Founder Cuoy Griffin Appeals Public Office Ban. Katabella Roberts. 9/21/2022. theepochtimes.com

The Cult of Donald Trump has become a Death Cult. People who refuse to wear a mask are bolstering their sore egos. Their national motto is not 'E Pluribus Unum,' it's 'You're not the boss of me.' Tom Nichols. 7/25/2020. USAToday.com

Colorado Secretary of State Jena Griswold Expresses 'Disappointment' With Trump Supreme Court Victory. Stephen Katte. 3/5/2024. https://www.theepochtimes.com

BREAKING: Judge Schedules Trump Trial in the Middle of Primaries, Months Before Election. Chris. trendingpoliticsnews.com

Obama Admin Had No 'Actual Evidence' Of Collusion By Trump When It Launched Crossfire Hurricane Investigation. Shawn Fleetwood. https://thepricklypear.org

Biden's DOJ Will Trigger A Major Crisis If Trump Is Indicted For Jan. 6. John Daniel Davidson. https://thepricklypear.org

Attorney Lays Out Why Fani Willis' Case Implicates 'Conspiracy' of 72 Million Trump Voters. Melinda Davies. NewsAddicts.com.

The Biggest Revelation From the Durham Report. Hans Mahncke. 5/22/2023. theepochtimes.com

Alan Dershowitz Turns Tables, Reveals 'Jack Smith Can Be Indicted' If Trump Wins Case. David Hawkins. SlayNews.com

Alan Dershowitz Issues Warning: Biden's America 'Looks Like Banana Republic Land.' David Hawkins. SlayNews.com.

'Absolutely Unprecedented': Trump Gag Orders Test Judges' Powers. Sam Dorman. 10/31/2023. https://www.theepochtimes.com

Supreme Court of the State of New York, County of New York, People of the State of New York, by Letitia James, Attorney General of the State of New York, against Donald J. Trump . . . Index No. 452564/2022. Received NYS-CEF: 09/21/2022

Summary of Election Fraud. twitter.com/KanekoaTheGreat/thread/1742670648433090764

2020 US Presidential Election Related Lawsuits. https://election-integrity.info/2020_Election_Cases.htm

16 Trump Supporters Charged with 'Conspiracy' in Michigan Over Alleged Alternate Electors Scheme. Chris. trendingpoliticsnews.com

'Never Trump' Billionaires Lead Nikki Haley's 2023 Fundraising. Austin Alonzo. 2/9/2024. https://www.theepochtimes.com

WAR

Winning the Second Cold War. Sohrab Ahmari & Matthew Schmitz. https://compactmag.com

What We Left Behind in Afghanistan. Roger Kimball. 8/29/2021. https://www.theepochtimes.com

War Waste. Sinclair Broadcast Group. 7/1/2018. The Defense Department did not respond to our questions about why so much information about the situation in Afghanistan was recently classified or who was responsible for the decision to classify the information. https://fullmeasure.news

War Is Always Inflationary. Michael Wilkerson. 1/23/2024. https://www.theepochtimes.com

U.S. Spends Billions on Overseas Wars, But Who Really Benefits? Andrew Thornebrooke. https://www.theepochtimes.com

The Pentagon fails its fifth audit in a row. Connor Echols. 11/22/2022. responsiblestatecraft.org

The Pentagon Failed Its Audit Again, But Says Bots Could Change That. Lauren C. Williams. 11/2022. DefenseOne.com

A List of American Taxpayer Funds sent to Ukraine since the start of the Russian-Ukrainian Conflict. @JoeyMannarinoUS. 9/7/2023

GOP Lawmaker Calls Pentagon Audit Situation "Unacceptable." On Wednesday, the Department of Defense's Chief Financial Officer announced that the Pentagon has failed its annual audit for the sixth time in a row. Bosun. 11/18/2023. wltreport.com

Defense Contractors Benefited From Nearly Half of $14 Trillion Spent for Afghan War: Study.

Mary Ellen Cagnassola. 9/13/2021. Newsweek.com

Costs of the 20-year war on terror: $8 trillion and 900,000 deaths. 1/9/2021. Watson Institute, Brown University. www.brown.edu

Blood and Treasure: United States Budgetary Costs and Human Costs of 20 Years of War in Iraq and Syria, 2003-2023. Neta C. Crawford. 3/15/2023. Watson Institute. watson.brown.edu

America's Controversial Stealth Fighter Jet Can Now Carry Nukes. John Haughey. 3/31/2024. https://www.theepochtimes.com

U.S Military Spending: The Cost of Wars. Anthony H. Cordesman. 7/10/2017. csis.org/burke/reports.

Killing Hope: US Military and CIA Interventions since World War II. William Blum. 1995. Common Courage Press. ISBN 1-56751-053-1, or ISBN 1-56751-052-3

"Any member of Congress who doesn't vote for the funds we need to defend this country will be looking for a new job after next November." Defense Contractors Benefited From Nearly Half of $14 Trillion Spent for Afghan War: Study: 9/13/2021. Mary Ellen Cagnassola. Newsweek.com

Rand Paul, Chuck Grassley and Bernie Sanders team up to audit the Pentagon. Jack Hunter. 6/23/2023. based-politics.com

Letter from the Forbidden Land. Brownstone Institute. Michael J. Sutton. https://brownstone.org

Anyone Who Believes in the Hollywood Image of the CIA Should Come to Serbia — Where the Agency Has Long Aligned with One of the Country's Most Notorious Criminal Gangs. Olga Peterson. CovertActionMagazine.com.

INDEX

X

Y

Z

ABOUT THE AUTHOR

Joseph C. Jenkins, born in 1952, is a distinguished American author celebrated for his award-winning non-fiction titles. As an independent, self-published entrepreneur and world traveler, Jenkins has evolved from a lifelong Democrat to a Green Party organizer, and now identifies as "non-aligned," with no affiliations to any political party, government agency, academic institution, or religious organization.

More information is available at JosephJenkins.com.

OTHER BOOKS BY THE AUTHOR

The Slate Roof Bible, 3rd Edition, (2016), hardcover, full color, 374 pages, nearly 800 Illustrations. ISBN-13: 978-0964425828

The Humanure Handbook, 4th Edition: Shit in a Nutshell, (2019), 300 pages, 91 illustrations, paperback. ISBN-13: 978-0964425880.

The Compost Toilet Handbook, (2021), 254 pages, 161 color pages, hardcover, ISBN: 978-1-7336035-1-5

The Balance Point, (2018), 341 pages, paperback, ISBN-13: 978-0964425866

Self Publishing Top Ten Tips, (2022), 100 pages, paperback, ISBN: 978-1-7336035-3-9